KW-552-890

64285

Corporate Governance and Regulation

Corporate Governance and Regulation

An Irish Perspective

RONAN KEANE
Former Chief Justice of Ireland
and
AILBHE O'NEILL, B.L.

ROUND HALL

THOMSON REUTERS

Published in 2009 by
Thomson Reuters (Professional) Ireland Limited
(Registered in Ireland, Company No. 80867.
Registered Office and address for service
43 Fitzwilliam Place, Dublin 2)
trading as Round Hall

Typeset by
Carrigboy Typesetting Services

Printed by
MPG Books, Bodmin, Cornwall

ISBN 978–1–85800–519–5

A catalogue record for this book
is available from the British Library.

All rights reserved. No part of this publication may be reproduced or transmitted in any form or by any means, or stored in any retrieval system of any nature without prior written permission. Such written permission must also be obtained before any part of this publication is stored in a retrieval system of any nature.

Thomson Reuters and the Thomson Reuters Logo are trademarks of Thomson Reuters. Round Hall is a registered trademark of Thomson Reuters (Professional) Ireland Limited.

Views expressed by each author are the views of that author alone and do not necessarily represent the views of other authors or the editors.

LIBRARY I.T. CARLOW
ACC. NO 64285 DATE 19/1/11
346.417066
CLASS NO. PRICE 165.–
THOMSON ROWEN INV: 124133
VENDOR P.O 110052

© Thomson Reuters (Professional) Ireland Limited, 2009

FOREWORD

An invitation to become a non-executive director of a public company, in particular of a bank, was once prized and welcomed amongst the business community. It is doubtful that such an invitation continues to be so viewed. Family members and friends were often willing to act as a second director of a small private company in the belief that any duties would be nominal. Such belief is no longer well founded.

There have been significant changes in the legal and regulatory framework applicable to corporate governance of public and private companies since 1990. Even before current events, more changes were anticipated in the proposed Companies Consolidation and Reform Bill.

It is difficult to recall a time when "corporate governance and regulation" was more topical than at present. The international and domestic financial crises and failure of or almost total loss of shareholder value in companies previously regarded as "blue chip" have raised serious issues relating to the regulation of corporate governance.

In such a climate, there is a risk of over-reaction. It may well be that further reform of the legal rules and norms according to which companies are controlled and managed is required. However, it would be regrettable if this were done without debate and careful consideration of the appropriate balance between allowing entrepreneurs reasonable scope to risk-take with the benefit of limited liability, and a regulatory regime which requires compliance by directors and others with minimum mandatory obligations and specified norms and standards, and which protects employees, shareholders, creditors and others dealing with the corporate entity.

This collection of essays makes a valuable contribution to such a debate and consideration. It demonstrates the variety and complexity of the issues faced by those attempting to find the requisite balance. The essay by Dr Courtney in relation to directors' compliance statements and, in particular, the review conducted by the Company Law Review Group of s.45 of the Companies (Auditing and Accounting) Act 2003, highlights the difficulty in reaching a consensus as to the appropriate balance in company legislation and the perceived risks to the Irish economy of imposing too onerous obligations on directors. It remains to be seen whether the proposed new Companies Bill will remain as signposted in Mr Conroy's contribution.

The essays also provide many thoughtful analyses of the application to date of company law and other applicable provisions for directors, auditors, pension trustees and others and of potential reforms. The essays by Dr O'Neill and Professor Lynch Fannon contain useful insights and critical assessment of judicial application of ss.150 and 160 of the Companies Act 1990, in relation to restriction and disqualification of directors; provisions not devoid of difficulty in their practical application.

I am delighted to recommend this collection of universally high quality essays. It is not possible to mention each, but they are all essential reading for those who wish to participate in a debate about the future of corporate Ireland. They are also most useful for anyone with an interest in corporate governance, whether as a policy-maker or as a director, auditor, pension trustee or in legal practice or as an academic. I thank the Editors for the opportunity to read the essays and invitation to write this foreword.

MARY FINLAY GEOGHEGAN
The High Court
Dublin
March 30, 2009

For Irene, R.K.
For Eoin, A.O.N.

PREFACE

The editors would like to thank the contributors to this collection for their commitment to this book, which we hope will be of interest to the practitioner and academic alike.

Thanks are also due to Catherine Dolan, Kristiina Kojamo and Natalie Hegarty of Round Hall for their hard work, patience and unfailing enthusiasm in the editing of this collection.

Dublin, March 30, 2009

Ronan Keane
Ailbhe O'Neill

Views expressed by each author are the views of that author alone and do not necessarily represent the views of other authors or the editors.

INTRODUCTION

"The money changers have fled from their high seats in the temple of our civilisation ... There must be an end to a conduct in banking and in business which too often has given to a sacred trust the likeness of callous and selfish wrongdoing."

The words of Franklin D. Roosevelt in his first inaugural address as President of the United States in 1933 have obvious resonances for our era. As governments around the world seek to grapple with an economic crisis which knows no frontiers, there is a focus in Ireland as in other countries on the role played by commercial and banking concerns in our present woes. One does not have to join the ranks of those who claim that capitalism is in its death throes to acknowledge that, in Ireland as elsewhere, serious questions arise as to how our corporate structures should be regulated and, in particular, whether our law and practice are adequately reflecting principles of good corporate governance. The essays in this book approach these problems from an Irish perspective, while at the same time recognising that some of the issues need to be addressed in a wider context, not least because much of our law in this whole area is strongly influenced by our membership in the European Union.

Many lawyers, I suspect, would have been unfamiliar with the very notion of "corporate governance" until comparatively recent times. Nor, indeed, is it easy to formulate a definition of "corporate governance" which would command universal acceptance. In the United States, academic discussion of the topic goes as far back as the Wall Street crash of 1929 and the writings of scholars such as Berle and Means. Since the 1970s, there has been an emphasis on the dangers which flow from the separation of ownership and control in large companies, particularly so far as the interests of shareholders are concerned. But the concept has also expanded to embrace the interests of other stakeholders in corporations: employees, creditors, customers and government agencies concerned with various aspects of public welfare such as health and safety and the environment. Thus, corporate governance can be seen as the assembly of practices, some of which, but not all, are embodied in laws, and which are intended to ensure that the needs of all those stakeholders are served.

More recently, major financial scandals in large corporations such as Enron in the US and Parmalat in Italy heightened concerns that standards of corporate governance were being eroded, leading to more stringent controls in the US in the form of the Sarbanes-Oxley Act of 2002. At the time this collection is published, the worldwide malaise suffered by financial institutions has prompted fresh anxieties as to the adequacy of regulatory structures.

For many Irish businesses, corporate governance is a remote and even meaningless concept. The sole trader, even if he or she has taken advantage of limited liability by incorporating as a company, may have no significant stakeholders to worry about. The overwhelming majority of Irish companies are private companies limited by shares and hence in many respects are not affected by concerns as to corporate governance to the same extent as are public limited companies.

The fact remains that corporate governance is hugely relevant in Ireland. In the first place, although they are relatively small in number, the plcs whose shares are traded on the stock exchange play a major role in the Irish economy. Secondly, even in the case of the one-person company, the manner in which its affairs are conducted can have consequences for its creditors and customers; and there are, of course, larger private companies where the interests of employees are affected or where the management and the shareholders are not identical.

The belief that the existing legislation did not provide adequate safeguards for stakeholders in companies, large or small, led to a series of new acts from 1990 onwards which established more stringent controls of their activities. The extension of the personal liability of company officers for fraudulent trading to reckless trading and for failure to keep proper books of account had major implications for directors. So too did the stringent controls on loans by a company to its directors. The requirements that the accounts be independently audited were also strengthened.

All this apparatus of control would have been of little practical significance if its enforcement was as inadequate as had been the case in the past. There was a particularly glaring lacuna in the case of insolvent companies, the liquidators of which might have good reason to believe the directors to have been seriously at fault, but little incentive, financial or otherwise, to do anything about it. The establishment in 2001 of the Office of Director of Corporate Enforcement in accordance with the recommendations of the McDowell report was a major step forward in this area and it is somewhat ironic that the most frequently voiced criticism of the first holder of the office has been that he exercises his powers too often. Given the previous history of company law enforcement in Ireland, that could only be regarded as an error in the right direction.

One of the areas in which the Director has been most active has been in applications for orders by the High Court restricting or disqualifying directors. It is understandable that judges dealing with this new and developing area of the law have not found it easy to establish a principled and consistent jurisprudence in dealing with the many and diverse cases that have come before them. This is illuminatingly explored by Dr Ailbhe O'Neill and Professor Irene Lynch Fannon in their essays, the dilemma facing courts being neatly epitomised in the title of Professor Lynch Fannon's essay: "The Dynamic Entrepreneur or the Incompetent Fool?"

One of the problems which emerges from these cases is as to how much should be demanded by the law of part-time directors. This is quintessentially an example of where adherence to proper norms of corporate governance is of crucial relevance. Compliance with express requirements of the law in the case of such directors may seem undemanding. All who take on such roles should bear in mind, however, that they are under an obligation to keep themselves informed as to the company's activities and to ensure that the company has the benefit of the knowledge and any particular expertise that they enjoy. In the case of larger private companies and public companies where there is a separation of ownership and managerial control, the importance of part-time directors exercising a role independent of the management is an essential feature of good governance.

The attempt to ensure compliance by companies with all their obligations by requiring the directors to include in their annual report an elaborate "compliance statement" to be verified by the auditors, under s.45 of the Companies (Auditing and Accounting) Act 2003 (the "2003 Act"), caused much controversy, its critics claiming that it was a wholly disproportionate response, out of step with other jurisdictions and likely to affect Ireland's competitiveness. The section was, in the result, not implemented and the majority report of the Company Law Review Group (CLRG) has recommended its replacement by a less onerous provision. This incorporates the approach adopted by the EU Commission's Corporate Governance Forum, sometimes called the "comply or explain" principle, which takes as its starting point the fact that the statement is to be addressed by the directors to the shareholders alone and that it should suffice for the directors either to demonstrate that the company has complied or in any instance where it has not to give the reasons. The chairman of the CLRG, Dr Thomas Courtney, in his essay gives an authoritative account of how this compromise was reached which repays careful reading. While it remains to be seen what form the compliance statement will take in the comprehensive new legislation which is expected, it is difficult to disagree with his conclusion that a disproportionate and burdensome statutory regime may create rather than resolve problems.

Section 45 of the 2003 Act was one of the responses to the concern provoked by the widespread evasion of DIRT tax and the role of the banks in facilitating such evasion and also in other areas exploiting their privileged position to the detriment of their customers. Clearly recent events will reawaken the debates to which s.45 gave rise to. The 2003 Act also provided a new regime for the auditing of company's accounts which is critically surveyed by Dr Ciaran O'Kelly in his essay on auditors' duties. He also asks searching questions as to whether the legal and regulatory framework under which companies exist in Ireland and elsewhere in the common law world and, in particular, the role of independent auditors can be reconciled with what he calls "the realities of contemporary capitalism".

One form of regulation that seemed to have only a distant connection with the reality of Irish capitalism was that governing insider trading. It is hardly believable that until the *Fyffes* litigation came before the courts in 2005, there had been no case since the legislation was enacted in 1900 in which anyone profited from an Irish stock exchange dealing while in possession of inside information. Yet there had been no civil claim during that period and only one criminal prosecution, which was unsuccessful. It seems more likely that the legislation was extraordinarily difficult to police.

It is also clear from the analysis by Stephen Dowling and Conor Feeney of *Fyffes plc v DCC and others* that some questions remain unanswered after that case. On the crucial issue of what constitutes "price sensitive information", the test of what would have influenced "the reasonable investor" was applied by Laffoy J. at first instance, but unanimously rejected by the Supreme Court. However, it was expressly adopted in reg.2 of the Market Abuse Regulations 2005 (the "2005 Regulations"), which replaced Pt V of the Companies Act 1990 under which *Fyffes* was decided. As the writers point out, the wording in the Directive to which the 2005 Regulations purportedly give effect omits the "reasonable investor" expression from the definition. It would seem that a nice problem of interpretation may confront the courts in the future—assuming, of course, that there are any cases to decide. It will be interesting to see how the extensive provisions in the 2005 Regulations designed to prevent market manipulation, which had no equivalent in the replaced legislation, will fare.

While the extent of take-over activity in the Irish stock exchange is obviously limited because of the size of the market, it is nevertheless regulated by two sets of legislation. The Irish Takeover Panel Act 1997 was rendered necessary by the separation of the Irish and London stock exchanges, prior to which take-over activity was controlled on a non-statutory basis by the City Code. In addition, regulations were introduced in 2006 to give effect to an EU directive on take-over bids. Professor Blanaid Clarke explores the underlying principles of the relevant legislation, which ideally should ensure that, in the case of the target company, with which her essay is concerned, the shareholders receive such information and advice as are necessary to enable them to make an informed decision on the offer. It is also the duty of the directors not to do anything which might frustrate the offer. She concludes that both the European and the national regulations in their present form do not go far enough in ensuring that the advice given by the directors is truly independent and objective. Thus, a cardinal feature of corporate governance is not fully present.

Questions of corporate governance also arise in the case of the trustees of Irish pension schemes which are considered by Orla Ormsby in her essay. This has become of acute importance as problems have arisen with many such schemes. Poor investment decisions may have calamitous consequences for the employees, and there is also the danger of fraud as demonstrated in the *Maxwell* case. She draws lessons from the standards which can reasonably be expected from non-executive directors of companies in discussing the levels of expertise and competence which can be required of trustees. In a timely and provocative essay, Stephen Kinsella also argues for a new approach to governance and regulation of Irish financial institutions in the light of the crisis which has engulfed the entire Irish economy.

The final essay by Brian Conroy examines the General Scheme of the new Companies Consolidation and Reform Bill (the "Bill") which was approved by the government in July 2007 and which is expected to become law by 2011. This promises to be the most far-reaching legislation affecting companies since the foundation of the State. It will mark a radical departure from the present structures which, despite many changes over the years, have faithfully adhered to the original English model which treated the public company as the norm and the private company as a variant from that norm, in no way reflecting actual conditions in Ireland. The establishment of the private company limited by shares as the basic type of company, the abolition of the ultra vires doctrine in the case of such companies and the replacement of the memorandum and articles by a single document of incorporation, to mention only some of the major changes proposed, should give us a streamlined and intelligible system specifically tailored to Irish conditions.

It is, of course, the case that the Bill is beginning its necessarily protracted journey on to the Statute Book at a time when conditions could hardly be less favourable to the continuance in business of existing firms, let alone the emergence of new enterprises. However, if, as we all hope, the world emerges from the present recession in a relatively short time scale, as has happened before, the existence in Ireland of a simplified, modern company law code will be essential if we are to take advantage of the recovery.

At the same time, we would be foolish to ignore the more ominous warnings given by some of the contributors to this collection as to the problems facing the global capitalist system. While it is undoubtedly true that no system of regulation can hope to eliminate all the unwise and sometimes unsavoury practices which disfigure free markets, the onus remains on those in government, both at the national and international level, to ensure that our laws go as far as possible in reducing them. In that continuing struggle, as this book makes clear, the courts under our legal system should have a major role to play in ensuring that regulations are applied in a manner which adheres to the spirit, as well as to the letter, of good corporate governance.

RONAN KEANE

CONTRIBUTORS

Editors

Ronan Keane was Chief Justice of Ireland from 2000 to 2004. He was President of the Law Refom Commission from 1987 to 1992. His publications include *The Law of Local Government in the Republic of Ireland*, *Irish Company Law* and *Equity and the Law of Trusts in the Republic of Ireland*. He is an Adjunct Professor of Law in the University of Dublin.

Ailbhe O'Neill is a practising barrister. A graduate of Trinity College and Cambridge University, she has published widely in the Company Law area and lectures Corporate Governance at Trinity College Dublin.

Other Contributors

Dr Thomas B. Courtney is a graduate of NUI Galway (B.A. in 1987 and LL.B. in 1989). Tom qualified as a solicitor in 1992 and worked as in-house counsel and company secretary in the financial services sector for 11 years before returning to private practice to join Arthur Cox as Partner and Head of the Company Compliance and Governance Group which specialises in company law, company secretarial and corporate governance. Tom is the author of *The Law of Private Companies*, 2nd edn (Dublin: Tottel, 2002) and *Mareva Injunctions and Related Interlocutory Orders* (Dublin: Tottel, 1998) and is co-editor with Lyndon MacCann S.C. of *Companies Acts 1963–2006*, 2nd edn (Dublin: Tottel, 2008). In 2004 Tom was awarded the Higher Doctorate in Laws (the LL.D.) from the NUI for his published legal works. Tom was a member of the McDowell Group on *Company Law Compliance and Enforcement* (1998) and was appointed the first Chairman of the *Company Law Review Group* in 1999 when it was established on an ad hoc basis, before it became a statutory group following the passing of the Company Law Enforcement Act 2001. As Chairman of CLRG, Tom brokered the compromise on directors' compliance statements in 2005. The CLRG's proposals to simplify and consolidate company law have been accepted by Government and the Companies Consolidation and Reform Bill is in the process of being finalised. In 2005 he was appointed to the EU Commission's *Advisory Group on Corporate Governance and Company Law*.

Professor Blanaid Clarke, B.C.L., M.B.S. (Banking & Finance), Barrister at Law, Ph.D. is an Associate Professor of Corporate Law in the Law School in University College Dublin where she teaches at both undergraduate and postgraduate levels in Corporate Governance, Takeovers Law and Contract Law. She is a founding member of the Centre for Corporate Governance at University College Dublin and has been involved both at a national and international level in regulating takeovers. Blanaid has published several texts including *Contract Cases and Materials* (co-authored with R. Clark) 4th edn (Dublin: Gill & Macmillan, 2008) and *Takeovers and Mergers Law in Ireland* (Dublin: Roundhall Sweet & Maxwell, 1999). She has produced numerous articles including most recently B. Clarke, "Insider Dealing: Getting Under the Skin of Fyffes Plc v DCC Plc & Others" [2009] 1 *Journal of Business Law* 68–91 and "Takeover Regulation: Through the Regulatory Looking Glass" (2007) *CLPE Research Paper* No. 18, "Articles 9 and 11 of the Takeover Directive" (2004/25).

Irene Lynch Fannon is a graduate of UCD (B.C.L. 1982); Oxford University (B.C.L. 1986, Senior Scholar, Somerville College) and the University of Virginia (Doctor of Juridical Science 1999). She qualified as a solicitor in Ireland in 1985, and subsequently practised in London before becoming an academic lawyer. She has taught Company Law and Employment Law in the Department of Law at UCC since 1987. She was appointed Head of the Department of Law for the period 1999–2002. She was elected Dean of the Faculty of Law 2000–2002. She has published over 60 research pieces (the majority sole authored) including books, articles and chapters both in Ireland and internationally on Company Law, Corporate Insolvency and Employment and Labour Law, most recently in the area of comparative EU-US corporate governance models. Publications include *Corporate Insolvency and Rescue* (with Jane Marshall and Rory O'Ferrall, Butterworths, 1996); *Working within Two Kinds of Capitalism* (Hart Publications, 2003). She is currently interim Head of the College of Business and Law, University College Cork. She is a member of the High Level Group on Business Regulation.

Ciarán O'Kelly is a lecturer in financial architecture and director of the Postgraduate Programme in Corporate Governance and Public Policy, the School of Law, Queen's University Belfast. His research reflects an interest in corporate theory, theories of accountability and the corporate constitution.

Orla Ormsby graduated with a B.C.L. from University College Dublin in 2006 and completed an LL.M. at Trinity College Dublin in 2007. She is currently a trainee solicitor in Arthur Cox.

Stephen Kinsella, Ph.D. is a Junior Lecturer in the Economics Department of the Kemmy Business School, University of Limerick. His interests are in financial economics, corporate governance, Irish public policy, and mathematical economics. He has published a number of papers in these areas.

Stephen Dowling B.L. is a practising barrister specialising in commercial law. He is also author of *The Commercial Court* (Dublin: Thomson Round Hall, 2007).

Conor Feeney B.L. is a practising barrister, specialising in company and commercial law. He also teaches on the company law module of the degree course in the Honorable Society of King's Inns.

Brian Conroy B.L., LL.B. (ling. fr.), LL.M. (Cantab) is a practising barrister with a particular interest in company law. He has also qualified as a Registered Tax Consultant (AITI) and he formerly worked as a senior research assistant for the judges of the Irish courts.

CONTENTS

TABLE OF CASES

IRELAND

ENGLAND AND WALES

NORTHERN IRELAND

UNITED STATES OF AMERICA

AUSTRALIA

NEW ZEALAND

SINGAPORE CASES

TABLE OF LEGISLATION

THE IRISH CONSTITUTION

IRISH STATUTES

IRISH STATUTORY INSTRUMENTS

ENGLAND AND WALES STATUTES

UNITED STATES OF AMERICA STATUTES

AUSTRALIAN STATUTES

NEW ZEALAND STATUTES

SOUTH AFRICAN STATUTES

EUROPEAN UNION DIRECTIVES

Part I

Governance and the Role of the Company Director

LIBRARY
INSTITUTE OF TECHNOLOGY
CARLOW

CHAPTER 1

DIRECTORS' COMPLIANCE STATEMENTS: ATTESTING CORPORATE COMPLIANCE ON A "COMPLY OR EXPLAIN" BASIS

Dr Thomas B. Courtney, Partner, Arthur Cox

1. INTRODUCTION

Section 45 of the Companies (Auditing and Accounting) Act 2003 (the "2003 Act") amended the Companies Act 1990 (the "1990 Act") by inserting two new sections: ss.205E and 205F. The effect of this amendment to the 1990 Act is that there is a provision of Irish Company Law that requires the directors of certain companies to publicly attest their compliance with Company Law, Tax Law and certain other relevant enactments. Fortunately for Ireland Inc, s.45 has not been commenced and will not be commenced. Following a review of its effects by the Company Law Review Group ("CLRG") the Government accepted the recommendations in its Report[1] and decided to repeal s.45 and replace it with a more workable and less draconian provision, referred to by the CLRG in its Report as Section X.

In this essay, Directors' Compliance Statements ("DCS") are considered under the following headings:

- The Origins of a Directors' Compliance Statement
- Section 45 of the Companies (Auditing and Accounting) Act 2003
- The Identification of Problems with s.45
- The CLRG's Review of s.45
- Section X – The CLRG's Compromise Proposal
- The Future for Compliance Statements

2. THE ORIGINS OF A DIRECTORS' COMPLIANCE STATEMENT

(a) The Comptroller and Auditor General's Report

The origins of the DCS lie in the July 1999 Report of the Comptroller and Auditor General ("C&AG") into the administration of deposit interest retention

[1] *Report on Directors' Compliance Statements 2005*, Government Publications.

tax (DIRT) which was undertaken at the behest of the Public Accounts Committee of Dáil Éireann. That Report found that the evasion of DIRT by taxpayers was widespread, that it was facilitated by credit institutions and that the relevant State Authorities were well aware of the problem.

(b) The Public Accounts Committee's Report

The Public Accounts Committee (PAC) then issued its own Report in December 1999 which was based on the C&AG's Report but also relied upon oral evidence given to the PAC in Autumn 1999. In its Report the PAC found that the problem of DIRT evasion was a financial industry-wide phenomenon and that there were a number of serious defects and weaknesses in relation to the statutory external audit function which contributed to the continuance of, in the lingo of the time, bogus non-resident accounts. The PAC was critical not only of financial institutions and auditors, but also of the inaction of the Department of Finance, the Revenue Commissioners and the Central Bank. The PAC Report concluded that the Department of Enterprise, Trade and Employment should establish a review group to review identified key issues relating to the regulation and practice of auditing.

(c) The Review Group on Auditing's Report

In response to the PAC Report's call, the Tanaiste and then Minister for Enterprise, Trade and Employment, Ms Mary Harney TD, established an ad hoc review group called the Review Group on Auditing ("RGA"). The RGA met from February to June 2000 and published its report in July 2000.

The Report of the RGA contained 80 recommendations dealing with issues of self-regulation of the accountancy bodies, auditors' independence, the auditing of financial institutions and the compliance of auditors and company directors with statutory provisions. For present purposes, it is Recommendation 14.1, which recommended the introduction of a directors' compliance statement with which we are concerned. Recommendation 14.1 provided:

> "Directors of a company should be required to report on an annual basis to the shareholders on the company's compliance with its obligations under company law, taxation law or other relevant statutory or regulatory requirements. The report should confirm that any instances of non-compliance have been reported to the relevant regulatory authority and that in all other respects the company has complied with its obligations under company law, taxation law and other relevant statutory or regulatory requirements. The report should be appended to the annual financial statements."[2]

[2] *The Report of the Review Group on Auditing*, July 2000, at p.218.

The RGA were careful to note that detailed guidance on the application of this Recommendation would be required and that all relevant parties should be consulted to identify regulations and administrative provisions considered to be relevant in advance of enactment of legislation. The RGA also recommended[3] that companies' external auditors should also be required to opine on the reasonableness of the directors' compliance report.

(d) The Company Law Review Group's First Report

Independent of the establishment of the RGA, on December 8, 1999, the CLRG was established on an administrative basis.[4] The CLRG was aware of the establishment of a dedicated review body on auditing and believed that the most appropriate approach for it to take was to offer its views on the RGA's recommendations as part of the consultation process which took place following the publication of the RGA's Report. Mindful of its brief to simplify company law, the CLRG in its First Report,[5] expressed concern that small companies, especially those exempt from the audit requirement should not be imposed upon or unduly burdened by the legislation that would result from the RGA's Report, having particular regard to Recommendation 14.1.[6]

[3] *The Report of the Review Group on Auditing,* July 2000, Recommendation 14.2 at p.218.

[4] Following the enactment of the Company Law Enforcement Act 2001, the CLRG was established on a statutory basis pursuant to s.67 of that Act.

[5] Company Law Review Group, First Report, December 31, 2001, published on February 28, 2002.

[6] The CLRG's observations were: "With regard to recommendations 14.1 and 14.2 it is important to achieve a sensible and operable form of compliance. In particular, the emphasis ought to be on the identification for reporting purposes of non-compliance that is both material in nature and serious in form. Proposed offences specified in the Company Law Enforcement Bill 2000, the Criminal Justice (Theft and Fraud) Bill 2000 and to be included in the Bill which will give effect to the Review Group on Auditing were noted. Penalties and procedures should be consistent across all three Bills. Given potential 'vast range of offences' there is a case for spelling out a limited number of specified serious offences which would give rise to the disclosure obligation. An even more limited number could be specified for small and medium enterprises. It may be useful to ask a small task force to examine the possible interaction between the three Bills and possibilities for a targeted approach to reporting requirements in the interest of effective and coherent regulation. In general, the Company Law Review Group considered that company law and taxation were the appropriate areas and the only areas on which companies should report. Any reporting requirements for financial institutions should be addressed as set out in Chapter 15 of the Report of the Review Group on Auditing, which basically establishes a protocol for reporting. Reporting should cover the period of the annual report. The reporting obligation should be at the level of the group of companies rather than on each subsidiary in tandem with audit committee obligations. It might be appropriate to attain the desired ends of Chapter 14 through Turnbull-style guidelines on corporate controls. It was also noted that disclosure to shareholders could be damaging to company profitability and might affect the raising of capital abroad. The issue was raised as to whether reporting to members should be done only if the Director of Corporate Enforcement or other regulator was not notified of non-compliance. It was noted that the Review Group on Auditing did not recommend an exemption from this

Eventually, legislation was prepared to give effect to the RGA's recommendations and this resulted in the enactment of the Companies (Auditing and Accounting) Act 2003.

3. Section 45 of the Companies (Auditing and Accounting) Act 2003

Section 45 of the Companies (Auditing and Accounting) Act 2003 amends the Companies Act 1990 by the insertion of two new sections: ss.205E and 205F. The full text of s.45 is set out in *Appendix 1*.

The rationale for a Directors' Compliance Statement (DCS) is to encourage companies to be compliant by fostering a culture of compliance. Section 45 does not impose any new primary obligations on companies; rather it is a compliance-verification measure, intended to encourage companies to demonstrate their commitment to obeying the laws to which they are already subject. The key features of s.45 are:

Scope – Companies that would be affected	Section 45 applies to: • Public limited companies (whether listed or unlisted); and • Private companies limited by shares which have a balance sheet total above €7,618,428 or turnover in excess of €15,236,856. It was also proposed that securitisation special purpose vehicles were to be excluded.
Contents of DCS – "Relevant Obligations" which DCS must address	Section 45 requires directors of companies in scope to opine on their companies' compliance with three separate *limbs*: a) The Companies Acts; b) Tax Law (as defined – see *Appendix 1*); and c) Any other enactments that provide a legal framework within which the company operates and that may materially affect the company's financial statements.

requirement for small or medium sized companies or for companies exempt from audit requirements. It is suggested that companies exempt from audits should be exempt from these reporting requirements and indeed that consideration be given to excluding all SMEs from this provision. In the event that SMEs are not excluded consideration should be given to allowing directors in these companies to delegate reporting obligations to a nominated and appropriately qualified individual acting under the supervision of a specified director (Section 203(2) of the 1990 Act may provide something of a precedent)".

Contents of DCS – The extent of the prescribed requirements regarding the Compliance Policy Statement	Companies in scope must have a *Compliance Policy Statement* which must contain the following information concerning the company: a) its policies respecting compliance with its relevant obligations; b) its internal financial and other procedures for securing compliance with its relevant obligations; and c) its arrangements for implementing and reviewing the effectiveness of the policies and procedures referred to in paragraphs (a) and (b). Moreover, the *Compliance Policy Statement* must: a) be in writing; b) be submitted for approval by the board of directors; c) at least once in every three-year period following its approval by the board, be reviewed and, if necessary, revised by the directors; and d) be included in the directors' report under s.158 of the Principal Act.
Contents of DCS – The extent of the prescribed requirements regarding the Annual Compliance Statement	The directors of companies in scope must also include in the directors' annual report, an *Annual Compliance Statement*: a) acknowledging that they are responsible for securing the company's compliance with its relevant obligations; b) confirming that the company has internal financial and other procedures in place that are designed to secure compliance with its relevant obligations and, if this is not the case, specifying the reasons; and c) confirming that the directors have reviewed the effectiveness of the procedures referred to in paragraph (b) during the financial year to which the report relates, and, if this is not the case, specifying the reasons.

Verification of DCS	The auditor of a company in scope must undertake *an annual review* of: a) the directors' compliance policy statement; and b) the directors' annual compliance statement to determine whether, in the auditor's opinion, each statement is fair and reasonable having regard to information obtained by the auditor, or by an affiliate of the auditor, in the course of and by virtue of having carried out audit work, audit-related work or non-audit work for the company. In addition, the auditor must: (a) include in the auditor's report appended to the company's annual accounts a report on, and the conclusions of, the review undertaken under subs.(1); and (b) where any statement reviewed under subs.(1) is not, in the auditor's opinion, fair and reasonable— (i) make a report to that effect to the directors, and (ii) include that report in the auditor's report appended to the annual accounts. And, where in the auditor's opinion, the directors have failed: a) to prepare, or to cause to be prepared, a directors' compliance statement as required by s.205E(3) and (4)(*a*) to (*c*); b) to include a directors' compliance statement in the directors' report as required by s.205E(4)(*d*); or c) to comply with s.205E(5) and (6), the auditor shall report that opinion and the reasons for forming that opinion to the Director of Corporate Enforcement.

4. The Identification of Problems with s.45

Before the enactment of s.45, serious concerns had been raised regarding its implications for Irish business. The Bill, as initiated, was even more draconian than s.45 as enacted and it is worthwhile remembering that it was once provided that, except for instances of non-compliance of a minor or otherwise immaterial nature, the directors of a company in scope would have been obliged to state whether they are of the opinion that "the company has complied with its relevant obligations in that financial year". Ultimately, the rationale underpinning the privilege against self-incrimination prevailed and this aspect of s.45 was dropped.

After the enactment of s.45 it was the ODCE that first tried to bottom-out the requirements on companies in its Consultation Paper[7] entitled *Guidance on the Obligation of Company Directors to Prepare Compliance Policy and Annual Compliance Statements under the Companies (Auditing and Accounting) Act 2003*. A large number of organisations and individuals responded to that Consultation Paper and after submissions closed on September 30, 2004, the ODCE set about preparing a revised guidance paper. On December 16, 2004, the ODCE published its *Revised Guidance on the Directors' Compliance Statements to be Prepared under the Companies Acts*. This document, which ran to over 40 pages, was particularly useful in highlighting the degree of prescription involved in s.45. At the time the revised guidance was issued, the intention was to allow directors and others who would be affected by its provisions to continue to prepare for the commencement of s.45.

Despite these preparations for commencement, the concerns over the effects of s.45 on Irish businesses continued to grow and the call for a full substantial review and regulatory impact analysis became louder. The criticism of s.45 included:

1. It was neither proportionate nor appropriate to the achievement of its objectives having regard to the potential cost and other burdens it would place on Irish companies;
2. The circumstances that gave rise to the original recommendation of the RGA had changed considerably through the enactment of many different new laws and the establishment of new institutions so that a DCS would be excessive;
3. Such a measure would put Ireland out of step with comparator jurisdictions, the rest of the EU and international corporate governance best practice;
4. Ireland's competitiveness would be seriously compromised by such a measure which would discourage foreign direct investment and encourage companies to incorporate in other jurisdictions;
5. The legislation was unduly prescriptive; and
6. Good people would not go forward as non-executive directors on account of the burdens imposed by the DCS.

[7] ODCE Consultation Paper C/2004/1.

The myriad criticisms of s.45 can be seen in the many submissions received by the CLRG and which are summarised in Ch.6 of its report.

5. The CLRG's Review of s.45

On April 21, 2005 the Minister for Commerce and Trade, Mr Michael Ahern TD, referred the Directors' Compliance Statement required by s.45 of the Companies (Auditing and Accounting) Act 2003 to the CLRG for its views on the proportionality, efficacy and appropriateness of its requirements having regard to the following factors:

- Ensuring the integrity of the corporation's accounting and financial reporting systems, including the independent audit and that appropriate systems of control are in place, in particular, systems for risk management, financial and operational control and compliance with the law and relevant standards;
- The scope of application and the requirements of the proposed Directors' Compliance Statement;
- Potential cost issues;
- Potential competitiveness issues; and
- Potential implementation issues.

The CLRG reported back to the Minister in July 2005 and in November 2005 the Government accepted the CLRG's recommendation that, if a decision was taken by the Minister to have some form of compliance-verification measure, then it should be in the form set out in Section X in the CLRG's Report.

The CLRG had been requested to produce a report consistent with the goal of "making markets and regulation work better" and to conduct its analysis and structure its report consistent with the model of regulatory impact analysis developed by the Working Group on Regulatory Impact Analysis. In the period from April to the end of July 2005, the CLRG met seven times in steering group and four times in full plenary session. Outside of these meetings, there were numerous other meetings of the Chairman and the Secretariat with members and others in analysing and considering the facts and submissions that were made to the CLRG. The CLRG canvassed extensively and widely the views of all interested parties.

The CLRG carried out a risk analysis of s.45 and in particular the options of: leaving s.45 as enacted; repealing s.45 in its entirety and mitigating the obligations imposed by s.45. The CLRG also carried out a Screening Regulatory Impact Analysis (see Appendix 2) and the results of that RIA are detailed in Ch.9 of the CLRG's Report. In essence, the CLRG found that whilst s.45 was likely to give rise to a number of intangible benefits in terms of encouraging companies to be compliant and in *proving* how compliant they were, these positive results were greatly outweighed by serious negative and disproportional outcomes regarding costs and affecting national competitiveness. The CLRG also found that much of the policy underlying the enactment of s.45 was and would continue to be achieved by a plethora of new legislation and new agencies that had been enacted/established since the RGA's original recommendation for a DCS.

The CLRG considered the risks associated with commencing s.45 (as enacted) as against the risks of either repealing s.45 or modifying s.45 and concluded that the risks associated with not repealing or modifying s.45[8] greatly outweighed, in terms of seriousness, the risks associated with not commencing s.45.[9] The CLRG advanced the following reasons for so concluding:

1. The existing company law compliance regime currently in force would not be reduced or lessened: companies and their directors still had the same legal obligations to ensure compliance with legislative enactments;
2. There was a clear and imminent risk that the commencement of s.45 would result in a substantial cost to Irish companies in scope;
3. There was a clear and imminent risk that investment in the Irish economy through Irish registered companies would be curtailed;
4. There was a clear and imminent risk that companies that were the subject of Irish regulation would migrate to other EU or non-EU countries;
5. Following on from the previous reason, there was a clear and imminent risk that fewer companies would be answerable to the Irish agencies of enforcement, registration and supervision;
6. With the exception of additional embedding of a culture of compliance, there was no other material tangible benefit arising from the commencement of s.45;
7. There was no evidence to suggest that a stand, by Ireland, on corporate compliance that would be so far-reaching and apart from EU and international trends, would be accepted by the international community and it was likely that such would operate to encourage foreign companies to incorporate in an alternative jurisdiction; and
8. The Screening RIA in Ch.9 supported the foregoing conclusions.

[8] The risks of not repealing/modifying s.45 were identified as being: 1. There will be substantial additional costs to Irish registered companies in scope. 2. Ireland may lose investment and companies may not register in Ireland because they are or are perceived as being at a disadvantage vis-à-vis other countries and especially EU MS in terms of their regulatory requirements. This could seriously impact on Ireland as FDI location. 3. There is likely to be dysfunctional behaviour that may result in companies with present or prospective operations in Ireland, either leaving Ireland and incorporating elsewhere *or* not incorporating here de novo. 4. The existing enhanced corporate compliance regime (post-2001) and now subsisting in Ireland will be abandoned by existing and new entrants for other EU jurisdictions with less prescriptive and stringent regimes—outside the remit of ODCE and/or CRO—with a resulting non-compliance. 5. Listing on the ISE will involve compliance verification requirements significantly more onerous than those in other jurisdictions and are likely to cause companies to abandon the ISE.

[9] The risks of not commencing s.45 were identified as being: 1. Companies' legal obligations under company law and tax law will continue as is, without anything additional to promote or

By a majority of 11 out of 19 voting members, the CLRG recommended that the Government should repeal s.45 on the understanding that it was appropriate to await international, and especially European Union, developments before enacting such a uniquely prescriptive and stringent Irish compliance-verification regime. The majority's reasons for so recommending were:

1. There had been significant changes to company law and its regulation since the RGA first recommended the DCS which had diminished if not entirely obviated the need for such a belt-and-braces compliance measure;
2. There would be significant additional cost for companies on account of the very prescriptive nature of s.45 in the nature of internal procedure development, internal and external legal advice and the involvement of companies' auditors. Moreover, because of the diminished necessity for such a heavy-hand, the expenditure of such cost could not be objectively justified;
3. The effect of the increased costs on Irish companies in scope would be to reduce their competitiveness and it was likely to give rise to increased costs for the consumers of their goods and services;
4. Ireland would become less competitive and would not be as desirable a place for foreign companies to locate;
5. It was prudent to await EU and international developments and to follow these, as opposed to lead the way in circumstances where Ireland would be isolated and susceptible to being considered to be a less attractive location for foreign companies and where indigenous companies would have their cost base increased to the detriment of consumers, shareholders and employees.
6. The Screening RIA analysis contained in Ch.9 supported the foregoing reasoning.

6. Section x – The CLRG's Compromise Proposal

Although the CLRG recommended the repeal and non-replacement of s.45, it was necessary to be pragmatic and to recognise that a *realpolitik* had developed around the concept of a Directors' Compliance Statement. It could not be assumed that a bald recommendation to abolish s.45 without replacement would be acted upon by the Minister or Government, particularly when the Minister and Taoiseach had indicated in public that the Government was committed to some form of DCS. It was in these circumstances that the CLRG went on by an

encourage compliance therewith. 2. The emphasis remains on punitive sanction and enforcement rather than prevention of wrongdoing or negligence. 3. The proposed role of the auditor as "watchdog" of compliance procedures and practices is not fulfilled and no independent verification of compliance will be provided. 4. The tax compliance of companies is not subject to verification. 5. The use of company law to focus compliance with other legislation, e.g. Health and Safety and environmental law will be abandoned.

even stronger majority of 16 out of 19 voting members to recommend a form of compromise DCS (Section X) if the Minister was determined to retain a corporate compliance-verification regime.

The majority who supported the compromise in Section X identified the following six problems with s.45 as enacted:

1. The scope of the DCS, i.e. the number of companies to which s.45 was applicable;
2. The extensive definition of "relevant obligations";
3. The absence of a sufficiently prominent materiality requirement;
4. The prescriptive requirements for a Compliance Policy Statement and an Annual Statement in companies' Directors' Reports;
5. The involvement of companies' auditors; and
6. The immediacy of the implementation of any form of a DCS.

The CLRG's five recommendations, set out below, seek to address the problems associated with s.45:

(a) "1. The companies in-scope for the DCS should remain as is, with the qualification that the two monetary requirements for the test for the inclusion of large private companies should be increased in line with the CLRG's recommended limits for a company to be a large private company for accounting purposes i.e. a balance sheet of over €12,500,000 and a turnover of €25,000,000. In addition, the provision should be made, expressly, conjunctive so that for a large private company to be 'in scope' it must satisfy both monetary requirements."

It will be seen that it remains the case that the only companies that will be in scope for Section X will continue to be PLCs and certain large private companies. The following companies will continue to be outside the scope of Section X: all guarantee companies, all unlimited companies, private companies with balance sheet totals and turnover below the thresholds designated at subs.(6) of Section X, investment companies as defined in Pt XIII of the Companies Act 1990 and securitisation special purpose vehicles (this latter class of companies will need to be specified by the Minister but it is understood by the writer that the decision to exempt them has been taken in principle).

The most significant change recommended by the CLRG in terms of scope, is the increase in the monetary thresholds applicable to private companies that will be within or without scope. So it is provided in Section X that the monetary thresholds for determining whether a private company is in scope will be those thresholds that apply in determining whether a company qualifies as a large private company for the purposes of the accounting requirements. Accordingly, for a private company to be in-scope, it must have a balance sheet in excess of €12,500,000 *and* a turnover in excess of €25,000,000.

(b) "2. The definition of 'relevant obligations' should be amended by the removal of the 'third limb' and by introducing a degree of materiality by defining company law obligations as those being indictable offences and by introducing a materiality test for tax law."

The CLRG considered that it was both desirable and reasonable to include compliance with the Companies Acts as a "relevant obligation" for the purposes of the DCS. It was found, however, that whilst it seemed not to have been the intention to require a detailed consideration of every single provision of the Companies Acts, in practice, this was how it had been interpreted. For that reason the CLRG recommended the introduction of a materiality proviso which limits a company's "relevant obligations" to those provisions of the Companies Acts, the contravention of which gives rise to an indictable offence. This formulation has the advantage of relative certainty because lists of indictable offences under the Companies Acts have been already published by the ODCE since company auditors were obliged to report indictable offences to the ODCE.

Although recommending, on balance, to retain the second limb—tax law—the CLRG considered that some form of materiality requirement should be introduced. Accordingly, it was recommended that the reference to "relevant obligations" itself was amenable to a materiality test which should be applied in the operative part of the new section (see Section X(3) and (4) in Appendix 3). What will be "material" will clearly vary from company to company.

More significantly, the CLRG recommended the repeal of the so-called "third limb" of the definition of "relevant obligations" contained in s.45. The rationale for this was the high cost of verifying compliance with "any other enactments that provide a legal framework within which the company operates and that may materially affect the company's financial statements." Not only was such a formulation considered to be too vague, but it was considered inappropriate to use company law to police laws and regulations applicable generally to all persons, be they companies or other bodies corporate such as cooperatives or, indeed, to natural persons. The CLRG also concluded that the exclusion of the third limb from its proposed new DCS would not adversely affect the completeness or value of companies' financial statements and noted that no other jurisdiction required companies to speculate on contingent eventualities that may or may not affect their financial statements. All in all, to require Irish companies to so speculate was considered to be inappropriate and disproportional to the aims of a DCS.

(c) "3. The removal of the prescription surrounding companies' 'Compliance Policy Statements' and the mitigation of the representations that must be made in the Annual Statement on Compliance in Directors' Reports and the requirement that appropriate representations are expressed to be made in the 'directors' opinion', coupled with a materiality requirement, all on a comply or explain basis."

The very high cost of *evidencing* or *proving* compliance was probably the most significant factor in the CLRG's reasoning that s.45 should be repealed entirely or replaced by a less onerous provision. CLRG was satisfied that one of the chief factors giving rise to those costs was the specificity and prescription surrounding the requirement to have a compliance policy statement and "procedures" designed to ensure compliance with a company's "relevant obligations".

The CLRG recommended that the requirement to have and the prescription surrounding compliance policy statements should be removed and it recommended the application of a statutory "comply or explain" approach to the DCS. Instead of the regime created by s.45, CLRG proposed that the directors of each company that is in scope must, in their annual Directors' Report:

- acknowledge that they are responsible for securing the company's compliance with its relevant obligations; and
- confirm that the company has in place a compliance policy statement, considered by the directors to be appropriate for that particular company or, if the company does not have a compliance policy statement, explain why not; and
- confirm that the company has in place, appropriate arrangements or structures that are, in the directors' opinion, designed to secure material compliance with its relevant obligations, which arrangements or structures may (at the discretion of the directors) include the company's reliance upon internal and or external advisors who have thc requisite knowledge and experience to advise the company on compliance with its relevant obligations); and, if this is not the case, explaining why not, and
- confirm that the company's arrangements or structures last referred to have been reviewed in that financial year and if not, explain why not.

The CLRG said that it believed that its suggested wording would allow companies sufficient flexibility in how they approach compliance verification through the use of words such as "in the directors' opinion" and the express statutory acknowledgement that directors may rely upon internal and external advisors. CLRG went on to identify another of the other primary cost drivers in s.45, namely the use of the word "procedures" since it is highly prescriptive and its ordinary dictionary meaning requires that companies institutionalise an "established or official way of doing something" and refers to "a series of actions conducted in a *certain order or manner*".[10] It was said that it was "unsurprising, therefore, that companies have received legal advice that a forensic examination of their 'relevant obligations' is required and that prescriptive procedures are demanded by 45/2003."

The CLRG went on to say that its use of the words "appropriate arrangements or structures" had been deliberately chosen to permit companies maximum

[10] *Concise Oxford English Dictionary*, 10th edn (Oxford: Oxford University Press, 2002), p.1139.

flexibility in demonstrating their commitment to securing compliance with their relevant obligations if they chose to do so and it was opined that companies that currently adhere to Turnbull Guidance may rely upon that fact in demonstrating their commitment to securing compliance.

Of particular importance here is the fact that CLRG recommended, and the Government accepted, the appropriateness of a "comply or explain" regime to Directors' Compliance Statements. The "comply or explain" concept is relatively new to Irish statutory law, its first appearance in Irish company law being in the context of audit committees in large private companies, introduced by the Companies (Auditing and Accounting) Act 2003.[11] The requirement that a company either "complies or explains" is one which is found in many codes on Corporate Governance throughout the world. In essence, it is designed to facilitate a debate between a company (represented by its directors) and the company's shareholders and nobody else. After all, the company's shareholders are its owners and the addressees of the Directors' Report.

This is indeed the position that has been adopted by the EU Commission's European Corporate Governance Forum in its statement on the "comply-or-explain" principle, dated February 22, 2006 and released on March 6, 2006 (see Appendix 4). At point 3 of its statement, and in the context of the proposed *EU Corporate Governance Statement*, it is said that the Forum:

> "… [I]nclines to the view that regulatory authorities should limit their role to checking the existence of the statement, and to reacting to blatant mis-representation of facts. They should not try and second-guess the judgement of the board(s) or the value of its/ their explanations. This is a matter for the company's shareholders.
>
> Similarly, the auditors should not be supposed to evaluate the judgement of the board(s), but may within their duties be called upon to review some element of facts contained in the statement".

It is significant that in the accompanying press release Internal Market and Services Commissioner Charlie McCreevy is reported as having said:

> "The principle of 'comply or explain' is a central element of EU corporate governance. So it is important to have a common understanding of the principle's scope and of the conditions that need to be put in place for it to work effectively. I welcome the Forum's findings, which will help everyone to approach these questions in the right way."[12]

(d) "4. The removal of the requirement that a company's auditors must specifically opine on the reasonableness or otherwise of the proposed revised Annual Statement on Compliance in Directors' Reports."

[11] See s.205B(4) of the Companies Act 1990, inserted by s.42 of the 2003 Act.
[12] See IP/06/269.

The CLRG recommended and the Government accepted that companies' auditors should not be required to opine on the reasonableness or otherwise of the proposed annual compliance statement in the Directors' Report. It should be noted that companies' auditors are not precluded from commenting upon the proposed annual compliance statement in Section X because auditors will continue to have responsibility to consider it under both company law and auditing standards:

- "*company law*: as the Statement is to be included in the Directors' Report, it will fall within the ambit of the auditor's obligation under section 15 of the Companies (Amendment) Act 1986 to consider whether the contents of a Directors' Report is consistent with the audited financial accounts and to report their opinion on that matter. Any inconsistency that remains unresolved by the directors will result in a qualification of that opinion;
- *auditing standards*: ISA (UK and Ireland) 720 requires auditors to read all other information accompanying audited accounts and to take action to seek correction of any material misstatement that they consider exists in that information. If the directors do not make appropriate amendments, the ISA requires them to consider highlighting the issue in their report on the financial accounts."

(e) "5. The non-commencement of Section 45 and the enactment of the Review Group's proposed alternative Annual Statement on Compliance as part of the *Companies Bill*, 2006, the heads of which the Review Group is in the process of finalising for submission to the Minister."

The CLRG's final recommendation was that Section X should become a provision in what will be the Companies Bill and not commenced before this for the sensible reason that the new Bill will introduce sweeping changes to Irish company law and so the new compliance-verification regime should be commenced contemporaneously. Whereas the original aspiration that the Bill would be published in 2006 has not been achieved, drafting of the Bill, which will be the largest in the history of the State, is at an advanced stage.

7. The Future for Compliance Statements

The times in which we live are characterised by an aversion to risk. When things go wrong the immediate reaction is to attempt to apportion blame and to seek legislative changes to ensure that "this kind of thing cannot happen again". There are limits to what can be legislated for and, indeed, as the CLRG's Report bears out, there is a real risk that disproportionate and burdensome legislation can itself become the problem. It is likely that the calls for a directors' compliance statement which arose from the indignation caused by the evasion of DIRT will get a second wind following the ongoing revelations concerning governance in the banking sector. It is thought, however, that the conclusions reached by the CLRG in 2005 remain as valid today as they were when accepted by the Government in 2005 and that when enacted Section X will provide a proportionate compliance verification measure.

Appendix 1

"205E.—(1) In this section—

'amount of turnover' and 'balance sheet total' have the same meanings as in section 8 of the Companies (Amendment) Act 1986;

'relevant obligations', in relation to a company, means the company's obligations under—

(a) the Companies Acts,
(b) tax law, and
(c) any other enactments that provide a legal framework within which the company operates and that may materially affect the company's financial statements;

'tax law' means—

(a) the Customs Acts,
(b) the statutes relating to the duties of excise and to the management of those duties,
(c) the Tax Acts,
(d) the Capital Gains Tax Acts,
(e) the Value-Added Tax Act 1972 and the enactments amending or extending that Act,
(f) the Capital Acquisitions Tax Act 1976 and the enactments amending or extending that Act,
(g) the statutes relating to stamp duty and to the management of that duty, and
(h) any instruments made under an enactment referred to in any of paragraphs (a) to (g) or made under any other enactment and relating to tax.

(2) This section applies to—

(a) a public limited company (whether listed or unlisted), and
(b) a private company limited by shares,

but it does not apply to a company referred to in paragraph (a) or (b) that is of a class exempted under section 48(1)(j) of the Act of 2003 from this section or to a company referred to in paragraph (b) while that company qualifies for an exemption under subsection (9).

(3) The directors of a company to which this section applies shall, as soon as possible after the commencement of this section or after this section becomes applicable to the company, prepare or cause to be prepared a directors' compliance statement containing the following information concerning the company:

(a) its policies respecting compliance with its relevant obligations;
(b) its internal financial and other procedures for securing compliance with its relevant obligations;
(c) its arrangements for implementing and reviewing the effectiveness of the policies and procedures referred to in paragraphs (a) and (b).

(4) The directors' compliance statement (including any revisions) must—

(a) be in writing,
(b) be submitted for approval by the board of directors,
(c) at least once in every 3 year period following its approval by the board, be reviewed and, if necessary, revised by the directors, and
(d) be included in the directors' report under section 158 of the Principal Act.

(5) The directors of a company to which this section applies shall also include in their report under section 158 of the Principal Act a statement—

(a) acknowledging that they are responsible for securing the company's compliance with its relevant obligations,
(b) confirming that the company has internal financial and other procedures in place that are designed to secure compliance with its relevant obligations, and, if this is not the case, specifying the reasons, and
(c) confirming that the directors have reviewed the effectiveness of the procedures referred to in paragraph (b) during the financial year to which the report relates, and, if this is not the case, specifying the reasons.

(6) In addition, the directors of a company to which this section applies shall in the statement required under subsection (5)—

(a) specify whether, based on the procedures referred to in that subsection and their review of those procedures, they are of the opinion that they used all reasonable endeavours to secure the company's compliance with its relevant obligations in the financial year to which the annual report relates, and
(b) if they are not of that opinion, specify the reasons.

(7) For the purposes of this section, a company's internal financial and other procedures are considered to be designed to secure compliance with its relevant obligations and to be effective for that purpose if they provide a reasonable assurance of compliance in all material respects with those obligations.

(8) Where the directors of a company to which this section applies fail—

(a) to prepare, or to cause to be prepared, a directors' compliance statement as required by subsections (3) and (4)(a) to (c),
(b) to include a directors' compliance statement in the directors' report as required by subsection (4)(d), or
(c) to comply with subsections (5) and (6),

each director to whom the failure is attributable is guilty of an offence.

(9) A private company limited by shares qualifies for an exemption from this section in respect of any financial year of the company if—

(a) its balance sheet total for the year does not exceed—
   (i) €7,618,428, or
   (ii) if an amount is prescribed under section 48(1)(l) of the Act of 2003 for the purpose of this provision, the prescribed amount, and
(b) the amount of its turnover for the year does not exceed—
   (i) €15,236,856, or
   (ii) if an amount is prescribed under section 48(1)(l) of the Act of 2003 for the purpose of this provision, the prescribed amount.

205F.—(1) The auditor of a company to which section 205E applies shall undertake an annual review of—

(a) the directors' compliance statement under subsections (3) and (4) of that section, and
(b) the directors' statement under subsections (5) and (6) of that section, to determine whether, in the auditor's opinion, each statement is fair and reasonable having regard to information obtained by the auditor, or by an affiliate of the auditor within the meaning of section 205D, in the course of and by virtue of having carried out audit work, audit-related work or non-audit work for the company.

(2) The auditor shall—

(a) include in the auditor's report appended to the company's annual accounts a report on, and the conclusions of, the review undertaken under subsection (1), and
(b) where any statement reviewed under subsection (1) is not, in the auditor's opinion, fair and reasonable—

(i) make a report to that effect to the directors, and
(ii) include that report in the auditor's report appended to the annual accounts.

(3) Where, in the auditor's opinion, the directors have failed—

(a) to prepare, or to cause to be prepared, a directors' compliance statement as required by section 205E(3) and (4)(a) to (c),
(b) to include a directors' compliance statement in the directors' report as required by section 205E(4)(d), or
(c) to comply with section 205E(5) and (6),

the auditor shall report that opinion and the reasons for forming that opinion to the Director of Corporate Enforcement.

(4) Section 194(6) applies, with the necessary modifications, in relation to an auditor's compliance with an obligation imposed on him by or under this section as it applies in relation to an obligation imposed by or under section 194.

(5) A person who contravenes this section is guilty of an offence."

Appendix 2

"Screening RIA

1. Description of policy context, objectives and options (e.g. different forms of regulation.
(i) A brief description of the policy context.
(ii) An explicit statement of the objectives that are being pursued.
(iii) An identification of the various policy options or choices which are under consideration.

2. Identification of costs, benefits and other impacts of any options which are being considered.
(i) Identification of likely costs, an estimation of their magnitude and to whom they fall.
(ii) A description of expected benefits and where these will fall.
(iii) Verification that there will not be disproportionately negative impacts on:
(a) national competitiveness;
(b) the socially excluded or vulnerable groups;
(c) the environment

and that the regulations do not:
(d) involve a significant policy change in an economic market;
(e) impinge disproportionately on the rights of citizens;
(f) impost a disproportionate compliance burden on third parties

64285

and other criteria to be decided from time to time by Government.

(iv) Summary of costs, benefits and impacts of each option identified in 1. identifying preferred option where appropriate.

3. Consultation

Summary of the views of any key stakeholders consulted – which must include any relevant consumer interests and other Government Departments.

4. Enforcement and Compliance

Brief Description of how enforcement and compliance will be achieved.

5. Review

Identify mechanisms for review and specify indicators which would demonstrate the success of the policy proposal."

Appendix 3

"Section X.—(1) In this section—

'amount of turnover' and 'balance sheet total' have the same meanings as in section 8 of Companies (Amendment) Act 1986;

'relevant obligations', in relation to a company, means the company's obligations under—

(*a*) the Companies Acts, where the failure to comply with any such obligation is an indictable offence under the Companies Acts, and

(*b*) tax law,

'tax law' means—

(*a*) the Customs Acts,

(*b*) the statutes relating to the duties of excise and to the management of those duties,

(*c*) the Tax Acts,

(*d*) the Capital Gains Tax Acts,

(*e*) the Value-Added Tax Act 1972 and the enactments amending or extending that Act,

(*f*) the Capital Acquisitions Tax Act 1976 and the enactments amending or extending that Act,

(*g*) the statutes relating to stamp duty and to the management of that duty, and

(*h*) any instruments made under an enactment referred to in any of paragraphs (*a*)to (*g*) or made under any other enactment and relating to tax.

(2) This section applies to—

(*a*) a public limited company (whether listed or unlisted), and

(*b*) a private company limited by shares, but it does not apply to a company referred to in paragraph (*a*) or (*b*) that is of a class exempted under *section 48(1)(j)* of the *Act of 2003* from this section or to a company referred to in paragraph (*b*) while that company qualifies for an exemption under subsection (6).

(3) The directors of a company to which this section applies shall also include in their report under section 158 of the Principal Act a statement—

(*a*) acknowledging that they are responsible for securing the company's compliance with its relevant obligations, and

(*b*) confirming that the company has in place a compliance policy statement that is, in the opinion of the directors, appropriate for the company; and, if this is not the case, specifying the reasons, and

(*c*) confirming that the company has in place, appropriate arrangements or structures that are, in the opinion of the directors, designed to secure material compliance with its relevant obligations, which arrangements or structures may (at the discretion of the directors) include the company's reliance upon internal and or external advisors who appear to the directors to have the requisite knowledge and experience to advise the company on compliance with its relevant obligations); and, if this is not the case, specifying the reasons, and

(*d*) confirming that the company's arrangements or structures referred to in paragraph (*c*), have been reviewed during the financial year to which the report relates, and, if this is not the case, specifying the reasons.

(4) For the purposes of this section, a company's arrangements or structures are considered to be designed to secure material compliance with its relevant obligations if they provide a reasonable assurance of compliance in all material respects with those obligations.

(5) Where the directors of a company to which this section applies fail to comply with subsection (3), each director to whom the failure is attributable is guilty of an offence.

(6) A private company limited by shares qualifies for an exemption from this section in respect of any financial year of the company if, either—

(*a*) its balance sheet total for the year does not exceed—

(i) €12,500,000, or

(ii) if an amount is prescribed under *section 48(1)(l)* of the *Act of 2003* for the purpose of this provision, the prescribed amount,

or, in the alternative to the provisions in (*a*),

(*b*) the amount of its turnover for the year does not exceed—

(i) €25,000,000, or

(ii) if an amount is prescribed under *section 48(1)(l)* of the Act of 2003 for the purpose of this provision, the prescribed amount."

Appendix 4

"22/02/2006

Statement of the European Corporate Governance Forum on the comply-or-explain principle

1—The 'comply or explain' principle has become a feature of Europe's approach to corporate governance. National Corporate governance codes lay down rules or recommendations which are not of mandatory application, but companies must either comply with them or explain publicly why they are not complying with some of their provisions.

The Forum strongly and unanimously supports this approach, which is best suited to take into account the variety of situations of individual companies, and fits well with the differences between national legal and governance frameworks. The Forum believes that, when it is effectively implemented, this is a better and more efficient approach than detailed regulation.

The experience of countries which have implemented this approach for several years shows that it does lead to a movement of convergence towards better governance practices.

2—For this approach to be effective, however, there has to be:

- a real obligation to comply or explain. Depending on the countries, this obligation can result from corporate law, from the regulatory authority, or from listing standards
- a high level of transparency, with coherent and focused disclosures
- a way for shareholders to hold company boards (unitary or dual) ultimately accountable for their decisions to comply-or-explain and the quality of their disclosures.

The comply-or-explain approach depends therefore on the appropriate regulatory framework, and on the existence and practice of sufficient shareholders rights.

3—Different approaches to the role of regulators and auditors have been proposed, or implemented in different countries. The Forum believes lessons should be drawn from these approaches before any general conclusion can be drawn.

However, the Forum believes the corporate governance statement which explains the areas of compliance as well as the reasons for non-compliance, is the responsibility of the company's board(s), for review and discussion with the shareholders.

It therefore inclines to the view that regulatory authorities should limit their role to checking the existence of the statement, and to reacting to blatant misrepresentation of facts. They should not try and second-guess the judgement of the board(s) or the value of its/their explanations. This is a matter for the company's shareholders.

Similarly, the auditors should not be supposed to evaluate the judgement of the board(s), but may within their duties be called upon to review some element of facts contained in the statement.

4—Evaluation by shareholders of the corporate governance statement should be an element of their voting decision at the shareholders' meetings. The Forum recommends that the services, which advise shareholders on these votes, consider the corporate governance statement of each company on its merits, and not only by "box-ticking". Ultimately it is shareholders, not these services, which are responsible for voting decisions. But this also requires of companies to give meaningful explanations for deviations of code provisions.

5—Particular attention should be given to the case of companies controlled by one or a few large shareholders. In that case, it is advisable that in particular independent directors should have a specific and identifiable role in the approval of the corporate governance statement.

6—The Forum urges Member States to set up processes that allow for the monitoring of the application of corporate governance codes. Such monitoring processes will increase our understanding of the effectiveness of corporate governance codes, and highlight what issues appear to be complicated, where developments are satisfactory and where they are not.

7—Where a company is incorporated in one Member State but its shares are listed in one or more other Member States, the result may be that either more than one corporate governance code applies to that company or no code at all. The Forum takes the view that in such cases at least one code should be applied by the company, but double application is to be avoided. The Forum will further work with the Commission on ways how to implement this principle.

8—The Forum urges Member States who have not yet adopted a code to do so. It intends to continue monitoring the implementation of the comply-or-explain approach in the countries of the European Union. The Forum will set up links with national organisations within the Member States charged with the responsibility for corporate governance codes and the monitoring of their application. It will report from time to time about progress made or outstanding issues."

CHAPTER 2

TAMING DIRECTORS: IN SEARCH OF A PRINCIPLED APPROACH

Dr Ailbhe O'Neill, Barrister-at-Law

1. INTRODUCTION

A number of jurisdictions have adopted corporate enforcement regimes which include sanctions for company directors which preclude prospectively their involvement with companies—usually referred to as disqualification orders. This article explores the legislative regimes and the approach taken by courts imposing these sanctions in Ireland, the United Kingdom, New Zealand and Australia. In so doing, it seeks to identify a rationale for these measures and to assess their role in contributing to good standards of corporate governance.

2. THE LEGISLATIVE FRAMEWORK

Modern corporate enforcement regimes in each of the jurisdictions analysed below are supported by legislation which is striking in its similarity. The legislative approach in these common law legal systems has generally been to adopt rules which provide effectively for the exclusion of directors from continuing to act in that capacity going forward on the basis of certain past conduct.

(a) Ireland

In Ireland, the relevant provisions are contained in ss.159–160 of the Companies Act 1990 which provide for the disqualification of directors. While the tendency is to view these provisions as applying only to directors, the provisions of s.160, which set out the grounds upon which a disqualification order may be made, in fact apply to a broader category of individual. Section 160(1) allows for the deemed disqualification for five years of "a person convicted on indictment of any indictable offence in relation to a company, or involving fraud or dishonesty". Section 160(2)(a), (b) and (d) concerns the conduct of an individual "while a promoter, officer, auditor, receiver, liquidator or examiner of a company". The conduct caught by these paragraphs, respectively, is fraud (in relation to the company, its members or creditors), breach of duty and conduct which makes one unfit to be concerned in the management of a company.

Subparagraph (e) provides for disqualification in the case of unfitness where, in consequence of a report from inspectors appointed to the company under Pt II of the Companies Act 1990, "the conduct of any person makes him unfit to be concerned in the management of a company." A person who "has been persistently in default in relation to the relevant requirements" (which relate to filing and notice requirements)[1] is caught by s.160(2)(f).

Section 160(2)(c) renders liable to disqualification any person against whom a declaration of reckless or fraudulent trading has been made under s.297A of the Companies Act 1963.[2]

These grounds for disqualification were added to in the Company Law Enforcement Act 2001 which inserted new provisions in respect of deemed disqualification[3] and added three grounds upon which an application to disqualify may be made. These are: (g) where a person has been guilty of two or more offences of failing to keep proper books of account[4]; (h) a person was a director of a company which was struck off the register for failing to make annual returns; and (i) the person has been disqualified under the law of another state and the court is satisfied that the conduct/circumstances giving rise to the disqualification would be sufficient to give rise to disqualification in this jurisdiction.

The original disqualification provisions lay dormant in the Companies Act 1990 due to the lack of any funded enforcement agency. The original provisions allowed for an application for disqualification to be made by the prosecutor in the context of an offence under s.160(1) and the Director of Public Prosecutions in respect of the provisions of s.160(2)(a)-(f). The Registrar of Companies could also make an application under s.160(2)(f). Applications under s.160(2)(a)–(d) may also be made by any member, contributory, officer, employee, receiver, liquidator, examiner or creditor of any company in which the person the subject of the application is acting, has been acting or is proposing to act as an officer, auditor, receiver, liquidator or examiner. The same parties may apply for a disqualification order against a person who has been, is or is proposing to take part in the promotion, formation or management of such a company.

The Company Law Enforcement Act 2001 effected a sea change in the enforcement of Company Law in Ireland through the creation of the Office of the Director of Corporate Enforcement (ODCE). The establishment of a dedicated regulator with powers to enforce the provisions relating to disqualification (and various other provisions under the Companies Acts) has seen the

[1] The definition of "relevant requirements" is set out in s.159 as meaning "any provision of the Companies Acts (including a provision repealed by this Act) which requires or required any return, account or other document to be filed with, delivered or sent to, or notice of any matter to be given to, the registrar of companies."
[2] This provision was inserted by s.138 of the Companies Act 1990.
[3] See s.42 of the Company Law Enforcement Act 2001.
[4] Under s.202(10).

revitalisation of the civil sanctioning regime and lead to the development, through enforcement proceedings, of a body of case law which reflects on the purpose of those legislative provisions.

(b) The United Kingdom

In the United Kingdom, disqualification is dealt with under the Company Directors Disqualification Act 1986. The grounds for disqualification are similar to those under the Irish legislation. Section 3 refers to persistent default in relation to returns, filings and notice requirements. Section 4 covers fraudulent trading, fraud and breach of duty. Provision is also made in ss.2 and 5 for disqualification in respect of certain summary and indictable offences. Disqualification for unfitness is dealt with in s.6 and s.8 concerns disqualification on that ground following an investigation into the affairs of a company. Section 9 of the Act, read with Pt I of Sch.1, sets out the matters to which the court in which an application to disqualify is made should have regard. As with their Irish counterparts, these include: misfeasance and breach of fiduciary or other duty. They also include any misapplication or retention of money or property of the company or any conduct by the director giving rise to a liability to account for company property or money. The Schedule also lists a number of statutory provisions and provides that the extent of a director's responsibility for failure to comply with same is a matter to be taken into account in the context of unfitness. These provisions apply in all applications for disqualification. Where a company is insolvent, further provisions apply including the director's responsibility for the causes of insolvency and for any failure by the company to supply goods or services for which payment has been received as well as a number of other breaches of statute. Under s.9A, a director may be disqualified for infringements of Competition Law.

The Secretary of State for Business, Enterprise and Regulatory Reform or in the case of a compulsory winding up, the Official Receiver, makes the application for a disqualification order. A change was made to the regime in the Insolvency Act 2000 which allows Secretary of State to accept "disqualification undertakings" and obviates the necessity for court proceedings. Such undertakings have the same effect as court made disqualification orders.[5] There is a minimum period of two years and a maximum of 15 years.

(c) Australia

In Australia, the Corporations Act 2001 provides for "banning orders". Under s.206(B)(1), a director may be automatically banned from managing a

[5] For a discussion of the impact of disqualification undertakings, see Cocks, "The efficacy of directors' disqualification undertakings" (2007) 23 *Tolley's Insolvency Law and Practice* 100.

corporation for a period of five years if they are convicted of certain offences. On application by Australian Securities and Investments Commission (ASIC), the period of five years may be extended by up to an additional 15 years.[6] Under s.206(C), a banning order may be made on application by ASIC to the court where a director has contravened a civil penalty provision and the court believes the disqualification is justified. In determining whether disqualification is justified, the court may have regard to "the person's conduct in relation to the management, business or property of any corporation" and "any other matters that the Court considers appropriate". Section 206(B) replaced previous provisions which required a court to be satisfied that a person had contravened a civil penalty provision and that he or she was not a fit and proper person to manage a corporation before making a banning order. The change in language introduced by the Corporate Law Economic Reform Program Act 1999 (CLERP) does not appear to have altered the approach taken in the case law.[7]

(d) New Zealand

Corporate enforcement is carried out in New Zealand by the National Enforcement Unit which is part of the Ministry of Economic Development. The closest equivalent to the concept of disqualification is s.385 of the Companies Act 1993. This falls short of the UK/Irish/Australian model in that it applies only where a person has been involved in a company that has failed and there is a maximum prohibition period of five years. There has been relatively little judicial consideration of these statutory provisions.

3. Protection of the Public—the *Lo-Line* Approach

The early approach taken by the English courts emphasised the prophylactic nature of the disqualification regime and identified its primary purpose as being to protect the public from future abuses. The most authoritative judicial statement to this effect appeared in *Re Lo-Line Electric Motors and Others*,[8] decided shortly after the Company Directors Disqualification Act 1986 came into force. In considering the unfitness ground for disqualification, Browne-Wilkinson V.C. stated as follows:

6 Corporations Act 2001, s.206BA.

7 See Welsh, "Adler, Whitlam, Elliott and others: Judicial interpretation of the civil penalty provisions of the Corporations Act 2001 (Cth)" (2005) 18 *Australian Journal of Corporate Law* 243. See also *Tasmanian Spastics Assoc; ASIC v Nandan* (1997) 23 A.C.S.R. 743, *ASIC v Plymin (No 2)*, (2003) 21 A.C.L.C. 1237, *ASIC; Re QLS Superannuation v Parker* (2003) 21 A.C.L.C. 888, *ASIC v Adler (No 5)* (2002) 20 A.C.L.C. 1146; 42 A.C.S.R. 80, *ASIC v Forem-Freeway Enterprises Pty Ltd* (1999) 17 A.C.L.C. 511; 30 A.C.S.R. 339, *ASIC v Rich (No 3)*, (2003) 21 A.C.L.C. 920; 45 A.C.S.R. 305.

8 [1988] Ch. 477.

"What is the proper approach to deciding whether someone is unfit to be a director? The approach adopted in all the cases to which I have been referred is broadly the same. The primary purpose of the section is not to punish the individual but to protect the public against the future conduct of companies by persons whose past records as directors of insolvent companies have shown them to be a danger to creditors and others. Therefore, the power is not fundamentally penal. But if the power to disqualify is exercised, disqualification does involve a substantial interference with the freedom of the individual. It follows that the rights of the individual must be fully protected. Ordinary commercial misjudgment is in itself not sufficient to justify disqualification. In the normal case, the conduct complained of must display a lack of commercial probity, although I have no doubt that in an extreme case of gross negligence or total incompetence disqualification could be appropriate."[9]

He also noted that "the making of a disqualification order involves penal consequences for the director".[10]

Thus a distinction between the punitive effect and the protective purpose of the disqualification regime was recognised at an early stage in the United Kingdom. The above extract from *Re Lo-Line* has been approved of in a number of Irish cases both in the context of disqualification proceedings under s.160[11] and restriction orders under s.150.[12]

The purpose of disqualification arose for consideration in the Northern Irish High Court in *Re McQuillan.*[13] This case concerned an application by a person disqualified as an undischarged bankrupt for leave to act as a director. Murray J. approved the following passage from the judgment of Street J. in the New South Wales case of *Re Altim Pty. Ltd*[14]:

"The section under which this application is made proceeds upon the basis that a person who is an undischarged bankrupt is prima facie not to be permitted to act as a director or to take part in the management of a company. The court is given jurisdiction to grant leave for such activities to be carried on, but an applicant who comes to the court seeking such leave must bear the onus of establishing that the general policy of the legislature laid down in this section

9 [1988] Ch. 477 at 485–486.

10 [1988] Ch. 477 at 486.

11 *Re Readymix Limited (in liquidation)* [2002] 1 I.R. 372; *Director of Corporate Enforcement v D'Arcy*, unreported, High Court, October 26, 2005; *Director of Corporate Enforcement v Collery* [2006] IEHC 67; unreported, High Court, Finlay Geoghegan J., March 9, 2006.

12 See, for example, *Kavanagh v Kelly* [2005] IEHC 421; unreported, High Court, July 28, 2005; *La Moselle Clothing Limited v Soualhi* [1998] 2 I.L.R.M. 345; *Re Squash (Ireland)* [2001] 3 I.R. 35; *In the matter of Club Tivoli Ltd (in voluntary liquidation); Foster v Davis and another* [2005] IEHC 468; unreported, High Court, MacMenamin J., December 21, 2005; *Fitzpatrick v Henley and another* [2006] IEHC 179; unreported, High Court, MacMenamin J., April 4, 2006.

13 (1989) 5 B.C.C. 137.

14 [1968] 2 N.S.W.R. 762.

> ought to be made the subject of an exception in his case. It should be borne in mind that the section is not in any sense a punishment of the bankrupt. Nor should a refusal to grant leave under that section be regarded as punitive. The prohibition is entirely protective, and the power of the court to grant leave is to be exercised with this consideration also in the forefront."[15]

A similar view was expressed by Dillon L.J. in the context of disqualification for unfitness in *Re Sevenoaks Stationers (Retail) Ltd*[16] where he noted:

> "It is beyond dispute that the purpose of section 6 is to protect the public, and in particular potential creditors of companies, from losing money through companies becoming insolvent when the directors of those companies are people unfit to be concerned in the management of a company."[17]

Both the statement from *Lo-Line* and that from *Sevenoaks* reproduced above were approved of in *Re Tansoft Ltd*[18] where Warner J. stated: "It is well established that the purpose of a disqualification order is not primarily to punish the individual concerned …"[19]

In *Re Moorgate Metals Ltd*,[20] the same judge held that:

> "Logically perhaps, since the purpose of a disqualification order is not to punish the director concerned but to protect the public from him, he should be disqualified for ever. But Parliament has been merciful."[21]

Judicial support for the protective purpose of disqualification orders can be discerned also from the case of *Re Gibson Davies Limited*.[22] This case concerned an application by a disqualified person for leave to act as a director. (In this instance the applicant had been disqualified due to unfitness.) Sir Mervyn Davies approved both *Lo-Line*, *McQuillan* and *Altim*.[23] He also approved the decision in *Re Cargo Agency Ltd*[24] where Harman J. had stated:

> "It seems to be that Mr. Newey must be right that applications for leave pursuant to s.1 [the relief provision] should only be granted where there is a need for them to be granted, and should only be granted upon evidence of adequate protection from danger."[25]

15 [1968] 2 N.S.W.R. 762 at 764. Cited in (1989) 5 B.C.C. 137 at 141.
16 [1991] Ch. 164.
17 [1991] Ch. 164, at 176.
18 [1991] B.C.L.C. 339.
19 [1991] B.C.L.C. 339 at 357.
20 [1995] 1 B.C.L.C. 503.
21 [1995] 1 B.C.L.C. 503 at 517.
22 [1995] B.C.C. 11.
23 [1995] B.C.C. 11 at 15.
24 [1992] B.C.C. 388.
25 [1992] B.C.C. 388 at 393.

In *Gibson*, the judge was granted leave on the basis of a number of safeguards which the applicant offered to the court.

In a subsequent case, *In Re Unicomp Holdings (UK) Limited and in Re the Companies (Northern Ireland) Order 1989; Forsythe v Department of Economic Development*,[26] the same approach was taken. Again, this case concerned an application by a person disqualified on the basis of unfitness for leave to act as a director. The High Court judge noted:

> "As I understand it, the overriding purpose of a disqualification order is not so much punitive of the respondent as protective of the public (see per Dillon LJ in Re Sevenoaks Stationers (Retail) Limited [1991] Ch 164 at page 176A). If that is so, the power of the court, in its discretion, to make an exception to that order should be exercised pre-eminently with the same consideration in view (see Street J in Re Altim Pty Limited (1968) 2 NSWR 762, 764; per Sir Nicolas Brown-Wilkinson V-C in Re Lo-Line Electric Motors Limited (1988) 4 BCC 415, 419 (also [1988] BCLC 698) where he refers to the need to balance protection of the public with a measure of protection for the rights of the individual; per Murray J in Re McQuillan (1989) 5 BCC 137; per Sir Mervyn Davies in Re Gibson Davies Limited (1995) BCC 11."[27]

4. *Lo-Line* and the Irish Case Law—from "Good Governance" to "Bad Directors"

A similar approach to the line of authority considered above can be seen in the Irish case law.[28] In *Cahill v Grimes*,[29] the Supreme Court approved the dicta of Browne-Wilkinson V.C. reproduced above, noting that it had been adopted in a number of High Court cases.[30]

The High Court cases after *Cahill* take less clear cut approach, often focusing on the blameworthiness of the individual director's conduct as well as the protection of the public which seems to be a secondary consideration. These cases make it difficult to identify a coherent sanctioning rationale. In *Kentford Securities Limited (under investigation) v Companies Act*,[31] Peart J. considered an application to disqualify an individual who had acted as an auditor of a company while he also held the position of director of that company. To hold both positions at the same time is prohibited under s.163 of the Companies Act

26 Unreported, High Court of England and Wales Chancery Division, January 15, 1998.

27 Unreported, High Court of England and Wales Chancery Division, January 15, 1998.

28 See discussion in Cahill, *Company Law Compliance and Enforcement* (Dublin: Tottel, 2008) at 957–960.

29 [2002] 1 I.R. 372.

30 Fennelly J. referred to *La Moselle Clothing Limited v Soualhi* [1998] 2 I.L.R.M. 345; *Re Squash (Ireland)* [2001] 3 I.R. 35; *Re Newcastle Timber Ltd*, unreported, High Court, McCracken J., October 16, 2001.

31 [2007] IEHC 1; unreported, High Court, Peart J., January 23, 2007.

1963. Peart J. found that the breach of s.163 had been neither deliberate nor conscious and declined to disqualify him on that basis. In response to a further allegation made by the ODCE that the respondent had failed in his duty as an auditor by signing unqualified reports on financial statements for a number of years, the court found that while he had breached his duty as an auditor in by accepting certain assurances and not looking behind them, he was unaware of the illegality in the activities of the company which were subsequently uncovered in the course of an investigation into its affairs.

In refusing to make a disqualification order on the basis of the breaches of duty, the judge placed heavy emphasis on the blameworthiness of the respondent's conduct, taking into account matters such as his relative inexperience at the time of the events complained of and the fact that the respondent had not profited from the illegal activities of the company. He also took into consideration the behaviour of the respondent after he left the company.

The assessment of such mitigating factors indicates a focus on the moral quality of the respondent's activities. This is redolent of the approach traditionally taken in criminal sentencing and sits more easily with a conception of the disqualification order as a punitive sanction of some sort. Later in his judgment, however, Peart J. stated that s.160 orders were "not punitive in nature, but rather protective of the community". He also pointed out that a disqualification order should only be made where the respondent is shown to be a current risk to the public.

The rationale for disqualification arose again in *Director of Corporate Enforcement v Seymour*.[32] This case concerned disqualification proceedings taken against the respondent who was formerly the executive director of National Irish Bank during a period where DIRT (Deposit Interest Retention Tax) was not paid to the Revenue Commissioners. The main evidence in the case was the report of inspectors who had investigated the company and made a number of findings adverse to the respondent. Murphy J. imposed a disqualification order based on these findings.

In deciding the length of the period of disqualification, the court considered the serious nature of the irregularities that were permitted to continue and the senior position of the respondent and decided on a period of 12 years. The court then went on to consider the mitigating factors in this case which were the age of the respondent, the fact that he was retired and no longer involved in any banking or commercial activities as well as the fact that he made some effort to address the compliance issues in the bank. These factors appear to take into consideration the moral quality of the director's actions in the past (in his attempt to address compliance issues) as well as the possible threat he might pose in the future. Taking these factors into account, the court reduced the period of disqualification by three years.

32 Unreported, High Court, Murphy J., January 20, 2007.

The same judge in *Director of Corporate Enforcement v Curran*[33] considered an application to disqualify another respondent who had held a number of senior management positions in National Irish Bank. Again, the application was based on an inspectors' report which made a number of findings against the respondent. The findings against him in the report were characterised by the court as findings of "omission" rather than "commission". In other words, the court accepted that the conduct at issue involved failure to prevent wrongdoing rather than any positive wrongful acts on the part of the respondent himself. The court also noted that the respondent was not in a position within the bank which would have enabled him to put a stop to the practices disclosed in the inspectors' report and refused to make a disqualification order against him.

In line with this focus on the blameworthiness of individual director's conduct, some of the recent disqualification cases, have emphasised the seniority of the director concerned in making the order for disqualification. *Director of Corporate Enforcement v Brennan*,[34] for example, concerned disqualification proceeding arising out of the report of inspectors appointed under Pt II of the Companies Act 1990 to investigate the affairs of National Irish Bank and the evasion of Deposit Interest Retention Tax through the establishment of bogus non-resident accounts.[35]

The inspectors had made a number of findings in their report against senior executives in National Irish Bank as to their knowledge and responsibility for the irregularities uncovered by the inspectors during the course of their investigation. Brennan had been the General Manager in charge of Retail Banking between May 1988 and June 1991 and had held a number of other senior executive posts in the bank after that.

In making a disqualification order under s.160(2)(d) and (e) of the Companies Act 1990, Murphy J. emphasised the very senior position of the respondent in the bank. In that context, the claims by the respondent that he was ignorant as to the ongoing tax evasion and other issues in National Irish Bank were seen by the court as being indicative of a failure of his management and control role within the bank. This failure rendered him unfit to be concerned in the management of a company.

The linking of culpability with seniority is also apparent in the case of *Director of Corporate Enforcement v Keane*.[36] Like *Brennan*, this case arose out of the National Irish Bank scandal. The respondent in this case had been the General Manager of Banking and the inspectors has been critical of his role in the context of a crucial audit meeting. Findings were also made against him in respect of his role in the sale of insurance services at the bank.

[33] [2007] IEHC 181; unreported, High Court, Murphy J., May 23, 2007.

[34] [2008] IEHC 132; unreported, High Court, Murphy J., April 22, 2008.

[35] See *Re NIB Ltd: Director of Corporate Enforcement v D'Arcy* [2006] 2 I.R. 163, *Re NIB Ltd: Director of Corporate Enforcement v Seymour* [2007] IEHC 102 and *Re NIB Ltd: Director of Corporate Enforcement v Curran* [2007] IEHC 181.

[36] Unreported, High Court, Murphy J., May 26, 2008.

Murphy J. made an order under s.160(2)(d) and (e) disqualifying the respondent on the grounds of unfitness to be concerned in the management of a company. In so doing, Murphy J. emphasised the very senior role held by the respondent within the bank.

Director of Corporate Enforcement v Byrne[37] arose out of the same circumstances as *Keane*. The respondent in this case had been the head of Financial Planning and Head of Finance at the bank. The court noted that Byrne was an accountant and that he had the means to inquire and refers concerns to the Board and other relevant bodies. In assessing whether his conduct should attract a disqualification order, Murphy J. posed the following questions:

> "Did this failure amount to a lack of commercial probity? Does it go far enough that it should be categorised as being grossly irresponsible or being a danger to the public? Or is such failure ordinary commercial misjudgement?"

Murphy J. took the view that, when considering unfitness in this context, he ought to have regard to the standard of ordinary conduct in the context of the facts of the case. Here, the court found that the respondent had a responsibility to raise issues after a key meeting and that his failure to do so was evidence of a lack of commercial probity sufficient to merit a disqualification order.

The approach taken in *Keane*, while it mentions a threat to the public, appears to make that reference retrospectively as part of an overall assessment of the conduct of the director at the time of the conduct complained of rather than looking into the future.

5. Developments in the United Kingdom Case Law after *Lo-Line*

As mentioned above, the *Lo-Line* and *Sevenoaks* cases, and the subsequent authorities endorsing them, suggest a strong focus in the UK case law on the protective purpose of disqualification orders. Consistent with this, later cases have emphasised the deterrent effect of disqualification both on the individual director being disqualified and other directors who might potentially engage in misconduct.

In *Re Atlantic Computers PLC*,[38] Lloyd J. noted that:

> "In order to disqualify a respondent the court has to be satisfied that he or she 'has fallen below the standards of probity and competence appropriate for persons fit to be directors of companies' … This is a minimum standard … It is also appropriate to recall that the purpose of the legislation is to improve the standard of conduct of company directors … The point of a disqualification

[37] [2008] IEHC 149; unreported, High Court, Murphy J., May 26, 2008.

[38] Unreported, High Court of England, Lloyd J., June 15, 1998.

> order is, by depriving the respondent of the liberty to take part in the management of a business carried on with the privilege of limited liability, to protect the public both from misconduct of a business by that director and also by a deterrent effect in relation to other company directors ..."[39]

This approach as also taken by the Court of Appeal in *Re Westmid Packing Services Ltd*[40] where Lord Woolf M.R., after referring to *Lo-Line*, went on to state:

> "[O]ther factors come into play in the wider interests of protecting the public, i.e. a deterrent element in relation to the director himself and a deterrent element as far as other directors are concerned. Despite the fact that the courts have said disqualification is not a 'punishment', in truth the exercise that is being engaged in is little different from any sentencing exercise. The period of disqualification must reflect the gravity of the offence. It must contain deterrent elements. That is what sentencing is all about, and that is what fixing the appropriate period of the disqualification is all about. What Vinelott J. (in re: Pamstock Limited [1994] 1 B.C.L.C. 716 at 737) called 'tunnel vision', i.e. concentration on the facts of the offence, is necessary when considering whether a director is unfit. In relation to the period of disqualification the facts of the offence are still obviously important but many other factors ought and (in reality do) come into play."[41]

This passage has been approved of in some of the recent Irish case law considered below.[42] It suggests that the primary purpose of the disqualification regime is as a mechanism to improve good governance. The deterrence referred to in the above extracts is general deterrence rather than the deterrence of the individual director himself. The "other factors" referred to by Lord Woolf M.R. may have little to do with the individual conduct of the director and more to do with the public interest and the interests of "innocent" third parties such as the employees and creditors of a company. This implication of the *Atlantic Computers/ Westmid* case law is realised in the most recent Irish Supreme Court case in this area, discussed below. The other aspect of *Westmid* is that it accepts that the courts in these cases are engaged in a sentencing exercise. The reference to the "gravity of the offence" suggest a focus on individual culpability which is more naturally linked with punishment on a retributive rather than a deterrent basis.

39 Cited with approval in *Secretary of State for Business Enterprise and Regulatory Reform v Sullman and another* [2008] EWHC 3179; unreported, High Court, Norris J., December 19, 2008.

40 [1998] 2 All E.R. 124.

41 [1998] 2 All E.R. 124 at 131–132.

42 *Director of Corporate Enforcement v D'Arcy*, unreported, High Court, Kelly J., October 26, 2005; *Director of Corporate Enforcement v Collery*, unreported, High Court, Finlay Geoghegan J., March 9, 2006.

6. The Approach in New Zealand

As noted above, the New Zealand regime differs from the other common law jurisdictions examined in that it provides for banning orders only where a company has failed and only for a maximum period of five years. In *Ramsay v Sumich*,[43] the respondent had been disqualified from being a company director for five years without leave of court following his conviction for a crime involving dishonesty. Within those five years, the respondent breached that order and acted as director of two companies both of which failed, causing substantial losses to creditors. The prosecutor was dissatisfied with the sentence imposed by the District Court in respect of acting while disqualified and appealed to the High Court. In the course of considering the appropriate penalty to be applied, Sinclair J., in the High Court, referred to the relevant criteria when considering an application by a disqualified person for leave to act as a director. Referring to an earlier decision of the court, *Minimix Industries Ltd*,[44] he quoted from the judgment of Cook J. in that case as follows:

> "Clearly there is a substantial onus on an applicant to demonstrate that his case is such as to warrant leave being granted as an exception to the general rule and, while one readily accepts that the section is not a punishment, in deciding whether or not leave should be granted one must have concern for the interests of the public, ie those who have dealings with the company and are entitled to find that they are dealing with persons of integrity, those who become creditors and are entitled to expect that the funds of the company are not dissipated by dishonest action; no doubt shareholders also who have delegated the management of the company to the directors and those in the company's employment."

Sinclair J. also referred to a judgment of Street J. in the Australian case of *Re Ferrari Furniture Co Pty Ltd*,[45] where that judge quoted with approval the extract from *Altim* reproduced above.
Sinclair J. went on to note that:

> "It must be remembered that both the Minimix and Ferrari decisions were concerned with applications for leave to become involved in the management of a company, and it is evident that the Courts considered that the protective element of the legislation was that which came to the forefront."

The protective aspect of the legislation appears to be that to the forefront of the approach taken by the regulator in New Zealand also. In its description of the s.385 jurisdiction, the National Enforcement Unit notes that, "Action by the

[43] [1989] 3 N.Z.L.R. 628.
[44] (1982) 1 B.C.R. 390.
[45] [1972] 2 N.S.W.L.R. 790.

Registrar under s.385 is discretionary, and the Registrar will consider whether there is a possible risk to the public in allowing the person to act as a director, manager or promoter of a company."[46]

It goes on to point out that:

> "The object is not, however, to use it against merely unsuccessful entrepreneurs so as to stifle all enterprise. It is not so much a penalty for past misconduct but a method of protecting the public from future misconduct."[47]

The New Zealand approach, therefore, seems to concur with that taken by Browne-Wilkinson V.C. in *Lo-Line*.

7. The Disqualification Rationale in Australia

(a) Focusing on good governance

There have been a number of Australian cases which have considered the purpose of disqualification. Much of the earlier case law emphasises the protective purpose of disqualification and emphasises the role of deterrence as a factor protecting the public going forward.

Chew v NCSC[48] concerned an application for leave to act as a director of a company by an individual disqualified from acting as a director as a result of his conviction of an offence in relation to the acquisition of shares. The relevant legislation provided for automatic disqualification once convicted with no discretion as to the time period. Olney J., in the Supreme Court of Western Australia, held that:

> "Given that the disqualification imposed by s 227(2) [of the Companies (Western Australia) Code] is not part of the punishment or the offence the conviction for which gives rise to the disqualification, the only conclusion one can draw in the total context of the Code is that this provision is inserted for the purpose of either deterring would be offenders or for protecting the public from exposure to persons who have offended and who might re-offend if not restrained or (as I think is more likely) both."[49]

Ultimately he emphasised the protective aspect of the provision, granting the application on the basis that:

> "… [F]or the present the interests of the public at large will not be placed in jeopardy and indeed the interests of a significant section of the investing

46 *http://www.companies.govt.nz/cms/your-legal-responsibilities/enforcement#selection-of-cases* Last accessed January 30, 2009.

47 *http://www.enforcement.med.govt.nz/BanDirs-fs.htm* Last accessed January 30, 2009.

48 9 A.C.L.R. 527, Supreme Court of Western Australia, March 6, 1985.

49 Supreme Court of Western Australia, March 6, 1985.

> public will be better served by allowing the applicant to resume without restriction his former role in the business community."[50]

In *Australian Securities and Investments Commission v Roussi*,[51] Einfeld J., in setting the period of disqualification, referred to a number of earlier authorities:

> "It has been held that the purpose of banning orders under s 230 [of the Corperation Law (Australia)] is protective not punitive: Re Minimix Industries Ltd (1982) 1 ACLC 511 at 512; Re Marsden (1981) 29 SASR 454 5 ACLR 694 at 699. Those included in the protective umbrella are the public who are seen by the Law as interested in the transparency and accountability of companies and in the suitability of directors to hold office: Commissioner for Corporate Affairs (WA) v Ekamper (1987) 12 ACLR 519 at 525."[52]

The *Minimix case* referred to in the preceding quotation has been cited approvingly in a number of other decisions concerning banning orders.[53]

The case law discussed above demonstrates an understanding of the disqualification regime as being part of an overall strategy to improve standards in corporate life and to protect the public from directorial misconduct. This focus on governance is reflected in the tendency in the case law to focus on the prospective effect of a banning order rather than to look back at the conduct of the individual director and assess its blameworthiness.

One issue which has arisen in the Australian case law is the time at which the director's conduct should be assessed. If the purpose of a disqualification order is to protect the public going forward, then there may be an argument that only the potential future actions of the director are relevant to a decision to make a banning order. That argument was considered in *ASIC; Re QLS Superannuation v Parker*.[54] It was argued in that case that the unfitness of the defendant to manage corporations should be assessed at the time of the court hearing rather than at the time the contraventions occurred. Counsel for the director argued that there was no evidence before the court that established that the director was unfit to manage corporations at the time that the orders were being made. His contraventions related to activities he had been engaged in while managing superannuation funds from late-1996 to mid-1997. He had been subjected to civil penalties for contraventions of the statute in 2003 by which time he was no longer involved in the management of superannuation funds. Drummond J.

50 Supreme Court of Western Australia, March 6, 1985.

51 32 A.C.S.R. 568 (Federal Court of Australia, May 11, 1999).

52 32 A.C.S.R. 568 (Federal Court of Australia, May 11, 1999).

53 Other cases citing *Minimix* include *Re C. & J. Holdings Pty Ltd.* 4 A.S.C.R. 703 (May 27, 1991, Supreme Court of Tasmania); *Australian Securities and Investments Commission v Papotto* 35 A.S.C.R. 107; Supreme Court of Western Australia, August 22, 2000; *Australian Securities and Investments Commission v Platcher* 44 A.S.C.R. 277; Federal Court of Australia, January 13, 2003.

54 (2003) 21 A.C.L.C. 888.

LIBRARY
INSTITUTE OF TECHNOLOGY
CARLOW

rejected this argument, stating that the discretion to disqualify was available to him even if the director had not caused persons involved with superannuation funds to suffer any harm since the commission of the contraventions of the Act. The quality of the director's conduct that had constituted the contraventions established in the current proceedings was enough to indicate that Parker was still unfit to manage corporations as at the date that the banning order was imposed.

In *ASIC v Forem-Freeway Enterprises Pty Ltd*,[55] Madgwick J. recognised that the capacity of the defendant to cause harm to the public must be given consideration by the court when it is deciding whether or not to impose a banning order because the aim of the banning order is to protect the public. Similarly, in *ASIC v Rich (No 3)*,[56] Austin J. stated that the claim that the purpose of banning orders is to provide protection to the public:

> "is usually made by way of guidance for the setting of an appropriate term of disqualification. Since the purpose of disqualification is to protect the public, rather than to punish, conduct that severely damages the financial interests of investors might attract a long period of disqualification even though it is not culpable conduct in a moral sense."

This Australian case law on banning orders thus seems to have a clear cut rationale. The factors to be taken into account in this context were summarised by Santow J. in the Supreme Court of New South Wales decision in *Re HIH Insurance Ltd; Australian Securities and Investments Commission v Adler*.[57] He reviewed the case law concerning the circumstances in which disqualification orders should be made and distilled from this body of case law a number of propositions:

> "(i) Disqualification orders are designed to protect the public from the harmful use of the corporate structure or from use that is contrary to proper commercial standards
> (ii) The banning order is designed to protect the public by seeking to safeguard the public interest in the transparency and accountability of companies and in the suitability of directors to hold office
> (iii) Protection of the public also envisages protection of individuals that deal with companies, including consumers, creditors, shareholders and investors.
> (iv) The banning order is protective against present and future misuse of the corporate structure.
> (v) The order has a motive of personal deterrence, though it is not punitive.
> (vi) The objects of general deterrence are also sought to be achieved.

55 (1999) 17 A.C.L.C. 511; 30 A.C.S.R. 339.
56 (2003) 21 A.C.L.C. 920; 45 A.C.S.R. 305.
57 (2002) 42 A.C.S.R. 80; Supreme Court of New South Wales, May 20, 2002.

(vii) In assessing the fitness of an individual to manage a company, it is necessary that they have an understanding of the proper role of the company director and the duty of due diligence that is owed to the company.

(viii) Longer periods of disqualification are reserved for cases where contraventions have been of a serious nature such as those involving dishonesty.

(ix) In assessing an appropriate length of prohibition, consideration has been given to the degree of seriousness of the contraventions, the propensity that the defendant may engage in similar conduct in the future and the likely harm that may be caused to the public.

(x) It is necessary to balance the personal hardship to the defendant against the public interest and the need for protection of the public from any repeat of the conduct.

(xi) A mitigating factor in considering a period of disqualification is the likelihood of the defendant reforming.

(xii) The eight criteria to govern the exercise of the court's powers of disqualification set out in *Commissioner for Corporate Affairs v Ekamper* (1987) 12 ACLR 519 have been influential. It was held that in making such an order it is necessary to assess:

- Character of the offenders;
- Nature of the breaches;
- Structure of the companies and the nature of their business;
- Interests of shareholders, creditors and employees;
- Risk to others from the continuation of offenders as company directors;
- Honesty and competence of offenders;
- Hardship to offenders and their personal and commercial interests; and
- Offenders' appreciation that future breaches could result in future proceedings;

(xiii) Factors which led to the imposition of the longest periods of disqualification (that is disqualifications of 25 years or more) were:

- Large financial losses;
- High propensity that defendants may engage in similar activities or conduct;
- Activities undertaken in fields in which there was potential to do great financial damage such as in management and financial consultancy;
- Lack of contrition or remorse;
- Disregard for law and compliance with corporate regulations;
- Dishonesty and intent to defraud; and
- Previous convictions and contraventions for similar activities;

(xiv) In cases in which the period of disqualification ranged from 7 years to 12 years, the factors evident and which led to the conclusion that these cases were serious though not 'worst cases', included:

- Serious incompetence and irresponsibility;
- Substantial loss;

- Defendants had engaged in deliberate courses of conduct to enrich themselves at others' expense, but with lesser degrees of dishonesty;
- Continued, knowing and wilful contraventions of the law and disregard for legal obligations; and
- Lack of contrition or acceptance of responsibility, but as against that, the prospect that the individual may reform;

(xv) The factors leading to the shortest disqualifications, that is disqualifications for up to 3 years, were:

- Although the defendants had personally gained from the conduct, they had endeavoured to repay or partially repay the amount misappropriated;
- The defendants had no immediate or discernible future intention to hold a position as manager of a company; and
- … the respondent had expressed remorse and contrition, acted on advice of professionals and had not contested the proceedings." [References omitted]

Santow J.'s approach, in its synthesis of earlier Australian authority, views deterrence (both personal and general) as being part of the protective agenda of the banning order regime. *Adler* was approved by the Supreme Court of Victoria Court of Appeal in *Elliott v ASIC*[58] which also emphasised the link between the protective and deterrent purposes behind disqualification orders.

The Australian case law thus seems to opt clearly for promoting good governance as opposed to punishing the misconduct of directors. Santow J.'s principles do include reference to matters entailing an assessment of blameworthiness, but these factors are linked to the possible future threat posed to the public, e.g. lack of contrition. Even where no direct link is drawn, it seems from the context in which these blameworthy aspects of conduct are considered that they are referred to due to their relevance to possible future breaches, i.e. the focus is prospective and protective rather than retrospective and punitive. The subsequent case of *Rich v Australian Securities and Investments Commission*[59] required the High Court of Australia to revisit this issue, albeit in a case which did not concern the imposition or duration of a banning order.

(b) Disqualification in the High Court of Australia

In *Rich*, the High Court of Australia considered the protective/punitive nature of disqualification in the context of a claim by appellant directors that they were entitled to the privilege against penalties in the response to orders for discovery made against them. The respondent (the ASIC) claimed that no such privilege applied as the purpose of the disqualification proceedings was protective rather than punitive. The High Court was critical of the distinction being made in order to determine that specific issue.

[58] 205 A.L.R. 594; Supreme Court of Victoria Court of Appeal, April 7, 2004.

[59] (2004) 209 A.L.R. 271.

Gleeson C.J. (joined by Gummow, Hayne, Callinan and Heydon JJ.) delivered the majority judgment of the court. He stated as follows:

> "The question is how should the general principles of the privileges against exposure to penalties and forfeiture find application in the particular circumstances of these proceedings. That inquiry is not assisted by examining why the orders sought in the proceedings might be made or what purposes might be achieved by their making. Rather, attention must be focused upon the nature of the orders that are sought.
>
> That it may be possible to characterise proceedings as having a purpose of protecting the public is not determinative. And to begin the inquiry from an *a priori* classification of proceedings as either protective or penal invites error. It invites error primarily because the classification adopted assumes mutual exclusivity of the categories chosen when they are not, and because the classification is itself unstable. To assume mutual exclusivity of the categories is to fall into the same kind of error as was identified in the constitutional context in Actors and Announcers Equity Assn v Fontana Films Pty Ltd [(1982) 150 C.L.R. 169; 40 A.L.R. 609]. Just as a law may bear several characters, a proceeding may seek relief which, if granted, would protect the public but would also penalise the person against whom it is granted. That a proceeding may bear several characters does not deny that it bears each of those characters."[60]

The majority judgment rejects the punitive/protective dichotomy—at least as a means of determining the availability of the privilege at issue in the case. It thus rejects implicitly the idea that there is one underlying rationale for the imposition of a banning order and refuses to categorise such orders as being punitive or protective. It seems, however, to implicitly draw the distinction made in *Lo-Line* between the protective purpose and punitive effect of disqualification orders.

McHugh J., in his minority concurring judgment, also took the view that disqualification orders were not purely protective in nature. Comparing them to sentencing orders in the context of criminal matters, he identified elements of retribution, deterrence and mitigation in the Australian disqualification case law. He also made the point that if the sole purpose of disqualification was protective, fixed terms of disqualification made little sense—stating that an indefinite period with the possibility of application to the court would be the solution if protection were the only agenda.[61] Thus, unlike the majority, McHugh J. appears to see the purposes of disqualification as being partly punitive rather than punishment being a mere side effect of such orders.

60 Paragraphs 34–35.

61 Paragraph 41. McHugh J.'s judgment, it should be noted, focused on the legislative history of the relevant provisions (ss.206C and E of the Corporations Act 2001). These, he found, evolved from earlier "civil penalty" provisions and this affected his approach to the punitive/protective issue.

(c) Dissent in the High Court—a return to *Lo-Line*?

Kirby J.'s dissenting judgment in *Rich* endorsed the protective nature of the banning order regime. Rejecting the application of the privilege against penalties in the context of disqualification proceedings, he firmly endorsed the idea that disqualification orders are protective rather than punitive. Referring to "the fundamental duty of the court [to] ... interpret, and give effect to, the Act [Corporations Act 2001 (Australia)] according to its true meaning", he went on to state that:

> "[I]n fulfilling that duty, this court could scarcely minimise the indications in the Act, and in the corporate context to which the Act responds, of the serious problems which the provisions of the Act were designed to address. These have both an Australian and global character. When those problems are remembered, the provisions of the Act can be better understood. They were designed to fulfil very important purposes concerned with corporate governance.
>
> Those purposes are part of a very detailed regulatory scheme enacted to contribute to the improved management and control of Australian corporations. They are not, as such, 'inflicted' as a 'penalty', on the appellants. Getting the character of the provisions of the Act right is essential to the proper application in this context of any residual rule of the common law as to penalty privilege ..."[62]

Later in his judgment, he went on to state:

> "Of its nature, disqualification looks to the future; not to the past. It protects the investing public, shareholders and others by immobilising the proved contravener and depriving him or her, for the specified period, of the position of trust and power that office in a corporation involves. Of course, the order has a serious economic and reputational consequence for the officer who is disqualified. But its purpose is not, as such, to impose criminal punishment. If it were punitive, it would say so and it would have been placed in a different part of the Act."[63]

(d) Australian case law post-*Rich*

Later interpretations of *Rich* in lower courts in Australia have emphasised the deterrent nature of disqualification and have also read that case as accepting that there is an element of punishment in these cases. In a subsequent case before the

[62] Paragraphs 62–63.

[63] Paragraph 87. See also later in the dissent where he stated at para.114:
"[T]he purpose and character of the Act in this respect, enlivened by the commission's application for disqualification orders against the appellants, is not, as such, punishment of the appellants or something of that nature. True, a consequence is a burden on the appellants. However, viewed in the particular context of corporations law, that is not the character of the provisions in issue. Properly characterised, they constitute part of a law for the regulation of acceptable corporate management in Australia. It is a regulatory law to be applied in

Federal Court of Australia, *Australian Securities and Investments Commission v Vizard*,[64] Finklestein J. emphasised the deterrent nature of disqualification orders, making reference to both specific and general deterrence:

> "This brings me to the issue of disqualification. It is my view that a disqualification for 5 years as suggested by ASIC is not sufficient. Although specific deterrence is generally not in issue here, general deterrence is of primary importance in cases of this kind. A message must be sent to the business community that for white collar offences 'the game is not worth the candle'. That is, the period of disqualification should reflect the need to protect society from the kind of unlawful conduct engaged in by the defendant."[65]

In a later passage, he referred to the judgment in *Rich* which he interpreted as allowing for an element of punishment of the director:

> "It may be accepted that the principal object to be achieved by a disqualification order is protective: protection of the company and its shareholders against the likelihood of repetition of the offending conduct. The mistake is to treat this as the sole purpose of a disqualification order. That error has now been exposed. In Rich v Australian Securities and Investments Commission (2004) 209 ALR 271; 50 ACSR 242[2004] HCA 42 the High Court made it clear that a disqualification order can be imposed not only to protect the company's shareholders against further abuse, but also by way of punishment and, importantly, for general deterrence."[66]

Unlike the *Lo-Line* approach, this approach sees punishment as a justification for disqualification instead of a mere inevitable consequence of it.

In *Australian Securities and Investment Commission v Vines*,[67] the Supreme Court of New South Wales referred to the 15 principles set out by Santow J. in *Adler* and held that:

> "The High Court's decision, that proceedings in which an application is made for a disqualification order are proceedings for the imposition of a penalty, for the purposes of the privilege against exposure to a penalty, has very little effect on the propositions. It directly affects only proposition (v), to the extent that a disqualification order should now be regarded as involving the imposition of a penalty.
>
> The majority judges in the High Court did not directly consider the principles to be applied by the court when considering whether to make a

accordance with civil procedures. That incorporates obligations of verified discovery by parties such as the appellants."

64 219 A.L.R. 714 (July 28, 2005).

65 Paragraph 11.

66 Paragraph 35.

67 58 A.C.S.R. 298; Supreme Court of New South Wales, August 2, 2006.

> disqualification order, and if so, the period of disqualification. However, McHugh J considered that topic at some length. His general thesis … was that although judges frequently said that the purpose of the disqualification provisions is protective, what they did in practice was little different from what judges do in determining what orders or penalty should be made for offences against the criminal law."[68]

Referring to the judgment of Finklestein J. in *Vizard*, and the references in that case to retribution and deterrence, the court in *Vines* took a similar approach, essentially endorsing that taken by McHugh J. in *Rich*.

8. An Inevitable Mixture?

The approach taken by Santow J. in *Re HIH Insurance Ltd; Australian Securities and Investments Commission v Adler*,[69] with its exposition of numerous principles, does not provide a neat and shorthand reference point for director disqualification. The development of the case law in Australia after *Rich* demonstrates that the courts in that jurisdiction have been unable to maintain a strict focus on protection alone in the imposition of banning orders and have developed an approach similar to that taken in the UK case of *Westmid* discussed above.

This multi-rationale approach is echoed in the Irish High Court decision in *Director of Corporate Enforcement v Collery*.[70] In that case, Finlay Geoghegan J. referred to *Westmid*[71] and went on to set out a number of principles to take into account when calculating the appropriate period of disqualification:

> "(1) The primary purpose of an order of disqualification is not to punish the individual but to protect the public against future conduct of companies by persons whose past record has shown them to be a danger to creditors and others.
> (2) The period of disqualification should reflect (in relation to and order under s. 160(2)(e)) the gravity of the conduct as found by the Inspectors which makes the respondent unfit to be concerned in the management of a company.
> (3) The period of disqualification should contain deterrent elements.
> (4) A period of disqualification in excess of ten years should be reserved for particularly serious cases.
> (5) The court should firstly assess the correct period in accordance with the foregoing and then take into account mitigating factors prior to fixing the actual period of disqualification."

[68] Paragraphs 35–36.
[69] (2002) 42 ACSR 80; Supreme Court of New South Wales, May 20, 2002.
[70] [2006] IEHC 67; unreported, High Court, Finlay Geoghegan J., March 9, 2006.
[71] See discussion above.

This multifactor approach adopts a position not unlike that taken by Santow J. in *Adler*. Considering the Irish case law, it has been suggested that:

> "While the primary purpose of a disqualification order is to protect the public, rather than to punish the respondent, the period of disqualification that is imposed should 'contain deterrent elements'. Even if it is apparent that a person is unlikely to pose a future risk to the public, the severity of the wrongdoing may nonetheless warrant a substantial period of disqualification, to deter the recurrence of such wrongdoing."[72]

New Zealand alone appears to have maintained a focus solely on the protective purpose of this aspect of corporate enforcement.

9. A Return to Good Governance in the Irish Courts?

The Irish Supreme Court has recently indicated its current understanding of the purpose of disqualification in *Director of Corporate Enforcement v McGowan*,[73] where it considered disqualification under s.160(2)(f) of the Companies Act 1990. This provides for the making of a disqualification order where a respondent has been "persistently in default in relation to the relevant requirements". The directors in this case had failed over a period of 13 consecutive years to make any of the annual returns required by the Companies Registration Office under ss.125 and 12 of the Companies Act 1963 as amended by the Company Law Enforcement Act 2001. Laffoy J., in the High Court, found that persistent default could only be established where there had been a court finding in respect of the failure to make returns.

In the Supreme Court, Fennelly J. disagreed with the above interpretation of s.160(2)(f). He found that the failure to make returns as described above constituted a persistent failure even in the absence of any court sanctions during the relevant period of time.

The High Court had also considered the possibility of making an order under s.160(2)(d) or (e) on the unfitness ground. Laffoy J. had taken the view that, while the respondent's conduct here was deserving of serious criticism, it narrowly fell short of the threshold for making a disqualification order on this ground.

Fennelly J., in the Supreme Court, appeared to emphasise heavily the protective nature of disqualification orders. In discussing the discretion of the court in deciding whether to make a disqualification order, he found that the High Court had been correct in this case to take into account the interests of employees and third parties. Fennelly J. pointed out that a disqualification order

72 Cahill, *Company Law Compliance and Enforcement* at 960.

73 [2008] IESC 28; unreported, Supreme Court, Denham, Geoghegan and Fennelly JJ., May 6, 2008.

in this case would serve no useful purpose and would disrupt the ongoing business of the company. Similar comments were made the context of the decision in this case not to make a restriction order under s.150. The Supreme Court pointed out that, quite apart from the disruption to the business itself, an order under either provision would have the side effect of precluding the company from discharging its obligations to the Revenue Commissioners.

This approach appears to focus primarily on the protective purpose of disqualification. although the comment was qualified by an observation that the same approach might not necessarily apply in a situation where some allegation of unfitness was made.

Referring to *Lo-Line*, the Supreme Court also accepted the submission of the ODCE that an element of deterrence was relevant to s.160, stating that:

> "It is part of the policy of the section to improve corporate governance. Courts have become increasingly vigilant and less tolerant in relation to lax standards and disregard of the law also in its policy of promoting good governance."

10. Conclusion

The Irish Supreme Court's most recent comments on the rationale for disqualification seem to locate it firmly within a corporate governance context. An exploration of the approach taken to disqualification in the common law jurisdictions analysed above demonstrates a marked similarity in the vacillation between sanctioning rationales. Each jurisdiction has been keen to emphasise the public interest that is protected by disqualifying rogue directors from further involvement in corporate life. Similarly, each jurisdiction has emphasised the relevance of deterrence (personal and general) to promoting good standards of governance. Despite this, there is a tendency to hone in on personal blameworthiness when assessing the period of disqualification in manner which suggests that the *purpose* rather than the just the *effect* of disqualification is punitive as well as protective. Of course there can be a logical connection between blameworthiness and the risk a director poses into the future. This connection, however, is not often made explicit and is absent in many of the Irish cases after *Cahill* discussed above. Furthermore, the Australian case law post-*Rich*, with its reference to retribution, demonstrates how difficult it is to identify good governance as the sole rationale for director disqualification. The most recent Irish Supreme Court pronouncement appears to herald a return to the focus on protection rather than punishment. It may be that the court is uneasy with the idea of retribution and punishment as being relevant in a civil context.

The recent case of *In the Matter of Tralee Beef and Lamb Ltd (In Liquidation) Kavanagh v Delaney*[74] contains an analysis of the restriction regime under s.150

[74] [2008] IESC 1.

of the Companies Act 1990 which suggests that the Irish Supreme Court views corporate enforcement legislation as ideally balancing the protection of the public against the impact on the individual. In that case, Hardiman J. was highly critical of the s.150 procedure, noting that it entailed significant stigma for the individual which was is arguably not justified by any appreciable contribution to good governance due to the limited parameters of restriction orders.

Even if the promotion of good governance alone is identified as the rationale for disqualification, the fact of the punitive effect of such orders remains. It may be that this is simply part of the cost of a regime that seeks to ensure good standards of directorial conduct. A distaste for such consequentialism and a desire to link the punitive effect of disqualification orders with the blameworthiness of the individual undoubtedly underlies much of the emphasis on culpability in the case law. If general deterrence is the primary explanation for these orders, then matters such as the profile of the director involved should arguably be of more relevance that his/her personal level of misconduct. Such an approach is, of course, unlikely to recommend itself to all but the most utilitarian decision maker.

CHAPTER 3

THE ROLE OF THE BOARD OF THE TARGET COMPANY DURING A TAKEOVER BID

Professor Blanaid Clarke, School of Law, University College Dublin[*]

1. INTRODUCTION

When a takeover bid is made, or when such a bid is imminent, the board of directors of the target company may react positively or negatively. Where the bid is welcome, the board can facilitate the process by providing all the relevant information to the bidder and encouraging its shareholders to accept the offer. Alternatively, where the bid is hostile, the board may seek to pre-empt or frustrate a bid. The board may consider taking positive action to ensure that the bid is not put before shareholders. Such action may include for example the introduction of poison pills or the sale of material corporate assets. Alternatively, action may take the form of persuading shareholders not to accept an offer which has been made. In this article, an examination will be undertaken of the regulatory framework for these actions in Ireland in order to determine what actions are permitted and the extent to which directors play a strategic role in the success or failure of that bid.

2. THE REGULATORY ENVIRONMENT

The Irish Takeover Panel (the "Panel") is the body responsible for the monitoring and supervision of takeovers and other relevant transactions in relation to securities in relevant companies in Ireland.[1] Prior to its establishment in 1997,

* This article is based in part on a paper presented at a workshop on Corporate Governance, Regulation and Development at the University of Manchester in November 2006. The proceedings for that workshop are available in J. Turner and A. Thankom (eds), *Corporate Governance, Regulation and Development* (Cheltenham: Elgar, forthcoming). Any opinions stated and interpretations suggested constitute personal opinions and interpretations and are not intended to represent the views or practices of any other person or body.

1 The terms "takeover" and "other relevant transaction" are defined in s.1(1) of the Irish Takeover Panel Act 1997. The term "relevant company" is defined by s.2 of the Act as amended by s.75 of the Investment Funds, Companies and Miscellaneous Provisions Act 2005 and s.26 of the Investment Funds, Companies and Miscellaneous Provisions Act 2006.

this role had been fulfilled by the London Panel on Takeovers and Mergers. The London Panel had been established by the market in 1968 and operated very successfully on the basis of a self-regulatory code—the City Code. Following the separation in 1995 of the London and Irish Stock Exchanges, it was agreed that a national supervisory authority would be established in Ireland. A decision was taken at this time that despite the attractions of a self-regulatory system, in order to ensure compliance with an Irish Panel's takeover rules and enforcement of its rulings, statutory powers would be required.[2] The Irish Takeover Panel Act 1997 (the "Act") was thus introduced to establish the Panel as the relevant supervisory authority for takeovers of Irish listed companies. The two principal objects of the Panel which are set out in s.5(1) of the Act are:

(a) to monitor and supervise takeovers and other relevant transactions in order to ensure compliance with the provisions of the Act and the Panel's rules; and
(b) to make rules under section 8 in relation to takeovers and other relevant transactions.

The current set of rules introduced pursuant to the Panel's powers under s.8 of the Act are the Irish Takeover Panel Act 1997 Takeover Rules 2008 (the "Rules") and the Irish Takeover Panel Act 1997 Substantial Acquisition Rules 2007. These rules provide a framework for the conduct of takeovers. In addition, the Schedule to the Act contains seven General Principles which serve to ensure that all shareholders are dealt with fairly and treated equally.[3] Parties to a takeover bid, including the board of the target company, must act in accordance with the relevant Rules and General Principles.

In addition to the domestic takeover legislation, takeovers are now regulated at a European level through Directive 2004/25/EC on Takeover Bids (the "Directive"). This piece of legislation was the subject of prolonged debate and disagreement between Member States since the announcement in 1985 of an intention to propose a directive on the approximation of Member States' regulations governing takeovers. In the early stage, the debate surrounded the nature of the Directive and in particular whether a directive should set out detailed rules or merely a general framework. Having opted for the latter, differences of opinion then arose about the viability of self-regulatory supervisory authorities, the necessity of mandatory general bids, the treatment of employees during a bid and importantly the possibility of defensive actions. Following a substantial number of failed proposals, the Conciliation Committee in 2001 reached a common agreed position.[4] Unfortunately, the text was rejected by the European Parliament on a tied vote. The Commission then established a

[2] Blanaid Clarke, *The Irish Takeover Panel Act, 1997 – A Further Cutting Of The Uk Regulatory Ties,* in Palmer's *In Company*, 1–3 (London: Sweet & Maxwell, 1998).

[3] The Schedule to the Act was amended by s.30 of the Investment Funds, Companies and Miscellaneous Provisions Act 2006.

[4] [2001] OJ C23/1.

High Level Group of Company Law Experts under the chairmanship of Jap Winter to review whether and to what extent a level playing field for takeover bids could and should be created with respect to the mechanisms and structures allowed and created under company law in Member States, which might frustrate or inhibit takeover bids. This Group's report (the "Winter Report") was published in January 2002[5] and heavily influenced the direction of subsequent negotiations. A further proposal was introduced in 2002 and following significant amendment, much of it last minute, the Directive was finally adopted in April 2004. The Directive was adopted with the stated aims of protecting the interests of a target's shareholders, creating EU-wide clarity and transparency in respect of the legal issues to be settled in the event of a takeover and preventing patterns of corporate restructuring within the EU from being distorted by arbitrary differences in governance and management cultures. The Directive contains a number of general requirements which Member States will have to respect through detailed implementing rules and six general principles with which Member States must ensure compliance. These principles are identical to the first six set out in the Schedule to the Act referred to above. Furthermore, art.3(2) expressly authorises Member States to lay down additional conditions and provisions more onerous than those of the Directive with a view to ensuring compliance with the General Principles. Within these limits, each Member State may introduce or retain its own particular rules. The Directive was implemented into Irish law by the European Communities (Takeover Bids (Directive 2004/25/EC) Regulations 2006 (the "Regulations"). The Investment Funds, Companies and Miscellaneous Provisions Act 2006 subsequently introduced a number of amendments to the Act and the Regulations.

It is appropriate to note at this juncture that the board of a target company is also subject to the usual fiduciary duties, Stock Exchange rules and corporate governance guidelines. Monitoring compliance with these regulations is not however part of the task of the Panel. Typically, fiduciary duties are enforced by the courts at the instance of the companies, Stock Exchange rules are enforced by the Stock Exchange itself and guidelines are, of course, merely optional. The relevant provisions are explored in greater detail below.

3. Defensive Action

(a) Rationale for takeovers

In the light of available economic evidence, the Winter Report stated that the availability of a mechanism which facilitates takeover bids is basically

[5] *Report of the High Level Group of Company Law Experts on Issues Related to Takeover Bids* (2002) *http://europa.eu.int/comm/internal_market/company/takeoverbids/index_en.htm* last accessed January 9, 2006.

beneficial.[6] It identified three specific reasons why this might be the case. Firstly, takeovers are a means for bidders to create wealth by exploiting synergies between their existing business and the target company. Secondly, takeover bids also offer shareholders the opportunity to sell their shares to bidders who are willing to offer a price above the prevailing market price. Finally, the market for corporate control suggests that actual and potential takeover bids are an important means to discipline the management of listed companies.[7] This theory is based on the idea that inefficient management leads to share price decreases and shareholders seeking to exit these companies. Opportunities thus arise for other persons to acquire the companies cheaply, to install new management and to achieve greater returns for the new shareholders. The theory suggests that not only do takeovers lead to the removal of under-performing directors but also that the threat of such takeovers encourages directors to perform to the best of their abilities in order to avoid losing their jobs following such takeovers. All that regulators must do in such a scenario is to ensure that the takeover market operates freely and without hindrance from the directors themselves.[8] The Winter Report was emphatic in its assertion that "such discipline of management and reallocation of resources is in the long term in the best interests of all stakeholders and society at large" and that these views "form the basis for the Directive".[9]

In the Irish market, the evidence supports the first two contentions but is weaker on the third. A study was undertaken of all 35 companies subjected to a takeover offer between 1997 (the inception of the Irish Takeover Panel) and 2006.[10] Of the documents studied, 49 per cent involved bids from established companies in the same industries, 36 per cent involved bids by MBO vehicles and a further 15 per cent involved bids by newly-established companies run by individuals often with experience in these areas. In the documentation, synergistic gains were stated to be the reason behind the acquisitions from companies in the same industry. In particular, the opportunity to expand in the Irish markets was emphasised. Interestingly, all the cross-border bids in the sample (28 per cent) fell into this category. In terms of premiums, the average

6 *Report of the High Level Group of Company Law Experts on Issues Related to Takeover Bids* (2002) p.9.

7 H. Manne, "Mergers and the Market for Corporate Control" (1965) 73 *Journal of Political Economics* 110; Jensen and Meckling, "Theory of the Firm: Managerial Behaviour, Agency Costs and Ownership Structure" (1976) 3 *Journal of Financial Economics* 305 and Fama, "Agency Problems and the Theory of the Firm" (1980) 88 *Journal of Political Economics* 288.

8 Though beyond the scope of this paper, it is submitted that the market for corporate control as a form of external market force suffers from its reliance on a number of disputable assumptions, limited application and ambiguous empirical support. See further B. Clarke, "Articles 9 and 11 of the Takeover Directive (2004/25) and the Market for Corporate Control" (2006) *Journal of Business Law* 355–374.

9 *Report of the High Level Group of Company Law Experts on Issues Related to Takeover Bids* (2002) p.19.

10 The study was based on the offer documents and response circulars of the 39 offers made from 1997 to 2006.

recorded for the bids was 33 per cent.[11] This is clearly attractive for the target company's shareholders. It also explains perhaps why all but one of the companies in the sample experienced a change in control following the bid. Finally, the evidence sheds some light on the health of the market for corporate control in Ireland. On a general level, only 5 per cent of relevant companies were subjected to a bid in any one year.[12] In considering which specific bids might be the result of inefficient management, the MBO situations would not appear relevant. Even if the poor share price was caused by inept management, it would seem to pervert the market for corporate control theory, if the management themselves were able to benefit from the fruits of their ineptitude. These bids were stated to be driven overwhelmingly by perceptions of "negative small cap sentiments" in the Irish market. Of the acquisitions from bidders in the same industry which disclosed these details,[13] only one involved all the target company's directors resigning and the remaining bids retained the CEO and/or at least half the board. Of the six bids from newly established bidding companies in the sample, one retained the CEO and finance director, four did not disclose whether any of the directors were resigning and only one declared that all directors were resigning. None of these companies cited poor management as the rational for the acquisition. However, before using this as evidence to question the existence of the market for corporate control, one must remember that the effect of the market for corporate control lies as much in the threat it poses to directors as the production of changes in control. It is arguable thus that where the threat operates effectively, there would not be high incidents of takeovers. All that one might conclude from the survey thus is that there does not seem to be substantial evidence of the stick aspect of the market for corporate control being used.

(b) The Directive

The Winter Report firmly acknowledged that there was a need for a level playing field for shareholders in the EU and that a directive on takeover bids was an important part of it. In this context, the Winter Report noted that:

> "[M]anagers are faced with a significant conflict of interests if a takeover bid is made. Often their own performance and plans are brought into question and their own jobs are in jeopardy. Their interest is in saving their jobs and reputation instead of maximising the value of the company for shareholders."[14]

[11] This does not include offers where there was no actual value for the share listing, e.g. because of a lack of a market, suspension or otherwise.

[12] The average number of relevant companies during the period 1997 to 2005 was 74. The term "relevant company" is determined in accordance with s.2 of the Irish Takeover Panel Act 1997.

[13] Six out of the 19 bids did not disclose any details of the resignations. A further one indicated the finance director and an undisclosed number of other directors were remaining.

[14] *Report of the High Level Group of Company Law Experts on Issues Related to Takeover Bids* (2002) p.21.

As a consequence of its deliberations, the Winter Report suggested that a guiding principle of any European company law regulation aimed at creating a level playing field should be the right of shareholders to make the ultimate decision in respect of whether to tender their shares and at what price. It concluded that the risk was too great that directors would negate the positive economic benefits of takeovers by engaging in actions which would frustrate hostile takeovers.[15] This is the view which is favoured by the Directive.

Recital 16 of the Directive states that:

> "in order to prevent operations which could frustrate a bid, the powers of the board of an offeree company to engage in operations of an exceptional nature should be limited, without unduly hindering the offeree company in carrying on its normal business activities".

This theme is continued in art.3(1)(c) which provides that:

> "the board of an offeree company must act in the interests of the company as a whole and must not deny the holders of securities the opportunity to decide on the merits of the bid".

Article 9(2), giving effect to this principle, requires the specific prior authorisation of shareholders for "any action ... which may result in the frustration of the bid other than seeking alternative bids"[16] and specifically "before issuing any shares" at least from the time the target company is approached. Article 9(3) introduces a requirement for shareholder approval of "decisions taken ... and not yet partly or fully implemented" before the beginning of the period during which r.9(2) applies where the decisions do not form part of the normal course of the company's business and where their implementation "may result in the frustration of the bid". The prohibition applies to all decisions which have a chance of frustrating the bid. Importantly, the identification of an alternative bidder is expressly excluded from the prohibition on the basis that in an auction shareholders are afforded an opportunity to sell their shares.

Article 11 of the Directive introduces a "break-through rule" to deal with what the Winter Report termed "pre-bid defenses".[17] These defences included differentiated voting rights, voting caps and other such structures deemed inconsistent with the recommended principles of shareholder decision-making and proportionality between risk-bearing capital and control. Article 11(2) and (3) dis-apply certain restrictions when a bid has been made public. During the

[15] *Report of the High Level Group of Company Law Experts on Issues Related to Takeover Bids*, n.2, p.2.

[16] Such an exemption is also consistent with practice in Ireland and the UK. Indeed in two of the three hostile bids made to Irish companies during the period of study, this was the successful form of defence utilised by management.

[17] *Report of the High Level Group of Company Law Experts on Issues Related to Takeover Bids*, p.29.

acceptance period, art.11(2) disapplies vis-à-vis the bidder restrictions on the transfer of securities provided for in the articles of association of the target company and restrictions on the transfer of securities in contracts between the target company and its shareholders or between shareholders entered after the adoption of the Directive. Article 11(3) provides that restrictions on voting rights provided for in the articles of association of the target company and restrictions on voting rights in contracts between the target company and its shareholders or between shareholders who entered after the adoption of the Directive shall not have effect at the general meeting of shareholders "deciding on any defensive measures" in accordance with art.9. In addition, art.11(3) provides that multiple-vote securities will carry one vote each at the general meeting of shareholders which "decides on any defensive measures" in accordance with art.9. Article 11(4) provides that where following a bid, the bidder holds 75 per cent or more of the capital carrying voting rights, none of the above restrictions and none of the "extraordinary rights" of shareholders in the articles of association concerning the appointment/removal of board members shall apply. Furthermore, multiple-vote securities will carry one vote each at the first general meeting of shareholders following closure of the bid, called by the bidder to amend the articles or appoint/remove directors. Article 11(6) and (7) provides an exception to the application of art.11(3) and (4) if the restrictions on voting rights are compensated for by "specific pecuniary advantages" or if the rights are held by Member States. The effect of this rule is to transform a bid on a company where there is one dominant blockholder into a bid for a company with dispersed ownership.[18]

Contrary to the spirit of arts 9 and 11 and arguably part of the price of achieving agreement on the Directive, art.12(1) provides that Member States may decide not to require companies registered in their jurisdiction to apply arts 9 and 11. The only concession is that if Member States "make use of this option" they must still grant companies the reversible option of applying the articles.[19] A further weakening of arts 9 and 11 is introduced by the reciprocity provision in art.12(3). This allows Member States "to exempt companies which apply" the articles "if they become the subject of an offer launched by a company which does not apply the same Articles as they do" or a company controlled by such a company. To do so, however, art.12(5) provides that they need the authorisation of their shareholders at a meeting granted no more than 18 months before the bid.

By February 2007, 18 of the 27 Member States had introduced, or were expected to introduce, art.9. Of these, only Malta had not previously provided for the board neutrality obligation in domestic legislation.[20] All the other Member States which had no strict board neutrality obligation before the

18 See however B. Clarke, "Articles 9 and 11 of the Takeover Directive (2004/25) and the Market for Corporate Control" (2006) *Journal of Business Law* 355–374.

19 Article 12(2). This decision must be taken by the shareholders in a general meeting in accordance with the rules applicable to the amendment of their articles of association.

20 Commission Staff Working Document, *Report on the Implementation of the Directive on Takeover Bids*, p.6. SEC (2007) 268, February 21, 2007.

implementation of the Directive, decided not to introduce one. What is more worrying however is that in five[21] of the 18 Member States where the obligation pre-dated the Directive, the reciprocity exception discussed below has also been introduced. Thus, in these five Member States, managements' power to take frustrating measures without the approval of shareholders has actually increased as a consequence of the Directive.[22] The Commission has noted that this development "will very likely hold back the emergence of an open takeover market, rather than promote it."[23] The vast majority of Member States have not imposed or, are unlikely to impose, the break-through rule choosing to make its application merely optional for companies. It is expected to be imposed only by the Baltic States and thus a mere 1 per cent of listed companies in the EU will apply this rule on a mandatory basis.[24] However, the majority of Member States have chosen to adopt the reciprocity provision in art.12(3). The Commission pragmatically concluded thus that, "taking into account the modalities of implementing the reciprocity rule, the main 'benefit' of reciprocity seems to be the fact that it gives management new powers to take frustrating action and makes it easier for companies to disapply the board neutrality or breakthrough rule".[25]

It seems that the implementation by a large number of Member States of the Directive in a protectionist manner[26] appears to have impeded the market for corporate control rather than facilitated it.[27] Commissioner McCreevy has admitted that the "protectionist attitude of a few seems to have had a knock-on effect on others" and that if this trend continues increased barriers to takeovers will result.[28] The Commission has indicated its intention to analyse the reasons

[21] France, Greece, Hungary, Portugal and Slovenia.

[22] A further two of the Member States which currently have board neutrality in place but had not transposed the Directive by the time of the publication of the report, Cyprus and Spain, informed the Commission about their intention to implement the Directive by introducing reciprocity.

[23] Commission Staff Working Document, *Report on the Implementation of the Directive on Takeover Bids*, p.6. SEC (2007) 268, February 21, 2007.

[24] Commission Staff Working Document, *Report on the Implementation of the Directive on Takeover Bids*, p.7. SEC (2007) 268, February 21, 2007.

[25] Commission Staff Working Document, *Report on the Implementation of the Directive on Takeover Bids*, p.9. SEC (2007) 268, February 21, 2007.

[26] Commission Staff Working Document, *Report on the Implementation of the Directive on Takeover Bids*, p.10. SEC (2007) 268, February 21, 2007.

[27] There may also be further reasons for this which are beyond the scope of this paper. For example, the UK Government recognised that the Directive might give rise to "an increased risk of litigation within the bid process, which could have the effect of delaying or frustrating a takeover bid and hindering the opportunity for shareholders to decide upon its merits." (DTI, *Company Law Implementation of the European Directive on Takeover Bids, A Consultative Document* (January 2005) para.1.8.) In addition, it may be the case that implementing the Directive's more opaque provisions will lead to uncertainty, delays in timetables and increased litigation. (B. Clarke, "Takeover Regulation – through the Regulatory Looking Glass" (2007) 8 *German Law Journal* No. 4).

[28] Press Release, February 27, 2007 (IP/07/251).

why Member States are so reluctant to endorse the fundamental rules of the Directive, and in light of this evaluation to bring forward the revision scheduled for 2011.[29]

(c) Irish Takeover Regulations

The provisions in the Directive relating to defensive actions have had limited practical effect in Irish law. Since the introduction of the first set of Takeover Rules in 1997, frustrating action has been prohibited without shareholder consent. The prohibition is set out in r.21 which gives effect to General Principle 3 of the Act which now repeats the wording of art.3(1)(c) set out above. Rule 21 sets out a list of actions specified which are permissible if shareholder approval is granted, if the actions are undertaken in pursuance of an earlier contract "not being a contract the purpose of which was to provide for the taking of frustrating action" or if the Panel is satisfied that the actions would not constitute frustrating action. The prohibition applies "during the course of an offer or at any earlier time at which the target company board has reason to believe that the making of an offer ... is or may be imminent". The list of actions include issuing shares and options, disposing of or acquiring assets of a material amount, entering into contracts otherwise than in the ordinary course of business and "taking any action, other than seeking alternative offers, which may result in the frustration of an offer or in the target company shareholders being denied the opportunity to decide on the merits of such an offer or possible offer". As a result of the implementation of the Directive an additional exception has been introduced to the list in r.21(a)(v). This allows the actions specified above, including frustrating action, where a decision to take the proposed action was made prior to the announcement of the offer or to any such earlier time and "such decision: (1) has been partly or fully implemented before that time; or (2) has not been partly or fully implemented before that time but is in the ordinary course of business." This extends the range of circumstances in which potentially frustrating action may be permissible. In regard to "pre-bid defenses", the structural barriers which the break-through rule was designed to deal with are rare in Irish companies. Part III of the Regulations does not thus make a break-through rule mandatory but rather provides, as it must under the Directive, that companies may choose to opt in to such a rule. To date however, no Irish company appears to have done this. Finally, it should be noted that the reciprocity provision was not applied in Ireland.

[29] Commission Staff Working Document, *Report on the Implementation of the Directive on Takeover Bids*, p.10. SEC (2007) 268, February 21, 2007.

4. The Provision of Advice

(a) The Directive

Despite the strict regulation of defensive actions, the mounting by the board of a target company of a robust defence is allowed. In practice this allows the board a significant opportunity to frustrate a hostile bid. The provision of advice by the board to shareholders is required by the Directive on the basis that the target company board's "insight into, and responsibility for, the strategy and day-to-day affairs of the company enable and require it to advise the shareholders on the takeover bid".[30] This advice plays a crucial role in persuading or dissuading shareholders to accept or reject a bid for the company. Empirical studies have consistently found that the recommendations of target company directors in takeovers are the most important variable in determining takeover outcome.[31] It is submitted that this increases the urgency of ensuring that effective corporate governance mechanisms exist to regulate the process of making these recommendations in order to ensure that directors are acting in the best interests of the company and its shareholders. One would have expected this subject to be included in the Directive. It would be consistent, for example, with its aim of creating a level playing field and preventing patterns of corporate restructuring within the EU from being distorted by arbitrary differences in governance and management cultures.[32] Yet on this subject, the Directive has surprisingly little to say.

There is a clear requirement in the Directive for the board of the target company to provide advice to shareholders. When an offer is made, art.9(5) requires the board to draw up and make public a document setting out its opinion of the bid and the reasons on which it is based. The directors are also required to include their views on the effects of the implementation of the bid on certain matters such as the company's interests, the company's strategic plans, employment and business locations. However, absolutely no reference is made to the composition of the board giving such advice. There is no requirement, for

30 *Report of the High Level Group of Company Law Experts on Issues Related to Takeover Bids* (2002), p.20.

31 N. O'Sullivan and P. Wong, "Board Composition, Ownership Structure and Hostile Takeovers: Some UK Evidence" (1999) 29 *Accounting and Business Research* 139–155; J.S. Cotter, A. Shivdasani and M. Zenner, "Do Independent Directors Enhance Target Shareholder Wealth During Tender Offers?"(1997) 39 *Journal of Financial Economics* 3–43; P. Holl and D. Kyriazis, "The Determinants of Outcome in UK Takeover Bids" (1996) 3 *International Journal of Economics and Business* 165–184; J.S. Cotter and M. Zenner, "How Managerial Wealth Affects the Tender Offer Process" (1994) 35 *Journal of Financial Economics* 63–97; P.H. Eddey and R.S. Casey, "Directors Recommendations in Response to Takeover Bids: Do They Act in their Own Interests" (1989) 14 *Australian Journal of Management* 1–28 and R. Walking, "Predicting Tender Offer Success: A Logistic Analysis" (1985) 20 *Journal of Financial and Quantitative Analysis* 461–478.

32 Recital 3.

example, for directors with a particular conflict of interest to stand down. The General Principles merely require that the board of the target company "act in the interest of the company as a whole".[33] While this duty clearly applies to the giving of advice to shareholders, it appears to amount to a restating of the traditional common law fiduciary duty.[34]

The Higgs Report (2003) acknowledged the "natural potential for conflict between the interests of executive management and shareholders" in the making of a range of routine decisions such as remuneration or audit.[35] In such circumstances, the Report noted that the legal duty on directors to act in the best interests of the company in itself is "insufficient to give full assurance that these potential conflicts will not impair objective board decision-making".[36] Yet, in the more extreme circumstance of a takeover bid, only this duty is prescribed by the Directive. It is submitted thus that by failing to regulate this crucial area of corporate governance, the Directive is failing in its objective to protect fully the interests of shareholders.

(b) Corporate Governance Regulations

The European Commission emphasised that a dynamic and flexible company law and corporate governance framework in the EU is essential for a modern, dynamic, interconnected industrialised society.[37] However, both a Commission-sponsored review of the main corporate governance codes relevant to the EU[38] and the High Level Group of Company Law Experts in its final report (the "final Winter Report")[39] advised against establishing an EU corporate governance code. The final Winter Report noted that while fixed rules in primary legislation may offer "the benefits of certainty, democratic legitimacy and strong possibilities of enforcement" this comes at "the cost of little or no flexibility, and disability to keep pace with changing circumstances." It recommended making use of alternative forms of regulation and identified corporate governance as the first area where this would be required. In the Action Plan on Modernising

33 Article 3(2)(c).

34 An argument might perhaps be made that unlike the traditional common law duties, this duty is owed to shareholders and other stakeholders.

35 D. Higgs, *Review of the Role and Effectiviness of Non-Executive Directors* (London: Department of Trade and Industry, January 2003), para.9.2.

36 D. Higgs, *Review of the Role and Effectiviness of Non-Executive Directors* (London: Department of Trade and Industry, January 2003), para.9.3.

37 Commission Communication. *Modernising Company Law and Enhancing Corporate Governance in the European Union – A Plan to Move Forward,* COM/2003/0284 final. Introduction.

38 Comparative Study of the Corporate Governance Codes relevant to the European Union and its Member States: *http://europa.eu.int/comm/internal_market/ en/company/company/news/corp-gov-codes-rpt_en.htm.*

39 *Final Report of the High Level Group of Company Law Experts on a Modern Regulatory Framework for Company Law in Europe* (November 4, 2002).

Company Law and Enhancing Corporate Governance in the European Union (2003) the Commission emphasised the need for any regulatory response at European Union level to be firm in the principles but flexible in application. It admitted that a self-regulatory market approach, based solely on non-binding recommendations, would not always be sufficient to guarantee the adoption of sound corporate governance practices. It stated that markets would only be able to play their disciplining role in an efficient way in the presence of a certain number of made-to-measure rules. The Commission thus decided against developing a EU corporate governance code on the basis that differences in underlying company law and securities regulation in Member States would mean either that such a code would involve a significant number of different options or it would have to confine itself to abstract principles. It decided thus to adopt a common approach at EU level with respect to these few essential rules and principles and to consider, where possible, the use of alternatives to legislation. In doing so, the Commission has expressed a preference for disclosure requirements viewing them as less intrusive in corporate life and yet a highly effective market-led way of rapidly achieving results.[40]

The presence of independent directors on the board, capable of challenging the decisions of the management, was identified in the Action Plan as a means of protecting the interests of shareholders and, where appropriate, other stakeholders. The Commission had expressly accepted that "in key areas where executive directors clearly have conflicts of interests ... decisions in listed companies should be made exclusively by non-executive or supervisory directors who are in the majority independent". It also indicated its intention to establish at an EU level certain minimum standards of what cannot be considered to be independent.[41] However, the EU Consultation Paper on the Role of Non-Executive or Supervisory Directors of Listed Companies and on the Committees of the (Supervisory) Board (2004) explained that precise definitions of "independence" vary in different codes and there is an absence of "a universal understanding of what independence precisely entails".[42] In February 2005, a non-binding Recommendation was duly published on the Role of Non-Executive or Supervisory Directors of Listed Companies and on the Committees of the (Supervisory) Board) ("The Recommendation").[43] The Recitals note the following:

> "In view of the complexity of many of the issues at stake, the adoption of

[40] Commission Communication. *Modernising Company Law and Enhancing Corporate Governance in the European Union - A Plan to Move Forward,* COM/2003/0284 final. Paragraph 12.

[41] Commission Communication. *Modernising Company Law and Enhancing Corporate Governance in the European Union - A Plan to Move Forward,* COM/2003/0284 final. Paragraph 3.1.3.

[42] Paragraph 2.2.3.

[43] 2005/162/EC.

> detailed binding rules is not necessarily the most desirable and efficient way of achieving the objectives pursued."[44]

Article 13 of the Recommendation deals with the issue of "independence". It provides that "a director should be considered to be independent only if he is free of any business, family or other relationship, with the company, its controlling shareholder or the management of either, that creates a conflict of interest such as to impair his judgment."[45] It also provides that a number of criteria for assessment of the independence of directors should be adopted at national level, taking into account the guidance set out in Annex II of the Recommendation, which identifies a number of situations reflecting the relationships or circumstances usually recognised as likely to generate material conflict of interest.[46] The Annex prefaces these circumstances with a comment that "it is widely understood that assessment of the independence of any particular director should be based on substance rather than form". Article 13 thus provides that the board may consider that, although a particular director meets all the criteria laid down at national level for assessment of the independence of directors, he cannot be considered independent owing to the specific circumstances of the person or the company, and the converse also applies.[47]

The EU Recommendation is consistent with the Combined Code (2006) which was adopted by both the London and the Irish Stock Exchanges on a "comply and explain" basis in their Listing Rules. It states that the board should include a balance of executive and non-executive directors and in particular independent non-executive directors.[48] It also provides that the decision as to whether a director is independent "in character and judgment" rests with the board which must decide whether there are "relationships or circumstances which are likely to affect, or could appear to affect, the director's judgment". Such relationships or circumstances include:

- The existing of "a material business relationship between the director and the company either directly, or as a partner, shareholder, director or senior employee of a body that has such a relationship with the company";
- The receipt by the director of "additional remuneration from the company apart from a director's fee";
- The existing of "close family ties with any of the company's advisers, directors or senior employees"; and
- The representation by the director of a significant shareholder.[49]

The inclusion of circumstances which "could appear to affect" a director's

[44] Recital 4.
[45] Article 13.1.
[46] Article 13.2.
[47] Article 13.2.
[48] A.3 Main Principle.
[49] A.3.1

independence is reduced somewhat by the statement in the Combined Code that where such relationships or circumstances exist which may appear relevant to its determination, i.e. which might appear to affect a director's judgment, the board may still decide that a director is independent but should state its reasons for doing so.[50]

A number of comments can be made about the application of the Combined Code rules in the context of a takeover. First, the rules may be avoided by merely explaining non-compliance. Secondly, it is easier to claim compliance because of the absence of a precise definition of the term "independent" or "conflict of interest". Like other forms of soft law, this leads to criticism that it lacks the clarity and precision needed to provide predictability and a reliable framework for action.[51] Thirdly, the Combined Code is further weakened by the statement that it is up to the Board itself to determine what constitutes "independence." The outcome of all of this is that in most cases where directors have been categorised as "independent" despite not meeting the Combined Code guidelines, the explanation given is that the Board was satisfied that they should be deemed so. This is sufficient to ensure compliance with the Combined Code. Finally, the provision in the Combined Code does not apply to specific decision making scenarios. It only applies to the general board position. What it refers to is independence from the company, not, for example, independence from a bidder. Although the Recommendation provides for periodic reconfirmation of independence,[52] it does not provide for reconfirmation on an issue by issue basis. For this reason, the guidelines pertaining to independence in the Combined Code and Recommendation might be said to be merely illustrative. All of this might be said to support a criticism which is often made of soft law—that it undermines EU legitimacy because it creates expectations but does not or cannot bring about change.[53]

(c) Takeover Rules

In keeping with its obligations under the Directive, rr.3.1 and 25 of the Rules require the target company's board to provide advice to shareholders and to set out the details which must be included in the offer document. However, both go further than the Directive in attempting to deal with the conflict of interest which arises in the context of a takeover. Rule 3.1 states clearly that any director with a conflict of interest should be excluded from the formulation and communication of advice to shareholders. Rule 25.1(d) reiterates this and states that the

[50] The Combined Code on Corporate Governance (July 2003), A.3.1.

[51] D. Trubek, P. Cottrell and M. Nance, "'Soft Law', 'Hard Law' and European Integration: Toward a Theory of Hybridity" (2005) *Legal Studies Research Papers Series* Paper No. 1002.

[52] Article 13.3.2.

[53] D. Trubek, P. Cottrell and M. Nance, "'Soft Law', 'Hard Law' and European Integration: Toward a Theory of Hybridity" (2005) *Legal Studies Research Papers Series* Paper No. 1002.

nature of the conflict should be explained clearly to the shareholders in any document issued by the target company.

Prior to the implementation of the Directive, the General Principles set out in the Schedule to the Act required competent independent advice to be provided to the shareholders of the target company. General Principle 8 in the Act originally stated that the directors of the target company owe a duty to the target company and its shareholders "to act in disregard to personal interest" when giving advice and furnishing information in relation to the offer."[54] However, when the General Principles in the Rules were subsequently replaced with the General Principles set out in the Directive,[55] the new provision was less helpful in this context. General Principle 2 now requires that the target company's shareholders "must have sufficient time and information to enable them to reach a properly informed decision on the offer" and General Principle 3 requires inter alia that the board of a target company must act in the interests of the company as a whole. While it is of course a strong argument to suggest that "sufficient" information includes independent advice, the removal of an express obligation on directors in this regard is significant.

In terms of what constitutes a conflict, the non-statutory Notes to the Rules give three examples of circumstances in which a conflict will exist:

- If there are significant cross shareholdings between an bidder and the target company;
- If a director is common to both companies; or
- If a person is a substantial shareholder in both companies.[56]

Significantly, the Notes state that "the Panel will normally consider in the absence of evidence to the contrary that it is appropriate for executive directors of the offeree to participate in giving advice to shareholders."[57] This deals with the contention that during a takeover, all directors are conflicted because they risk losing their jobs. However, it provides that such directors must satisfy themselves that they do not have a conflict of interest, and that if any director considers that he has a conflict of interest, he should withdraw from the independent board.[58] The Rules deal specifically with a takeover offer which constitutes an MBO. The Notes provide that a director will be regarded as having a conflict of interest if it is intended that he or she will have "a continuing role", whether in an executive or non-executive capacity, in either the bidder or

[54] It might be argued however that this seems somewhat to contradict the Rule prohibiting the director from involving himself or herself in the decision.

[55] With the exception of General Principle 12 dealing with the SARS which has remained.

[56] Note 2 on r.3.1.

[57] Note 2 on r.3.1.

[58] Note 2 on r.3.1.

[59] Note 3 on r.25.1.

target company if the offer is successful.[59] In this context, one issue which could be usefully imported from the corporate governance codes is the point made by Higgs that this new definition addresses not just relationships or circumstances that would affect the director's objectivity but also those that could appear to do so.[60]

A final point to note is that there are a number of clear differences in the categorisation of directors as independent as between these Rules and the various corporate governance codes. Some of these differences are set out in the table below:

	Takeover Rules	Combined Code
Hostile Takeover	Can Advise	No Conflict
Member of MBO Team	Cannot Advise	Conflict
Ongoing Role	Can Generally Advise	Conflict
Association with Shareholder in the Bidder	Generally Cannot Advise	Conflict
Association with Shareholder in the Target Company	Generally Can Advise	Conflict

In actual fact, the existence of these differences may be positively unhelpful in the determination of independence in the context of a takeover. The research undertaken to date explains the difficulty of applying consistent rules to this area. A study of the 39 offer documents reveals that while 31 per cent of directors declined to participate in the advisory team, 69 per cent felt able to give advice to shareholders. In 29 per cent of the bids made, it was declared that at least some of the advisers would become part of the new board or become consultants to the newly acquired company.[61] In a further 29 per cent of the bids, all advisers were expressly stated to have no further role. However, in the remaining 42 per cent of cases, there was no disclosure at all as to the future role, if any, of the directors. In these cases, the shareholders did not have the benefit of this information in evaluating the advice. Clearly, hard rules would be difficult to formulate in relation to independent directors as in practice "one size does not fit all" and there are a myriad of different definitions of independence

60 D. Higgs, *Review of the Role and Effectiviness of Non-Executive Directors* (January 2003), para.9.11.

61 In four of these cases, the majority of the advisers remained, in one an equal number remained, in five a minority remained (although often in an important role like CEO or financial director) and in one an unidentified minority remained.

62 D. Higgs, *Review of the Role and Effectiviness of Non-Executive Directors* (January 2003), para.9.8.

all with different criteria.[62] This is one of the consequences of operating within a hybrid system where hard and soft law operate in the same policy domain. The facets of soft law which appear to make it the appropriate form of regulation can also lead to significant difficulties in terms of application and enforcement.

5. Conclusion

From the foregoing, it seems clear that both national and domestic regulation concentrate almost exclusively on the prohibition of frustrating actions by directors and ignores the impact of directors' advice on the outcome of a takeover. The Directive requires the provision of advice to shareholders but only domestic regulation provides for the giving of independent advice. That said, even it does so in such a way as to allow the directors themselves significant discretion as to their role. In particular, the composition and objectivity of the committees of directors giving advice has largely been overlooked in both European and national regulation. It appears thus to have fallen between two regulatory stools. As a consequence, there exists independently and without reference to each other, systems of corporate governance and takeover regulation in this area which, when taken separately, are not fully effective and which, when combined, create new problems—a negative synergy. Clearly, hard rules would be difficult to formulate in this regard as in practice one can see that "one size does not fit all". As Higgs noted there exists a myriad of different definitions of independence all with different criteria.[63] Although the Rules do not attempt to set out all the circumstances in which a conflict arises, they do set out a number of circumstances in which they will exist. This is helpful because at the very least it shifts the onus of proof onto the directors in such cases to prove that no conflict arises. It is submitted that a solution, if one can be found, might exist in the finding of a compromise between hard and soft law. A description of the nature of independence could be set out clearly in the Rules or indeed in the Directive, which gives the relevant supervisory authorities greater control over the board in this regard. Unlike the Recommendation, the regulator not the board would become the final arbiter of independence. A somewhat similar treatment is given in the Directive and the Rules to the definition of "concert party". It is submitted that advice received from an independent board is crucial to the achievement of the positive economic benefits associated with takeovers and the failure to regulate this area reduces the opportunities for such benefits.

[63] D. Higgs, *Review of the Role and Effectiveness of Non-Executive Directors* (January 2003), para.9.8.

CHAPTER 4

THE DYNAMIC ENTREPRENEUR OR THE INCOMPETENT FOOL?

THE ROLE OF NORMS IN IDENTIFYING LEGITIMATE RISK-TAKING UNDER IRISH COMPANY LAW

Professor Irene Lynch Fannon, Faculty of Law, University College Cork[*]

1. INTRODUCTION

In the last eight years or so, since the establishment of the Office of the Director of Corporate Enforcement under the Company Law Enforcement Act 2001 and the consequent animation of applications to the High Court under ss.150 and 160 of the Companies Act 1990, the Irish judiciary and the commercial bar have had the opportunity to consider the issue of risk-taking in the corporate context. Because of the tightly drawn legislative framework which underpins applications for restriction orders and disqualification orders under ss.150 and 160[1] respectively, it has been possible for the judiciary to closely scrutinize managerial and directorial behaviour against a standard of acceptable risk-taking in a manner which has not occurred before in the history of Irish company law. In the course of their decisions the judiciary has expressed various views on the nature of entrepreneurship and risk-taking and on the issue of what is and what is not a legitimate business risk. This article will examine some of the most interesting of these judgments with two goals in mind. The first is to cast some light on the possibility of developing a set of "bright line" rules or standards as to legitimate commercial risk taking in this area. The second is to ask some interesting questions of an academic nature on the role of judicial rhetoric in Irish company law using the section 150 and 160 cases as illustrative of a broader discourse on the role of non-legally enforceable norms or NLERs as

* This article was prepared at the invitation of Dr Ailbhe O'Neill of Trinity College Dublin for this selection of essays. It was also presented in an abbreviated form at the Society of Legal Scholars Annual Conference at Durham University in September 2007. The author is grateful to Professor D.D. Prentice for an introduction to the literature on the role of norms in company law. Thanks are also due to Karole Cuddihy for invaluable and thorough research assistance. Responsibility for any errors rests solely with the author. Comments and views are most welcome. i.lynchfannon@ucc.ie.

1 See ss.150 and 160 of the Companies Act 1990, as amended by the Company Law Enforcement Act 2001.

they are sometimes described in the academic literature. Thus the paper will firstly provide a context for the author's interest in the role of norms in company law. Secondly it will briefly describe the academic literature on this question. Thirdly it will focus on the Irish section 150 and 160 cases where the role of norms seems evident and finally will proffer some concluding remarks.

2. Corporate Governance and the Role of Norms

Some time ago this author considered a transatlantic case which had arisen in relation to the loss of over €500 million by AIB in a rogue trading scandal.[2] Whilst some aspects of the unsuccessful investor litigation against directors and senior officers of AllFirst Bank (the subsidiary of AIB) and institutional defendants, AIB, AllFirst Bank and AllFirst Financial presented interesting issues concerning Irish and English company law on shareholder actions, in contrast to similar laws in the US,[3] one of the clear lessons to be learnt from a consideration of the entire series of events was that the corporate litigation had little potential to add to the resolution of the corporate governance questions which the case history raised. In fact, the litigation seemed almost irrelevant in light of other steps taken by management to resolve corporate governance concerns of the shareholders as a whole. These steps included commissioning an independent investigation on events,[4] making significant changes at senior management level and restructuring the bank's US investments.[5] Throughout the interesting but failed litigation and in the period afterwards, Allied Irish Banks continued to be a highly profitable company generating considerable income

[2] I. Lynch Fannon, "A Transatlantic Case: The Derivative Action as a Corporate Governance Tool" (2005) 27 D.U.L.J. 1.

[3] *Tomran Inc. v William M. Passano, Jr. et al.*, unreported, Baltimore City Circuit, Matricciani J., Case No. 24–C–02–002561. This case was a derivative action brought by the plaintiff, the holder of ADS representing shares in AIB quoted on the NYSE. In this case the primary relevant state law was either the law of New York or of Maryland, in both cases similar to the law of Delaware in relation to the issues at hand. For a discussion of the relevant law on this issue in these states see M. Dooley, *Fundamentals of Corporation Law* (New York: Foundation Press, 1995), 300ff.

[4] Promonotory Financial Group and Wachtell Lipton Rosen and Katz, "Report to Board of Directors of Allied Irish Banks P.L.C., AllFirst Financial Inc., and AllFirst Bank Concerning Currency Trading Losses" (March 2002) (hereinafter referred to as the "Ludwig Report"). See further *www.aib.ie*.

[5] These actions included selling the US subsidiary operations and before this securing the resignation of a number of key staff there. In addition AIB embarked on a significant buyback of its shares, including those traded on the NYSE. These actions and the Ludwig Report are discussed more fully in Lynch Fannon, "A Transatlantic Case: The Derivative Action as a Corporate Goverance Tool".

[6] In July 2004, the report of Allied Irish Banks on the half-year to June 2004 noted an increase in earnings per share of 10 per cent to €0.64.4 cents and an increase of 13 per cent in the profitability of, inter alia, its US operations. In 2005 after tax profits increased to US$1,387m from US$1,105m in the previous year. For the full text of the press release from Allied Irish Banks on July 27, 2004, see *www.aibgroup.com* (last accessed on July 29, 2004).

from its domestic banking operations.[6] Because of its profitability, in governance terms, the company continued to comply with the *primary imperative from its shareholders*.[7] (This was the case despite the trading losses suffered at the hands of John Rusnak and also despite considerable trading losses incurred by its other foreign operations, primarily in Poland).[8]

The centrally compelling narrative in this case history was that the corporate governance issues, which might have centred on oversight and monitoring by management of the bank's activities[9] were much more effectively managed and resolved outside the legal arena, through pro-active management of the matter by the board of directors and through the continued successful and profitable management of the banking operations as a whole.

> "Throughout the history of this trading scandal it is clear that the Board of AIB has been very proactive in seeking to allay investor fears in relation to the losses caused, underscored by the appointment of the investigating team, which led to the publication of the Ludwig report. The goal presumably is to achieve some sort of resolution of the issues which this scandal raised, and for the most part this strategy seems to have been effective. Most shareholders seem to be content with the resolution if one is to judge by investor confidence as reflected in share price and by various business and media reports. The shareholders have laid down their metaphorical swords and why should they not?"[10]

The story raises questions about the role of legal standards in company law and the relationship of those rules, whether statute-based or judicially developed, to what are generally described as norms or non-legally enforceable norms. The

[7] For a interesting development of academic thinking on current profit maximisation imperatives as experienced by management of public companies see L.E. Mitchell, *Corporate Irresponsibility: America's Newest Export* (New Haven and London: Yale University Press, 2001). Following publication of this text by the influential US corporate law scholar, Lawrence Mitchell, a collection of articles was published in the *George Washington Law Review* considering governance issues in the more somber post-Enron and Worldcom atmosphere which currently prevails. Consideration of concepts such as shareholder primacy and shareholder wealth maximisation in this new zeitgeist has clearly begun the quest for a new set of answers. See in particular D. Millon, "Why is Corporate Management Obsessed with Quarterly Earnings and What Should be Done About It?" (2002) 70 *George Washington Law Review* 890 and M. Gulati, "What are Larry's Criteria for Good Corporate Law?" (2002) *George Washington Law Review* 886.

[8] See the interim report from the company posted on July 29, 2003 which gave profit and loss statements for the half year to June 30, 2003. This report showed that whilst Allied Irish Bank figures improved from 2002 to 2003 in its domestic banking operations from 294 million to 310 million in 2003 and in its operations in Great Britain and Northern Ireland, from 117 million to 125 million it suffered losses in Poland, from 24 million to 8 million and in the United States, from 117 million to 66 million. The report summary also states that, "the profit and loss for half year to June 30, 2003 includes AllFirst up to March 31, 2003 and the Group's 22.5% share of M & T's profit from April 1, 2003." The trading occurred during 2002.

[9] See a somewhat similar scenario but with very significantly different outcomes for the bank and for senior management in the discussion of Barings Bank plc below.

[10] Lynch Fannon, "A Transatlantic Case: The Derivative Action as a Corporate Governance Tool", at p.26.

latter seem to have a particularly important role to play in the context of company law and its relationship to commercial activity. Naturally of course academics in the US[11] had already started considering this question some time ago and so a number of questions have already been raised which require consideration in the corporate law arena on this side of the Atlantic.

3. A Brief Discussion of the Academic Consideration of Norms in the Corporate Context

(a) The first kind of norm or non-legally enforceable rule (NLER)

The identification of NLERs seems to have begun with a consideration of the role of social norms in the economics field, where theories have been developed in the last decade recognising that not all economic transactions can be explained by reference to economic motivators and that social norms and values and other norms of behaviour play a role in transactional decisions.[12] This has been extended to the area of behavioural finance[13] and more recently into legal scholarship[14] and to the relationship between law and norms of behaviour, usually classified as non-legally enforceable norms. So at first glance these kinds of norms could amount to anything which motivates individuals to act in ways which may be ethical or moral but not necessarily mandated or required by law. This brings us to our first kind of norm which can include, for example, a social norm that it is expected that senior management act in accountable and responsible ways and that in some way this norm is internalized. Alternatively one could hypothesise that it is expected that senior management of large companies are seen to react in a dynamic way to corporate events such as the

[11] See further Lynch Fannon, "A Transatlantic Case: The Derivative Action as a Corporate Governance Tool", at p.26 for some references.

[12] See generally *http://cowles.econ.yale.edu*. See R.J. Shiller, *Behavioural Economics and Institutional Innovation* (2005) 72 *Southern Economic Journal* 269–283 on the impact of behavioural economics on the law and economics school. "The discovery of behavioural economics in the past decade or two is really a return to reality from an untenable position that the rational optimizing model is the only framework for economics." See further N. Mazar, and D. Ariely, "Dishonesty in Everyday Life and its Policy Implications" (2006) *Journal of Public Policy and Marketing* 1–21.

[13] R.J. Shiller, *Irrational Exuberance* (Princeton: Princeton University Press, 2000) which considers the dot.com bubble and the second edition of the same text (2005) which topically for Irish audiences considers the housing market bubble in the United States. *University of Pennsylavia Law Review*, 2001–2006/7.

[14] See Symposium, "Norms and Corporate Law" (2001) 149 Univ. Pa. L. Rev.1607; Symposium, "The Legal Construction of Norms" (2000), 86 Va.L. Rev. 1577 (commenting on a number of social norms which regulate civic acts, and the economic internalization affecting these civic acts); M.A. Eisenberg, "Corporate Law and Social Norms" (1999) 99 Colum. L. Rev.1253, 1254–55; see generally R. Ellickson, "Law and Economics Discovers Social Norms" (1998) 27 J. Legal Studies 537, 538–39 (noting the impact of legal scholarship on social norms); and "Symposium: Law, Economics and Norms" (1996) 144 U.Pa.L.Rev..

Rusnak trading matter. We can thus suppose that some of these kinds of norms motivated the management of AIB to take the steps that they took. There is no doubt that possible shareholder litigation and threats of similar actions would contribute to a proactive stance, but what is important in the context of norm scholarship is that many of the steps taken to "fix" the problem were not legally motivated, i.e. the officers of the bank were not obliged to act. One of the interesting points made by NLER scholars is that adherence to norms of behaviour seems to work particularly well when the nature of the community is closed and where reputational interests are extremely valuable. This is clearly a useful analysis in this case in view of the membership of the board of AIB, the importance of reputation to its members and the close knit character of the Irish business and financial community.[15]

Although this area of enquiry is of great interest, particularly in a multi-disciplinary context, these kinds of social norms will not be considered in any further detail in this paper.

(b) A second kind of NLER: the kind with the "judicial backstop"[16]

Another kind of NLER which has been identified in the US literature is the one that judges describe either when they are interpreting statutory standards or filling out obligations described in the common law. Here, academics in the US have noted that in the area of directors' duties it is quite common for judges to describe what directors and others *should and should not do* but without necessarily identifying a legal standard to go with it, and also without visiting any particularly significant legal consequences on the actors for not behaving in this way. A most recent example from the US which caused considerable interest arose in the case brought by minority shareholders regarding executive remuneration in the Walt Disney Corporation. In the Delaware Chancery Court Chancellor Chandler,[17] deciding the matter, had to consider allegations by shareholders of breaches of directors' duties and wasting of corporate funds in relation to the hiring and firing of Michael Ovitz. Here the court found that "many aspects of the defendant's conduct … fell significantly short of the best practices of ideal corporate governance" but went on to states that "Delaware law does not … hold fiduciaries liable for a failure to comply with *aspirational ideals of best practise*".[18] Even more interesting is the following statement from

[15] See further Symposium, "Norms and Corporate Law" (2001) 149 U.Pa.L.Rev. In this collection see in particular on this type of norm, J.C. Coffee, Jr., "Do Norms Matter? A Cross-Country Evaluation" (2001) 149 U.Pa.L.Rev. 2151. See further E.B. Rock and M.L. Wachter, "Norms and Corporate Law: Introduction" (2001) 149 U.Pa.L.Rev. 1607.

[16] Rock and Wachter, "Norms and Corporate Law:Introduction" (2001)149 U.Pa.L.Rev. 1607 at pp.1611–1613.

[17] *In re the Walt Disney Company Derivative Litigation*, No. 15452 (Del. Ch. Aug. 9, 2005).

[18] As Lyman Johnson has asked what do the judges think they are doing here? The judicial understanding of what exactly the purpose of their rhetoric is will be considered below. L.

the Delaware court which goes on to state in *Disney* that it recognises the importance and "essence of business risk" and also states that where decision-makers act "as faithful servants … the redress for failures … *must come from the markets*." In effect the court is indicating that the actions of the directors fell short of best practice but that they are not legally accountable. Nevertheless the court envisaged that if the directors were rendered accountable for their actions in the market through shareholder or other internal corporate actions, that this would be the appropriate vehicle for setting the higher standards aspired to in the judgment. In effect, there is a judicial deferral to the market; something which we will see is quite common in our own jurisprudence.

In the Delaware court in the United States, most of the judicial rhetoric about best practice, or about managerial and directorial standards of behaviour concerns the central corporate governance question, i.e. it focuses almost exclusively on the director-corporation-shareholder relationship. In contrast, cases on this side of the Atlantic arising from that particular relationship are few and far between. Instead the occasion for scrutinizing judicially-generated norms arises in the context of the director-corporation-creditor (and sometimes general public) relationship. The third part of this article, the central part, will consider Irish judicial activity in the context of section 150 and 160 applications.

(c) A third kind of NLER: The norm that replaces law

Before moving on to consider the role of judge-made norms in Part 3, we must finally describe a different school of norm scholarship which moves from a descriptive analysis of what is occurring to a prescriptive analysis. In this scholarship a broader definition of non-legally enforceable norms is argued for. This kind of norm scholarship seeks to proactively identify voluntarism and self-regulation as an effective way of monitoring corporate and directorial action exclusive of any legislative or judicial activity. A good example here is the attempt by this kind of norm scholarship to embrace the CSR movement (i.e. the Corporate Social Responsibility movement). Broadly speaking, CSR will consist of a body of non-legally enforceable norms of good behaviour, for example, pro-active environmental actions, community activism and other kinds of actions which will deliver beneficial results. Here, a school of thought puts forward the idea that norms will yield behaviour which is desirable but which, it is argued, law cannot and perhaps ought not to deliver.[19] This is a more difficult proposition. In this scholarship, regulation and law is viewed as hostile to business interests, enforcing non-voluntary standards that corporations will not accept. In a nutshell, a clear preference is expressed for voluntary policies over hard-core regulation sometimes justified by the argument that self-regulation or

Johnson, "After Enron: Remembering Loyalty Discourse In Corporate Law" (2003) 28 Del. J. Corp. L. 27.

[19] I. Lynch Fannon, "The Corporate Social Responsibility Movement and Law's Empire: Is there a Conflict?" (2007) 58 N.I.L.Q. 1.

voluntarily accepted codes will yield standards which are more acceptable and ultimately therefore more effective. What is most worrying is that this view of the efficacy of self-regulation will be hijacked by those who want to keep the regulators away, reflecting what Chomsky has described as the "American passion for de-regulation", a passion which reached its zenith of achievement in the late 1990s but perhaps is on the decline slightly since Sarbanes-Oxley was passed. For example, Coffee rather worryingly states that the idea that corporate behaviour "may be more shaped and determined by social norms than by legal rule seems to an idea whose time has come".[20] This may well be true in a socially descriptive way but Coffee does not shy away from the prescriptive position and goes on to state that commentators "have placed the relative efficacy of social norms as compared with legal rules at the center of the debate over the judicial role in corporate law." He also seems to express support for the argument that perhaps the courts should be less rigorous because social norms adequately govern behaviour.[21] In some of the judgments considered below, even though this approach is not overtly articulated, one can legitimately ascribe these sentiments to some of the judicial commentary on directorial behaviour. Unfortunately, a number of norm scholars make such robust arguments for the facilitative role of company law that one can only conclude that the agenda is to resist further regulation rather than explore the relationship between norms, corporate laws and good outcomes in any genuine way. Thus in his work, Coffee quite peculiarly identifies the Scandinavian countries as areas where norms seem to place an important role, but fails to acknowledge the equally if not more important fact that these jurisdictions are highly regulated. Norman Veasey similarly decries[22] further attempts at federal regulation as exemplified by Sarbanes Oxley and argues that norms have operated quite well against the backdrop of the common law, again seeming to advocate a hands-off approach for statutory regulators.

In conclusion of this part then, two cautionary notes must be sounded. The first is that non-legally enforceable norms will not yield uniform responses to issues which matter to us. Even though voluntarism can play a part in engaging in discourse with companies and their directors and managers on evolving standards of behaviour, legal standards must articulate what is desirable for all. It is argued here that law cannot be viewed as merely presenting a minimum standard, paving the way for voluntarily adopted standards of competence and socially responsible behaviour. The function of law is to yield high standards in its own right through high legislative standards, effective enforcement and penalties. The second cautionary note is about the danger that the movement towards self-regulation or voluntary codes will be hijacked by those who favour voluntarism in a cynical way. Those are descendants of the law and economics

[20] Coffee, "Do Norms Mater? A Cross-Country Evaluation" at p.2151.

[21] Coffee, "Do Norms Mater? A Cross-Country Evaluation" at p.2151.

[22] N. Veasey, "The Judiciary's Contribution to the Reform of Corporate Governance" [2004] *Journal of Corporate Law Studies* 225.

school of thought who see again a theoretical argument for resisting what they consider to be "big government". Both of these dangers are interrelated.

4. The Role of Norms in Irish Commercial Activity

Following from this brief analysis in Part 2, the rest of this article will focus primarily on the second kind of norm: that created with a judicial backstop.

It is clear that judges on this side of the Atlantic also engage in describing in a non-legally enforceable way aspects of *best practice* without visiting legal consequences for breach of them. As is well-known at this point, the application for restriction under s.150 of the Companies Act 1990 is based on a statutory reversal of the burden of proof so that the onus is on the respondent to show that he or she has acted responsibly and honestly in relation to the conduct of the affairs of the company. Under s.160 it is envisaged that applications can be brought to disqualify directors on a number of grounds, amongst which the ground that the respondent is "unfit to be concerned in the management of a company" has given rise to much commentary. Both the standards of responsibility and unfitness to manage have allowed the judiciary to expand on their ideas of acceptable risk-taking and provide an opportunity to address the broader questions surrounding the creation of norms based on a legal framework.

At the very beginning of the litigation on ss.150 and 160 the Irish judges relied on some English decisions for guidance as to how to delimit what was acceptable or unacceptable in the modern context for directors. So in cases such as *Business Communications Ltd. v Baxter,*[23] *Re Newcastle Timber Ltd*[24] and *Re La Moselle Clothing Ltd*[25] the High Court relied on the statements in *Re Lo-Line Motors Ltd*[26] referred to below. Thus in *Re Lo-Line* Browne Wilkinson V-C made the following statement[27]:

> "What is the proper approach to deciding whether someone is unfit to be a director? The approach adopted in all the cases to which I have been referred is broadly the same. The primary purpose of the section is not to punish the individual but to protect the public against the future conduct of companies by persons whose past records as directors of insolvent companies has shown them to be a danger to creditors and others. Therefore, the power is not fundamentally penal. But, if the power to disqualify is exercised, disqualification does involve a substantial interference with the freedom of the individual. It follows that the rights of the individual must be fully protected. Ordinary commercial misjudgment is in itself not sufficient to justify disqualification. In the normal case, the conduct complained of must display a lack

[23] Unreported, High Court, Murphy J., July 21, 1995.
[24] [2001] 4 I.R. 586.
[25] *La Moselle Clothing Ltd v Soualhi* [1998] 2 I.L.R.M. 345.
[26] (1988) B.C.L.C. 698.
[27] (1988) B.C.L.C. 698 at 703.

> of commercial probity, although I have no doubt that in an extreme case of gross negligence or total incompetence disqualification could be appropriate."

This approach was affirmed and also followed by the Supreme Court in *Re Squash (Ireland) Ltd.*[28]

With these standards in mind the Irish judiciary embarked on an attempt to distinguish between behaviour that was not ideal, that was in fact in some cases "incompetent" and "irresponsible", sometimes "unwise", but which nevertheless was not worthy of attracting legal consequences and, on the other hand, behaviour which was illegal because it went beyond mere commercial misjudgment and lacked "commercial probity". In addition, in some cases the courts quickly agreed with the idea that it was possible to identify behaviour which is between these two poles, behaviour which was "totally incompetent" or "grossly negligent" and therefore illegal. The spectrum of irresponsibility which could range from "totally" to "mildly"[29] irresponsible was similarly accepted as a spectrum of behaviour readily discernable through judicial scrutiny.

The courts have thus expressed a willingness to identify bad behaviour which is still legitimate and seem to have confidence in their ability to distinguish illegal bad behaviour from the more legitimate kind of bad behaviour. In addition, the judges express some confidence in the notion that they will be able to identify extreme cases of incompetence and irresponsibility which will similarly attract legal consequences. Sometimes we will see that the judiciary describes this kind of bad behaviour as total incompetence or total irresponsibility.

Despite the rhetoric, however, and even though the rhetoric might be helpful, the facts of each case seem to be very difficult to classify a priori. Thus it is not easy to predict what behaviour will be regarded by the judge to be just incompetent (or perhaps colloquially we could describe this as being "not great but not illegal") and totally incompetent (illegal), and what will be considered to amount to behaviour lacking in commercial judgment (not great) and lacking commercial probity (illegal). Four years on from the original group of decisions it is clear from the decision in *Re Barnroe Ltd; Director of Corporate Enforcement v Rogers*[30] that the courts continue to adhere to the essential dividing line as laid out in *Re Lo Line* as far as the rhetoric is concerned, but again the difficulty lies in how to classify a particular pattern of facts in accordance with the "guidelines".

Here, the respondents had been directors of the company named in the above-entitled proceedings. The applicant sought disqualification orders under s.160 against them both on the following grounds:

28 [2001] IESC 200.

29 For a consideration of this distinction see *Re Xnet information Systems (in voluntary liquidation)*; *Higgins v Stafford and the Director of Corporate Enforcement (notice party)*, unreported, High Court, O'Neill J., October 10, 2006, considered in more detail below.

30 [2005] IEHC 443; unreported, High Court, O'Leary J., December 21, 2005.

(a) The respondents had failed to keep proper books of account within the meaning of s.202 of the Companies Act 1990.
(b) The respondents operated a bank account for the Company which was not recorded in the Company's books or records and failed to notify the Company's auditor of its existence.
(c) The respondents misappropriated Company funds to personal bank accounts and used a Company bank account for the purposes of personal expenditure. Additionally the respondents caused the Company to expend monies in relation to property owned personally by them.
(d) The respondents maintained or created twin sets of financial statements for the same accounting periods for the purpose of giving a false impression of the Company's position.
(e) The Company failed to file revenue returns on a timely basis.
(f) The respondents caused the Company to trade over an extended period of time when the Company was insolvent.

The applicant submitted that such matters rendered the respondents unfit to be concerned in the management of a company.

O'Leary J. held that the breaches as outlined amounted to breaches of the directors' duties to the company, and that (b), (c), (d) and (f) "amount[ed] to fraud on the part of the respondents in connection with the operation of the Company." He went on to state that the matters outlined at b) and c) were "of the utmost seriousness [and] qualitatively different to the serious but more frequently occurring complaints at a), e) and f)".

O'Leary J. again referred to *Re Lo-line Electric Motors Ltd*[31] and also described the purpose of disqualifying directors as outlined in that decision as not being punitive in nature but primarily designed to protect the public. "Ordinary commercial misjudgment" per se was insufficient to justify disqualification: "the conduct complained of must display a lack of commercial probity, although … in an extreme case of gross negligence or total incompetence disqualification could be appropriate." As to the law on the appropriate period of disqualification, O'Leary J. cited the following passage from the judgment of Finlay Geoghegan J. in *Re Cautious Trading Ltd: Director of Corporate Enforcement v Forristal*,[32] to the effect that "in the absence of any relevant evidence in relation to a respondent, other that the minimum proofs to satisfy s.160 (2) (h) … a period of disqualification" was appropriate. O'Leary J., stating that, "a disqualification, no matter for how short a period, will be seen in the business community as a far greater sanction than a restriction", held that in the instant case disqualification for a period of five years was appropriate.

[31] [1988] 2 All E.R. 692 at 696.
[32] [2005] IEHC 85.

The corporate advisor might take heart in O'Leary J. distinguishing between bad behaviour of the utmost seriousness and bad behaviour that was serious but more common, such as not keeping proper books of account. He or she might be forgiven for thinking that perhaps if the respondents in Barnroe had only failed to keep books of account, things might not have gone so badly. However, the decision of the Supreme Court in *Cahill v Grimes*[33] illustrates the foolhardiness of such an approach. Referring to his own earlier statements in *Business Communications Ltd v Baxter & Anor*[34] which he describes as "fortuitous" Murphy J., delivering the judgment of the Supreme Court, emphasised the importance of the relatively ordinary and mundane activity of maintaining proper corporate documents, however, "*basic in form and modest in appearance*" such documents might be. The court expressed the view that the keeping of records is important to facilitate the orderly management of a company and most importantly, in this context, the orderly liquidation of the company. In the judgment of the court, the respondent's lack of malice and the fact that such destruction of documents seemed to be a one-off act of mismanagement were not sufficient to exonerate him[35]:

> "[A] ... significant feature of the judgment of Mr. Justice Smyth was his statement that he allowed time to Dr Grimes to reconsider the argument which he made to the court and notwithstanding the opportunity given to him he, Dr Grimes, '*continued in a vein as to betoken a total disregard in his conduct complained of*'. It was the fact that Dr Grimes could not then—and does not now—appreciate the gravity of his misconduct that justifies the conclusion that he is unfit to hold the office of liquidator and casts serious doubt upon his suitability to participate in the management of any company."[36]

The disqualification of the respondent for seven years was therefore upheld.

From a guidance or norm scholarship point of view it is possible to extrapolate that in O'Leary J.'s judgment there are matters which are so serious that legally they are beyond redemption, there are other matters which are also serious but more common and therefore perhaps more likely to be exonerated, but the Supreme Court has indicated that exoneration will not be possible even in the more milder instance of misbehaviour, where there is no remorse or consciousness of one's wrongdoing displayed.

33 *The Matter of CB Readymix; Cahill v Grimes* [2002] IESC 12; Supreme Court, March 1, 2002. See also the decision of Smyth J. in the same case in the High Court. *Re Readymix* [2002] 1 I.R. 372.

34 *Business Communications Ltd v Baxter & Anor*, unreported, High Court, Murphy J., July 21, 1995.

35 This is entirely appropriate in light of the fact that the statute makes no mention to the presence or absence of malice as a significant element and does not require any pattern of activity, nor does it exclude responsibility by reference to the frequency or infrequency of the behaviour in question.

36 Unreported, High Court, O'Neill J., October 10, 2006.

Another area of activity which the judiciary have endeavoured to provide guidance is in relation to decisions which may not have been wise but which cannot be considered to be legally blameworthy in hindsight. The difficulties presented by exercising too much hindsight in the commercial world were mentioned by Murphy J. in *Business Communications Ltd v Baxter and Or.*[37] and have recently been echoed by O'Leary J. in *Re Camoate Construction Ltd.*[38] This latter case concerned an application by liquidators of the named company for restriction orders against the three respondents. Liquidators claimed that a payment to the second respondent by the company in respect of his shares was contrary to s.60 of the Companies Act 1963. The respondents said they had received legal advice from a solicitor that the transaction was not contrary to s.60. O'Leary J. held that none of the respondents had acted irresponsibly or dishonestly. Although the actions of the first and third respondents in allowing the company continue to trade for three months after January 2003 were "not wise", O'Leary J. said he was mindful of the remark of Murphy J. in *Business Communications Ltd v Baxter* that the court "must be careful not to be wise after the event. There must be no 'witch-hunt' because the business failed, as businesses will."[39]

(a) The difference between delegation and abdication

The issue of managerial or directorial oversight is another area presenting judicial attempts to give guidance as to best practice. Again, on this side of the Atlantic, the occasion for considering the outer edges of what is in fact a duty of skill and care has taken place in the context of applications for disqualification of directors, rather than in the context of shareholder or investor litigation. A useful point of departure is the decision of Parker J. in *Re Barings Bank plc (No. 5)*.[40] The decision of the Chancery Court arose in relation to applications for the disqualifications of some of the directors of Barings Bank plc following its collapse through losses sustained in another rogue trading scandal. Unlike AIB, the losses were such that the bank could not sustain them and so, on insolvency, applications to disqualify various directors were made. The court had a number of observations to make about delegation and its consequences including the following:

> "But just as the duty of an individual director … does not mean that he may not delegate, neither does it mean that, having delegated a particular function,

[37] *Business Communications v Baxter and Another*, unreported, High Court, July 21, 1995.

[38] [2005] IEHC 346; High Court, July 29, 2005.

[39] In relation to the share transaction, the court was of the view that it was contrary to s.60, in that the company assisted in the purchase of its own shares. O'Leary J. said he was "astonished" that a solicitor could have advised otherwise, but the respondents were entitled to rely on such (erroneous) legal advice.

[40] *Re Barings plc. (No.5)* [1999] 1 B.C.L.C. 433. The latter summary (regarding delegation and oversight by directors) had been approved by the Court of Appeal ([2000] 1 B.C.L.C. 523).

> he is no longer under any duty in relation to the discharge of that function, notwithstanding that the person to whom the function has been delegated may appear both trustworthy and capable of discharging the function ..."

In his concluding remarks Parker J. stated:

> "... directors are entitled ... to delegate particular functions to those below them in the management chain, and to trust their competence and integrity to a reasonable extent [but] the exercise of the power of delegation does not absolve a director from the duty to supervise the discharge of the delegated function".[41]

These ideas certainly sound like good guidelines for appropriate governance not only in companies, but also in other organisations and in fact they have been approved in Ireland. In *Re SPH Ltd. (in vol. liq.)*; *Fennell v Shanahan*[42] orders under s.150 of the Companies Act 1990 were sought by the liquidators against the first and second respondents, who were husband and wife directors of the company. The husband was the "prime mover" behind the company; the wife was a non-executive director. The statement of affairs given by the directors estimated the ultimate deficiency of assets at over €1.7 million. There was a Revenue debt of approximately €25million.

Finlay Geoghegan J. noted that the onus lies on the director to establish that he or she acted honestly and reasonably. She cited the tests set out by Shanley J. in *La Moselle Clothing Ltd.*[43] (approved by the Supreme Court in *Re Squash (Ireland)*[44]) and in her own judgment in *Re Tralee Beef and Lamb Ltd.*[45] (wherein she had previously adopted the passage from the judgment of Parker J. and had held the court should have regard to the degree of compliance with a director's common law duties). Despite the facts that the company met its obligations regarding books and records, except for the year ended March 30, 2002, and that no issue regarding honesty was raised, it was held that there was a serious issue regarding the control and supervision exercised by the respondents over the company's financial affairs, having regard in particular to the amount of the Revenue debt and the manner in which it had been allowed to accumulate. These facts prevented the court from finding that the respondents had at all times acted responsibly and the orders sought were granted.

Interestingly Parker J. felt obliged to point out that "No rule of universal application can be formulated as to the duty referred to ... above." This seems to be borne out by the decision of Peart J. in *Kentford Securities* considered below.[46]

41 *Re Barings plc. (No.5)* [1999] 1 B.C.L.C. 433. The latter summary (regarding delegation and oversight by directors) had been approved by the Court of Appeal ([2000] 1 B.C.L.C. 523).

42 [2005] IEHC 152; High Court, May 25, 2005.

43 [1998] 2 I.L.R.M. 345.

44 [2001] IESC 200.

45 [2004] IEHC; July 20, 2004.

46 Below p.88.

Indeed sometimes the burden of identifying what is bad but not illegal and what is bad and illegal becomes extremely onerous as we can see when we consider Peart J.'s observations of the vagaries of human nature in *Re USIT World plc*[47] where an application was brought to restrict Gordon Colleary. In eventually exonerating Mr Colleary, having spent some time considering standards of directorial behaviour, Peart J. noted that, "it is the very essence of entrepreneurial activity that risks are taken" and that: "The intention of the legislature [in enacting restriction and disqualification provisions] is not to stultify risk taking or business life …". (This is not quite true because it was precisely the intention of the legislature to stultify certain kinds of risk-taking.)

For Peart J., the corporate director or officer can loosely be categorised as being one of two kinds of actor: firstly a well-intentioned but misguided individual who might have unfortunately caused losses because he or she was acting in ways which may have been "unintentional, ignorant, [resulting from] lack of education, naïve, over-enthusiastic, inexperienced, careless, unlucky …" (these surely can be categorised as types of motivations falling short of best practice without attracting legal consequences) or the director or officer can be something much less attractive, a person who is "calculating, callous, opportunistic to the point of criminality, contrived yet convincing … all these people can be restricted …". These activities fall into the category of illegal activity infringing legal standards. So as with the Delaware Court in the United States, and as with many other judges in the company law context, Peart J. acknowledged in this passage, that certain kinds of actions do not meet *best practice* but are well shy of attracting legal liability. In a closely reasoned judgment, Murphy J., in answering the question what does it mean to be unfit to be a director of a company leading to disqualification, similarly differentiated between ordinary commercial misjudgment (*again not meeting aspirational standards of best practice*) which is in itself not sufficient to attract disqualification and conduct displaying a lack of commercial probity which does attract legal consequences. However, Murphy J. also widened the scope of legal consequences by stating that sanctioned behaviour can include cases of gross negligence or total incompetence.[48]

5. The Possibility of Drawing some Bright Line Rules

The danger must be clear to the reader even after considering these few examples of judicial rhetoric in this area. Even though the possibility of providing guidance as to best practise is present there is also the possibility that the sheer volume of adjectives which have been employed to describe legally acceptable behaviour (unwise, incompetent, mildly irresponsible, naïve, ignorant

47 [2006] IEHC 285.
48 *Re Readymix Ltd* [2002] I.R. 372.

but always contrite) and the legally unacceptable (lacking in commercial probity, grossly negligent, totally incompetent, totally and wildly irresponsible and lacking in remorse) becomes overwhelming. For those advising directors and officers and others, the possibility of identifying accurately all of the ranges of behaviour which could be encompassed from case to case accordingly diminishes. Even the apparently straightforward issue of maintaining proper books of account falls into the realms of debatable standards of behaviour depending on the surrounding circumstances. One of the problems facing those wishing to analyse the extensive judicial statements in this area is whether there are any clear guidelines as to what will be considered behaviour which crosses over the line of not complying with aspirational guidelines of best practise to behaviour worthy of sanction. Moreover, even where the facts are made out which would justify a disqualification order, the legislative provisions provide expressly for judicial discretion in deciding not to disqualify and also provide for a discretionary decision as to the period of disqualification. This is clearly stated by the Supreme Court in *Cahill v Grimes*.[49] The identification of a bright line dividing such behaviour is further complicated in this area of law by the fact that in Irish company law we have the penalty of restriction operating at a lower or less serious level than disqualification. This allows the judiciary plenty of room for discretion in considering a broad spectrum of behaviour. In addition, the possibilities presented by applications for relief under the relevant provisions also provide further room for consideration and deliberation over types of behaviour as the following case illustrates.

In *Re Xnet Information Systems (in voluntary liquidation)*; *Higgins v Stafford and the Director of Corporate Enforcement (notice party)*,[50] the applicant sought relief under s.152 of the Companies Act 1990 from the declaration of restriction made by the High Court (Finlay Geoghegan J.) on May 24, 2004. The main ground on which Finlay Geoghegan J. had held that the applicant's conduct had been *irresponsible* (emphasis added)[51] and thus failed to meet the standard required by s.150 was that the applicant had (along with another director) taken three separate loans from the company for amounts totalling over €580,000 and purported to enter into a contract to sell to the company for over €150,000 business fixtures and fittings, all without bringing the matters to the attention of the other directors. This behaviour was held to be in breach of s.194 of the Companies Act 1963.[52]

[49] [2002] IESC 12.

[50] Unreported, High Court, O'Neill J., October 10, 2006.

[51] Obviously attracting sanction under the restriction order provisions but not otherwise where disqualification is at play or where directors' common law duties are at issue. Note that in this section the author seeks to italicize all references to either standards of behaviour or standard which increase the level of judicial discretion exercisable to illustrate the practical impossibility of drawing bright line rules.

[52] See judgment dated May 6, 2004. These actions also amount to a breach of fiduciary duties preventing conflict of interest. They are also potentially in breach of Pt III of the Companies Act 1990.

On behalf of the applicant seeking relief it was submitted that s.152, in contrast to the rigidity of s.150, gave the court a very broad discretion to intervene whenever it considers that it is *just and equitable* to do so.[53] It was submitted that the following factors should be taken into account by the court: the applicant's constitutional right to earn a livelihood; the absence of any finding of *dishonesty* against the applicant; *the applicant's conduct* since the winding up; s.150's role in protecting investors and the public and the effect, if any, on the deterrent value of the section 150 restriction. *Hardship suffered by the respondent* should also be considered, particularly in relation to the constitutional right to earn a livelihood. It was submitted that on an application under s.152, the court should consider whether the effect on the particular individual was arbitrary or excessive, having regard to the legitimate object of statutory restriction. In addition, it was argued that, whereas *all* conduct attracting restriction under s.150—"from the *worst dishonesty* to the *mildest irresponsibility*"—was treated in the same manner, the court was free upon a section 152 application to enquire into the gravity of the conduct, which, in the particular case, had led to the declaration of restriction. It was argued that the applicant had suffered in that he was *unable to engage in entrepreneurial activity* and had *to rely on his wife's income*, at a time when he bore significant personal financial losses resulting from the company's winding up. He had also repaid to the company €25,000. In relation to the deterrent effect of s.150 as a mechanism to protect investors and the public, it was submitted that this was much less engaged where, as here, there had been no finding of *dishonesty* or *bad motive*. In addition, the applicant had already had to *endure the stigma* attaching in the commercial world to a declaration of restriction, a factor referred to by Murphy J. in *Business Communications v Baxter*. In light of the two-year period for which the applicant had now been subject to the section 150 order, it was argued that to accede to the section 152 application would not undermine the deterrent effect of s.150.

The Director of Corporate Enforcement, in opposing the application for relief, argued that, though inexactly equivalent, the UK and Australian experience regarding relief of directors from orders of disqualification, was of considerable guidance and assistance. It was argued that the case law from those jurisdictions suggested the following propositions:

- It must be established that a particular company required a director in a prohibited capacity.
- The legislature must be taken to have been aware that every order of restriction or disqualification would result in a degree of hardship, but the legitimate object of protecting the public outweighed any punitive effect on a restricted individual.

[53] Reference was made to *In Re Ferngara Associates Ltd; F & R Robinson v Forrest* [1999] I.R. 426 and *Carolan and Cosgrave v Fennell* [2005] IEHC 340. (Arguably, in light of *Cahill v Grimes*, these actions could have grounded a disqualification application).

- More regard must be had to the interests of third parties, such as the prospective creditors, employees and directors of any company of which the applicant under s.152 wishes to act as director in future. The court should be satisfied, both that the concerns giving rise to the section 150 declaration have been addressed and that the deterrent value of s.150 was not undermined, before acceding to an application under s.152.
- In light of such considerations, and the mandatory five-year period of restriction enacted by the legislature, the court should be slow to allow an application under s.152. The court's prime focus should be whether a total or partial relief would protect the public.
- Relief, where granted, should generally be limited and conditional, unless the circumstances clearly warranted otherwise.[54]

The ODCE argued that the findings of Finlay Geoghegan J. were extremely serious (possibly echoing O'Leary J. in *Barnroe*) and had demonstrated an entirely inadequate understanding on the applicant's part of the role and duties of a director, particularly in the very sensitive area of dealings in which a director was personally interested. Alternatively, the ODCE also proposed a list of conditions which should be attached in the instant case, should the court be disposed to favour relief. These included that the share capital limit contained in s.150(3) should continue to apply, but be reduced to €40,000, and that a majority of the board of directors of any new company must be independent of the applicant, his wife and any other relative and that no board meeting should take place at which the applicant and his wife were a majority.

O'Neill J. held that the application must be viewed in light of the "fundamental purpose" of s.150, i.e. protection of the public. The wording of s.152(1)[55] meant that the five-year period was not to be considered as equivalent to a jail sentence, which a director *must serve out* or endure. O'Neill J. was further of the view that the relatively low capitalisation requirement contained in s.150(3) indicated that the legislature had been intent on the "relatively speedy rehabilitation" of directors in respect of restriction orders made. Furthermore, O'Neill J. said that the "low capitalisation threshold" in s.150(3) meant that as a practical matter the public would be "relatively unprotected from restricted directors who happen to have access to modest levels of wealth."[56] Accordingly, having regard to Art.40.1 of the Constitution, the statute must not be interpreted so as to "work an invidious discrimination against impecunious persons".

Applying these considerations to the instant case, O'Neill J. first looked to the reasons for the declaration of restriction. There was *a scale of wrongfulness*: At

[54] In the author's view the propositions of the ODCE are worth serious reflection, not least because they do attempt to provide a coherent set of guidelines which seem to be difficult to extract from the range of decisions available.

[55] (“*not more than one year after a declaration has been made in respect of him*”).

[56] Not everyone would describe €60,000 plus as "a relatively modest amount" as it is currently about 30 per cent more that an average annual salary for most.

the one end were actions such that no court would be satisfied to lift a restriction order, and at the other were actions such as had been involved in *Re Ferngara Ltd; F & R Robinson v Forrest*. Next the court should have regard to *the "need"* or *"interest*" of a director in having the restriction lifted. It would not be sufficient for an applicant simply to seek to have the restriction removed for the sake of his reputation; he must have a "plan or intention to re-engage in trade through the medium of a limited company". An applicant must also satisfy the court that, having regard to his impecuniosity, the capitalisation requirement is to him "an insurmountable obstacle". The requirement should be lowered, where it is shown that the level of risk to the public would be low. Hardship, while relevant, must remain secondary to the crucial consideration: protection of the public. According to O'Neill J., the conduct for which the applicant in the instant case had been restricted was somewhere between the two ends of the "*scale of turpitude*" and were *"serious matters*" but that it should also be borne in mind, that Finlay Geoghegan J. had found that the applicant had behaved responsibly for the greater part of the life of the company. Since the winding up of the company, also, the applicant had, despite straitened financial circumstances, abided by an agreement to repay monies due to the company by him.

O'Neill J. said he was satisfied that the applicant had received a "very expensive lesson" from the collapse of the company and the findings of Finlay Geoghegan J. The court was satisfied that the applicant had "absorbed guidance and instruction from these". He had been restricted since May 2004 and had to suffer the stigma attaching in the business community to such status, such stigma being a major part of the deterrent effect of s.150. The essence of the applicant's case was that he was an entrepreneur with an expertise in the computer industry and that he had developed ideas of commercial potential, which he would be unable to exploit without forming and being the director of a limited liability company. It was also submitted that it was beyond the applicant's capacity to raise the €63,000 required to benefit from the section 150(3) exemption and that, in any event, even if he were to attempt to exploit his ideas commercially, investors would be in a position to demand an unfair and disproportionate share of his enterprise, given his restricted status. The court accepted that it would be disproportionate and unfair to allow the applicant to remain in a position whereby he would be "compelled to concede to others a disproportionate and perhaps unfair share in the ownership in the exploitation of his ideas".

Therefore, the court concluded that it was appropriate to lift the restriction order on condition that the section 150(3) requirement on minimum capital would remain but be reduced to €7,500 and that the applicant must inform the notice party of any company in which he became director, secretary, or any position to which a declaration of restriction applies.

As a commentary on this case the following points are worth considering. First, the actual actions of the directors may not have in this case been described as dishonest but it might certainly be reasonable to regard them as being so, in light of the clear breach of fiduciary duties, breaches of Pt III of the Companies

Act 1990 and breaches of s.194 of the 1963 Act. It is fair to observe that if this much ink had been spilled worrying over the state of mind or standard of behaviour of the average petty thief in the criminal courts in addition to considering their constitutional right to earn a livelihood, the hardship they would endure, the stigma attaching to them after a penalty is imposed, it is very possible that levels of incarceration would be substantially reduced in the State. Another interesting point which underscores the possibility for disagreement amongst the judiciary as to where on the spectrum one can pin a particular action is that even as far as the minimum capital requirement imposed under s.150(3) was concerned, none of the parties could agree whether the sum is expensively devastating, relatively modest or prohibitive leading to three different amounts of minimum capital being argued for as the order continued, i.e. €60,000 (as the full amount required), €40,000 and €7,500 with various views expressed as to what sort of an amount of money these are.

In a similar vein trading whilst insolvent has attracted a five-year period of disqualification *In the matter of James Pierce & Sons Limited; Director of Corporate Enforcement v James Pierce and Rosemary Pierce*[57] but in *Newcastle* the view of the court was that trading whilst insolvent for a period of four years was a different matter. Here the court distinguished between the first and second two-year periods. McCracken J. observed that:

> "... To trade while insolvent for 1 year, or perhaps 2 years, in the hope that the company may trade out of its problems is understandable, but to have kept Newcastle trading insolvently for some 4 years, and allowing Revenue debts to build up, appears to me to be totally irresponsible. I do not have the same discretion under Section 150 as I have under Section 160, and the Directors have not satisfied me that they acted responsibly, and accordingly I think I am bound to make an Order under Section 150."

Similarly failing to supervise the issuing of blank cheques was sufficient in the view of Peart J. in *Foster v Swords* to warrant disqualification[58] whereas on a similar oversight issue the same judge was more lenient to a youthful, but nevertheless qualified accountant, who we will encounter in our consideration of the *Kentford* case below.

[57] Unreported, High Court, Finlay Geoghegan J., December 18, 2006. A note of this judgment is available on *www.odce.ie*.

[58] [2005] IEHC 434; unreported, High Court, December 21, 2005. This case concerned applications for orders under s.150 of the Companies Act 1990 against two directors of the named company. The second respondent, Mr Chambers consented to such an order being made against him. The issue was whether an order should be made against the first respondent. Inadequate books and records were kept for the 17 months preceding appointment of the liquidator. S stated that the maintenance of books and records had been C's responsibility; C claimed that the opposite was the case. Peart J. held directors had a duty to inform themselves as to whether books and records were being kept: it was not enough for S to say that he presumed all was being attended to by C. His failure to adequately concern himself was

(a) The importance of judicially created norms. So what ARE the judges doing?

A benign theory is that judges are sketching out best practice; either for future legislators to consider or for guidance on good governance for current directors and in so doing are creating something akin to voluntary codes of good corporate behaviour which will compliment existing legal standards and inform the creation of future legal standards. On a positive note, Lyman Johnson's observations on judicial rhetoric in the United States in the related area of directors' duty of loyalty are instructive. He states that the duty of loyalty can offer "a doctrinal avenue for addressing a potentially broader area of director misconduct than is commonly thought." In reviewing a range of US cases on directors' obligations to the company he hypothesizes that "rhetoric matters too precisely because it affects behaviour."[59] The same analysis can be applied to Irish judicial statements in the context of section 150 and 160 applications. Best practice can become a legal standard. For example many years ago Carroll J., in *Re Hunting Lodges Ltd*,[60] reprimanded the spouse/nominal director of that company in very trenchant terms:

> "The day has long since passed since married women were classified with infants and persons of unsound mind as suffering from a disability so far as responsibility for their acts was concerned … Mrs. P cannot evade liability by claiming that she was only concerned with minding her house and looking after her children. If that was the limit of responsibilities she wanted she should not have become a director of the company … A director who continues as director but abdicates all responsibility is not lightly to be excused."

Here, Carroll J. rendered what might have then been considered a norm of behaviour into a legally reprehensible omission when she remonstrated with the stay at home wife/nominal director of that company for not keeping abreast of company affairs. The consequence was that the nominal director was held personally liable for the debts of the company and it is clear that this principle has now become part of our law.[61] Similarly, to take an example from the English courts regarding the common law duty of skill and care, Hoffman J. in

irresponsible. Also, if it was indeed true, the fact that one director could sign 76 cheques without the other's knowledge was evidence that the company's affairs were not being conducted in a responsible manner. Peart J. was not satisfied that S had in all respects acted honestly and responsibly in relation to the affairs of the company, and so the order sought would be made.

[59] Johnson, "After Enron: Remembering Loyalty Discourse in Corporate Law" (2003) 28 *Delaware Journal of Corporate Law* 27.

[60] [1985] I.L.R.M. 75.

[61] At the time her decision was criticized by many not least Ussher in *Company Law in Ireland* (London: Sweet and Maxwell, 1986) pp.522–525. The author of this seminal text on Irish company law expressed the view that the orders made in the case were not entirely within the terms of the legislation. However, this decision of Carroll J. has withstood the test of time.

Norman v Theodore Goddard[62] and in a second decision in *Re D'Jan of London Ltd*[63] set out a twofold objective/subjective standard for the director's duty of care. The duty which a director owes will be considered to be that which a reasonably diligent person would owe given (a) the general knowledge skill and experience that may *reasonably* be expected of a person carrying out the same functions as are carried out by the director in relation to the company-objective and (b) the general knowledge skill and experience that that director has. Lord Hoffman himself acknowledged that in developing the element of reasonable expectation in (a) that he had overstated this duty in these cases, although the standard was not central to the cases in question. Under older authorities such as *Re City Equitable Fire Insurance Ltd*[64] and *Re Brazilian Rubber Plantations Ltd*[65] there was no objective standard at common law. (The standard of care that a director was required to meet under these authorities was the standard expected of another director with his skill and experience appointed to the same position as he or she had been appointed to by the company). Nevertheless, despite the fact that it was clearly accepted that Lord Hoffman had extended the scope of the duty in these decisions, the Law Commission report on Directors' Duties adopted these standards as "a remarkable example of the modernization of law by the judges".

A less benign theory, which raises more complex questions, is that judges are implicitly acceding to the "hands-off" requests explicitly made by many in the corporate world. Although this theory might be construed as proposing a conspiracy between the judiciary and a business elite,[66] there is a positive interpretation of the "hands-off" or laissez-faire approach. This interpretation can be encapsulated by two ideas proffered by NLER scholars, both of which implicitly posit that the realm of activity with which we are concerned, business risk-taking, and the possible sanctions and their consequences, loss of reputation, means of generating wealth and loss of livelihood present an area of enquiry that is peculiarly distinguishable from other areas of behaviour which are scrutinized by the courts, for example, in the context of criminal law.[67] The first is the idea that NLERS can be very or quite effective in monitoring managerial performance and guiding best practice in the corporate context. The second and more significant idea is that corporate law facilitates and perhaps should continue to facilitate the operation of NLERS in guiding good managerial behaviour towards shareholders.[68]

In the opinion of this author, it seems clear that members of the Irish judiciary may have adopted aspects of both these theories, the benign and less benign,

62 [1991] B.C.L.C. 1028.

63 [1994] B.C.L.C. 561.

64 [1925] Ch. 407.

65 [1911] 1 Ch. 425.

66 A conspiracy which might be of interest to those who engage in a certain kind of "judicial realism" analysis regarding the relationship of the judiciary to particular sectors in society.

67 The author acknowledges the possible contradiction between this observation and observations made earlier regarding the position of the petty thief.

68 See N. Veasey, "The Judiciary's Contribution to the Reform of Corporate Governance" [2004] J.C.L.S. 225 for summary.

without necessarily articulating it in these terms. Examples of the former are led by the statements of Carroll J. in *Re Hunting Lodges Ltd*, statements by Murphy J. referred to in this article regarding the keeping of corporate documents and, to some extent, by statements by O'Leary and Finlay Geoghegan JJ. in relation to standards of decision-making. In relation to the second theory, rhetoric of Peart J. in *USIT*, of O'Neill J. in granting relief in *Xnet* and statements of Peart J. in *Kentford* considered in this section, would seem to indicate that some members of the judiciary might continue to prefer a more facilitative role for company law in this area of activity. Their statements could be interpreted as acknowledging a preference for a "norm" driven approach providing guidelines as to best practice rather than a legally driven, sanctions-based approach which depends on uniformity of standards in all cases.

In *Re Kentford Securities Limited (under investigation); Director of Corporate Enforcement v Patrick McCann*,[69] the court declined to make an order under s.160 in respect of the respondent.

A report by an authorised officer (appointed by the Minister for Trade and Enterprise) found that Kentford was used by the late Des Traynor (who died in May 1994) as "a vehicle for withdrawing monies from and paying monies into the Ansbacher deposits on behalf of Irish resident individuals and companies, thereby facilitating the evasion of taxes". The respondent, who had acted as a director and auditor of the company, swore in an affidavit that the first occasion on which he became aware that Kentford had any connection to the so-called Ansbacher accounts was when he heard it emerge at the Moriarty Tribunal, that he was never party to any scheme to defraud the Revenue Commissioners, and that he never intended to commit any wrongful act. Peart J. accepted this evidence. There was, said Peart J., "no suggestion made on the present application that the respondent made any improper financial gain from his involvement with Kentford".

The applicant submitted that a number of matters rendered the respondent unfit to be concerned in the management of a company including the fact that the respondent had acted as auditor of Kentford while still a director thereof, in contravention of s.163 of the Companies Act 1990. In addition, company documents filed with the Registrar of Companies attempted to disguise this transgression by being deliberately backdated to March 14, 1989. The respondent, as auditor, issued reports on the company's financial statements for the years ending March 31, 1990, 1991, 1992 and 1993, at a time when he knew (or should have known) that the picture presented of a dormant company with £2 assets and share capital respectively was false and misleading, given that large transactions were going through the company's bank accounts, and that there were substantial balances in those accounts. The authorised officer was of the view that, by his conduct in this regard, the respondent had committed offences under s.22(3) of the Companies (Amendment) Act 1986 and s.242 of

[69] Unreported, High Court, Peart J., January 17, 2007. Written judgment available at *www.odce.ie* (pdf).

the Companies Act 1990 and thereby facilitated the defrauding of the Revenue Commissioners. Finally, the respondent knowingly submitted to the authorised officer a forged document, in support of an assertion that he (the respondent) had been assured by Mr Traynor that Kentford was a dormant company with no assets or liabilities.

Peart J. was satisfied that the resignation date of March 14, 1989 had been contrived in 1992 but was of the view that this was in keeping with a culture of signing blank documents and/or backdating documentation. As regards the auditor's reports for 1990–1993, Peart J. said he was satisfied that at the times he signed those reports, the respondent had not signed any form of resignation as a director but that "on the balance of probability this was not a deliberate or conscious breach of the law", noting that the respondent attached little importance to the requirement that he should not act as auditor without having formally resigned as a director. Peart J. said he had no doubt that the respondent "arranged for some backdating of documentation in order to correct the paper record." For a period of time, as a result of "a culture in which he was immersed", the respondent had signed without question any blank documents required of him. Peart J. held that the respondent had breached his duty as auditor by signing the unqualified reports for the years 1990–1993. It was no answer that he had accepted an assurance from Mr Traynor that Kentford was a dormant company with no assets or liabilities. It was not enough for an auditor simply to "go through the motions"; rather his duty was to "pro-actively satisfy himself that what he was told was in fact the situation". Finally, in relation to the forged document handed over to the authorised officer, Peart J. stated that the respondent must have been aware that it was a fabrication and held that the respondent had not acted in a bona fide manner in passing it to the authorised officer. However, Peart J. said he accepted that the respondent had not been aware of the illegal nature of Kentford's activities.

In relation to all matters complained of by the applicant, the court found against the respondent but surprisingly, the court declined to grant a disqualification order. Peart J. took into account that the events in question had occurred between 1988 and 1994, and had begun when the respondent was a very recently qualified accountant. It was also important to bear in mind that the respondent made no financial gain from the illegal activity of the company, "even his failure to observe proper standards as an auditor facilitated the scheme of tax evasion of which he was not aware." Peart J. expressed himself unable to avoid the conclusion that "the respondent was at the time a very small and insignificant cog in the larger wheel being turned by Mr Des Traynor". It was Traynor and his associates involved in the tax evasion scheme that had benefited from the respondent's naivety, lack of attention to his responsibilities and carelessness. Since that period, the respondent had been given a "clean bill of health" by his professional body. Peart J went on to state that "the consequences of a disqualification order being made against an accountant in private practice are devastating"—*"worse even"* (emphasis added) than restriction of a director under s.150. A person subject to a disqualification order would be unable to trade *via* the medium of a limited liability company. The court must balance the effect on a respondent's right to earn a livelihood with the legislative intent to protect the public from auditors who have "fallen short of the standards expected of such an important profession in the commercial life of the country".

Again the by now familiar refrain was re-iterated that the purpose of disqualification was not punitive, but protective of the public. The "only function of the Court" was to:

> "prevent a respondent from acting as an auditor or other officer of a company, *where the evidence is sufficient to demonstrate that as a matter of probability ... the person in question would present a current risk to members of the public who may be adversely affected*". (emphasis added)

Peart J. was satisfied that the respondent in the instant case presented no such current risk, emphasising "the use of the present tense" in relation to unfitness to be involved in the management of a company and noting that the statutory scheme was consistent with the court declining to make an order even where it has found that a respondent has breached his duty as auditor, and/or is unfit to be concerned in the management of a company. While the evidence of the respondent's past conduct disclosed many shortcomings, Peart J. declared himself satisfied that:

> "whatever irregular and improper conduct he was mixed up in all those years ago at the behest of his employer and Mr Traynor is a thing of the past, and that the experience of being caught up in other people's deceptions and illegality has been a chastening one for him and one to which he will never risk returning."

Since the respondent did not *currently* represent "a danger from which the public ought to be protected", the court would decline to grant the order sought.

6. Conclusion

This article will conclude by making two brief points, hopefully arriving at some clarity assisted by brevity.

Firstly, it is timely and important that the Irish judiciary express awareness of and perhaps articulate their intellectual interest in the exercise regarding rhetoric and norms in which they are engaged. The use of judicial rhetoric can be most instructive where it is thoughtfully designed to give clear guidance as to what is best practice, what is considered to fall short of such standards and what is considered to be beyond a mere failure to meet standards of best practice and therefore illegal and worthy of sanctions. These sanctions are admittedly serious for those engaged in commercial activity and this provides the single most compelling reason for clarity in this area. Our consideration at the beginning of this article of other kinds of norms allows us to acknowledge that not only are the sanctions serious in terms of inhibiting the ability to earn a livelihood through the medium of a limited liability company, but that the sanctions are also significant in non-legal ways, in particular in terms of loss of reputation which is particularly important in a relatively small and close-knit community.

For the judiciary, the goal is to pursue what Johnson has described in the context of judicial rhetoric in the US on the duty of loyalty, as a doctrinal avenue of intellectual engagement which will promote "creative-but still disciplined and historically faithful-discourse about where and how to draw … decidedly unsettled boundaries … in modern corporate law." It is easy to accept the role of norms or non-legally enforceable rules or standards, particularly in an emerging area of legal practice. There is no question that well-constructed judicial statements can operate to provide clear guidance to those involved in the management of companies and to their legal advisors. It is indeed helpful when the judiciary provide us with opinions of what behaviour might be considered to be indicative of "sailing windward of the law"[70] and to indicate to advisors and practitioners what is required to comply with aspirational ideals of best practice. However, the level of rhetoric currently surrounding s.150 and s.160 is overwhelming and would seem to operate against the provision of such guidance.

This brings the article to the second brief concluding point and that is that even though the original legislative provisions are comparatively admirably clear and have worked well, it is arguable that the level of argument and consequent rhetoric has in fact clouded that clarity. Guidelines issued by the Office of Director of Corporate Enforcement, although useful in "non-pathological" situations involving the majority of commercial men and women are reduced to points of argumentation in the case law. As a consequence it is not clear whether they can be relied on for any significant period. Timely reclarification and restatement of the basic legislative framework incorporating the best judicial guidelines might be very worthwhile.

[70] An interesting phrase used quite a long time ago by O'Hanlon J. in a decision regarding the behaviour of an auditor, one Des Traynor in a fraudulent trading action in *Re Kelly's Carpetdrome (No. 2)*, unreported, High Court, O'Hanlon J., July 13, 1984.

PART II

GOVERNANCE AND OTHER ACTORS

CHAPTER 5

ACCOUNTABILITY, AUDITOR LIABILITY AND THE POLITICS OF DISCLOSURE

Ciarán O'Kelly, School of Law, Queen's University, Belfast[*]

1. INTRODUCTION

The aim of the audit is to ameliorate the risk associated with company accounts. How can shareholders know whether the accounts tell the truth or not? After all, the directors who depend on a positive set of accounts to keep their jobs are also responsible for actually drawing them up. Independent gatekeepers' verifications of the directors' account of the business's success allow shareholders to discount some of the risk associated with delegating control over their investments to other people. In recent years, however, auditor reputations in Ireland, the UK, the US and elsewhere have been diminished by a series of crises. Beginning with the implosion of Enron and the collapse of Arthur Anderson in its wake and culminating in the global financial crisis from 2007–08, the global financialised economy has seemed to founder on the back of frauds and (more significantly for the system) catastrophic corporate decisions.

Ireland's "light touch" regulatory regime had contributed to its wealth being based on the globalisation of capitalism. The country's economy, ranked as one of the "most globalised" worldwide, has exploited its geographic and demographic position to attract foreign direct investment and to develop export industries. Policies aimed at maintaining a competitive position had Ireland keeping the costs of doing business somewhat less than those of key competitors. As well as more explicit costs, like corporation tax, the costs of doing business in Ireland are a function of disclosure and other regulatory rules. Ireland has, perhaps more than most countries, had to maintain a constant balance between high regulatory standards and the need to keep foreign business in the country.[1] This struggle takes place in the context of membership in the

* Dr Ciarán O'Kelly: c.okelly@qub.ac.uk. The research was facilitated by a research fellowship funded by the Economic and Social Research Council's World Economy and Finance Programme (RES No. 156–25–0033). My thanks go to Professor Justin O'Brien, the Australian National University, Professor Sally Wheeler, Queen's University Belfast and Professor Melvin Dubnick, the University of New Hampshire for many discussions that led to the ideas that are elaborated in this paper.

1 This need not mean that Ireland is always engaged in a "race to the bottom". High regulatory standards are a key component in attracting some reputation-driven businesses to the country. This is notable in terms of the Irish implementation of the reinsurance directive for instance.

European Union's regulatory regime. As a result, part of the trade-off involves the Irish competing with other Member States in terms of attracting investment (most notably the UK when it comes to financial services) but within the context of coordination between Member States on regulatory standards.

The Irish company law and regulatory regime must be understood in the context of these dynamics. At the same time, it seeks to answer questions and problems that recur across all Anglo-American regimes. The relationship between the audit function and corporate governance, for one thing, is not simply a matter of company law. It is also subject to how the idea of corporate accountability is formulated across the regulatory structure. This formulation is in turn not only influenced by the audit as a technical function, but by the audit *industry* as a profession and by the audit *firm* as a business.

This paper aims to explore the position of the audit in corporate governance as it has developed in the Irish economy. I focus on the issue of auditor liability, in terms of both the legal shifts that have shaped the liability regime and the policy debates and positions that have sought to influence the manner in which liability has been defined. I examine the dynamics described in the paragraphs above by looking at two closely related issues: the development of liability in company law and policy, most recently through the European Union, and debates over optimum levels of disclosure in Ireland in the last decade. My aim is to describe how the Irish regime has negotiated a line on the audit in the context of globalisation and Europeanisation and in the light of global dynamics in the audit industry itself. This issue is important in the context of the crisis from 2007–8 onwards because it highlights the difficulties Ireland as a small, open economy faces in finding a path through difficult economic times. It also serves to describe some of the issues that have brought the global financialised economy, of which Ireland is one part, to the impasse it finds itself in, as the gap has widened between incentives and expectations as imagined in the dominant corporate ideology and the realities of accumulation and appropriation in corporate economies, as they are.

One final note: one primary debate over the audit tends to relate to the "expectations gap", between the audit function in law and expectations of the audit, as imagined by members of the public, or politicians, or key stakeholders. My argument here is relevant to the expectations gap debate but I am more concerned with describing the legal regulation of the audit in the context of its relation to the demands of regulation, of commerce and the corporate person, and in relation to the demands that the audit and auditors place on them. Before debating the proper role of the audit, we need to develop a closer sense of how the audit fits into the superstructure of any particular regime.

The remainder of the paper is divided into four sections. In the first section I will address the idea of accountability in the corporation in general, especially as imagined in the "principal-agent" theory. I will then review auditor liability to third parties as it has developed in company law and as it continues to develop within the European regulatory regime. I will focus on the tensions and problems created by the multiple pressures to maintain gate-keeping standards where the audit function is dominated by four firms and where policy is driven by the fear of a catastrophic collapse in the industry (a fear, I should add, that is fuelled by the large audit firms).[2] Then, thirdly, I will give an account of one area where debate over audit liability and the regulatory regime spilled over into the public sphere: the debate over the Directors' Compliance Statement (DCS) requirement in s.45 of the Companies (Auditing and Accounting) Act 2003. I will highlight the manner in which the matter of international regulatory competition came to the fore in thinking about the Compliance Statement. Finally, I will make some remarks about the options open to the Irish regime in terms of the accountability components of the corporate economy.

2. Corporate Accountability

The public company is at base an accountability vehicle. Designed around the separation of ownership and control,[3] the legal, regulatory and governance regime surrounding the public corporation, at least according to the dominant principal-agent theory, enables the raising of capital and generation of revenue because it attends to the interests of diffuse bodies of shareholders while allowing managers to attend to the day-to-day running of the organisation.[4] Although the origins of the principal-agent model of the corporation are American, they are probably even better suited to how the corporation is imagined in the "Anglo" company law sphere, including in the Republic of Ireland. Whereas the company maintained a distinctly public flavour in American political culture until recently,[5] the British, Irish and other corporate models, developing as they did from nineteenth century partnership law, have to a greater or lesser extent always maintained a private tone.

2 Although they do not have standing in Irish law, standards that apply in practice through the Irish professional bodies are generally developed in the UK under the auspices of the Accounting Standards Board (ASB) and the Auditing Practices Board (APB). Accounting standards for companies are developed through the ASB and auditing guidelines through the APB. The ASB and APB are part of the Financial Reporting Council (FRC). The FRC's task is to promote sound financial reporting and the Irish government attended its meetings as an observer (this role has been handed over to the IAASA since its inception). The APB was established in 1991. It develops definitive standards and guidance for auditing practice in the UK and Ireland.

3 A. Berle and G. Means, *The Modern Corporation and Private Property* (New York: Macmillan, 1932), fn.3.

4 For some foundational texts, see M.C. Jensen and W.H. Meckling, "Theory of the Firm: Managerial Behavior, Agency Costs and Ownership Structure" (1976) *Journal Of Financial Economics* 3, 305–360; E.F. Fama, "Agency Problems and the Theory of the Firm" (1980) *The Journal of Political Economy* 88, 288–307; E.F. Fama and M.C. Jensen, "Separation of Ownership and Control" (1983) *Journal of Law and Economics* 26, 301–325; M.C. Jensen, "Value Maximization, Stakeholder Theory, and the Corporate Objective Function" (2001) *Journal of Applied Corporate Finance* 14; for a review of agency theory, see K. Eisenhardt, "Agency Theory: An Assessment and Review" (1989) *Academy of Management Review* 14, 57–74.

5 L.E. Mitchell, *The Speculation Economy* (San Francisco: Berrett-Koehler Publishers, 2007).

As such, accountability mechanisms are imagined in company law, regulation and in corporate governance codes as flows of information from the company to the body of shareholders.[6] Accountability, in these terms, is transparency.[7] The assumption is that, given their rights of control over the corporation, shareholders can discipline managers either directly by exercising their voices or indirectly by exiting the company (which, following a fall in share prices, will subject the managers to the market for corporate control).[8] Power, where the regime works well, lies with the shareholders.

The reliance upon the assumption that a self-regulatory system of accountability-as-transparency underpins a private relationship between the company's directors and its members, binding directors to their duties as well as is possible (in the context of corporate commerce) and allowing shareholders to manage their stake in the company. Furthermore, the privacy of corporate relationships is predicated on the centrality of a cadre of professional gatekeepers—auditors, lawyers and ratings agencies—who testify to the veracity of corporate disclosures.[9] Finally, the value of the gatekeeper system and the

6 See Financial Reporting Council, *The Combined Code on Corporate Governance* (London: Financial Reporting Council, 2008); The Institute of Chartered Accountants in England & Wales, *Internal Control: Guidance for Directors on the Combined Code (The Turnbull Report)* (London: The Institute of Chartered Accountants in England & Wales, 1999); Institutional Shareholders' Committee, *The Responsibilities of Institutional Shareholders and Agents – Statement of Principles* (London: Institutional Shareholders' Committee, 2007); OECD, *OECD Principles of Corporate Governance* (Paris: Organisation for Economic Cooperation and Development, 2004); see also L. Sheridan, E. Jones, and C. Marston, "Corporate Governance Codes and the Supply of Corporate Information in the UK" (2006) *Corporate Governance: An International Review* 14, 497–503; I.P. Dewing and P.O. Russell, "Regulation of UK Corporate Governance: lessons from accounting, audit and financial services" (2004) *Corporate Governance* 12, 107–115; R. Monks, "Modern Company Law for a Competitive Economy: the strategic framework" (2000) *Corporate Governance: An International Review* 8, 16–24; R.A. Monks, "Redesigning Corporate Governance Structures and Systems for the Twenty First Century" (2001) *Corporate Governance An International Review* 9, 142–147; J. Gray, "Lessons from the BCCI Saga for the Current Accountability Debate Surrounding Northern Rock?" (2008) *Journal of International Banking Law and Regulation* 23, 3743.

7 For an explicit conflation between accountability and transparency, see Company Law Review Steering Group, *Modern Company Law for a Competitive Economy: The Strategic Framework* (London: Department of Trade and Industry, 1999), 15: "A key role of company law is as a means of facilitating the operation of market forces, through contractual and other mutual relationships. These operate in markets and other arenas where accountability ('transparency') enables effective assertion of claims by external interests and appropriate response by managements and members (or shareholders)".

8 On exit and voice see A. Hirschman, *Exit, Voice, and Loyalty: Responses to Decline in Firms, Organizations, and States* (Cambridge, MA: Harvard University Press, 1970).

9 On gate-keeping, especially in the wake of the crisis caused by Enron's collapse, see J. Coffee, *Gatekeepers: The Professions and Corporate Governance* (Oxford: Oxford University Press, 2006); for an alternative response on Enron, see M. Aglietta and A. Rebérioux, *Corporate Governance Adrift: A Critique of Shareholder Value* (Cheltenham: Edward Elgar Publishing Ltd, 2005), 235–237 who argue that failures of monitoring must be seen in the light of the shareholder primacy system itself; see also L.A. Cunningham, "Beyond Liability: Rewarding

shareholder primacy-oriented corporate architecture in turn, is itself dependent upon the assumption that gatekeepers are oriented towards members, that members are capable of overseeing gatekeeper relationships to the firm and that shareholders are even *inclined* to oversee those relationships.[10] The shareholder primacy regime collapses if these premises do not hold.

Irish (and British) company law is predicated on the auditor as the primary gatekeeper in corporate accountability: they guarantee the quality of information flows.[11] Although their role is not explicitly set out in Irish company law, they are responsible for verifying that the (largely financial) statements of the company represent a "true and fair" view of the company's actual financial state. Auditors must be appointed by the general meeting and their job is to report to the body of shareholders as to whether the company's accounts have been prepared in accordance with the provisions of the Companies Acts 1963–2006 and give a true and fair view of the state of affairs of the company.[12] As such, the auditor's relationship with the company is primarily focused on a duty of care to the body of shareholders.[13]

Unfortunately, the principal-agent theory approach is predicated on two errors. First, we must understand the implications of the conflation of accountability and transparency in the principal-agent worldview. Agency theorists acknowledge that perfect corporate governance is not attainable. They aim instead to find a best fit between the alleviating of costs associated with delegated agency and the costs of enforcing compliance.[14] Nevertheless, the limits of the contractual or formal formulation of compliance have been shown again and again, whether it was through the disjuncture between Enron's gold-plated board-centred corporate governance standards and the actual position of the board in the company's power structures or through the collapse in the self-regulation of risk in the banking industry that preceded the global financial crisis from 2007–2008. The character of accountability in the agency frame is very narrow indeed. Rather than producing honesty, in other words, accountability-as-transparency seems on occasion to simply produce better liars.

Following from that, second, the defining relationships between auditors and companies are in fact between auditors and *directors*. This has especially been

Effective Gatekeepers" (2007) *Minnesota Law Review* 92, 323–386; S. Deakin and S. Konzelmann, "Learning from Enron" (2004) *Corporate Governance: An International Review* 12, 134–142; M. Klock, "Two Possible Answers to the Enron Experience: Will it be Regulation of Fortune Tellers or Rebirth of Secondary Liability" (2002) *Journal of Corporation Law* 28, 69–109.

10 While imputed versus actual shareholder inclinations are important, I will not address them here. The focus here is on external gatekeepers.

11 For a discussion of the audit as envisaged in the consolidated Irish Companies Bill 2007, see B. Conroy, "Revolutionising Irish Company Law—The Proposed New Companies Consolidation And Reform Act" in this volume, Ch.9.

12 Companies Act 1990, s.193.

13 Not to individual shareholders: more on that below.

14 Jensen and Meckling, "Theory of the Firm" (1976) *Journal Of Financial Economics* 3, 305–360.

the case given the increasing centrality of non-audit services as revenue-generators for audit firms. As the Cadbury Committee put it:

> "Although the shareholders formally appoint the auditors, and the audit is carried out in their interests, the shareholders have no effective say in the audit negotiation and have no direct link with the auditors. Indeed the Committee can see no practicable way of establishing one. Auditors do, however, have to work closely with those in management who have prepared the financial statements which they are auditing in order to carry out their task, and audit firms, like any other business, will wish to have a constructive relationship with their clients."[15]

"Audit firms compete on price and on meeting the needs of their clients (the companies they audit)", the report continues. "This may be at the expense of meeting the needs of the shareholders."[16]

From the 1990s onwards, the five big audit firms (as were) transformed the audit into a loss-leader, designed to provide access to company directors and from which taxation and management consultancy products could be sold. Formal accountability in the guise of reporting requirements and the hiring of gatekeepers does not easily translate into any substantive ceding of power over corporate governance to shareholders.[17]

If the gatekeeper system is captured by corporate managers, then the use of incentives to align the interests of directors with those of shareholders—stock options, bonuses etc.—risks actually exacerbating the problems those incentives were designed to solve. As well as verifying the formal elements in the legal architecture of corporate reporting and governance, gatekeepers can play a role in the moderation of the necessary risk-taking activity upon which a firm must grow. Without gatekeepers, directors might be tempted to design structures that encourage combining the taking of high risks with the capacity to cash in when those risks pay off (and pass losses on to others where necessary).

The conflicts of interest produced by non-audit services lay at the root of the root of the dysfunctional relationship between Arthur Anderson and Enron, although Arthur Anderson's Houston office was not just beholden to Enron for non-audit fees but also for the audit fees that made up 27 per cent of their audit income from public clients.[18] Indeed, partners in Arthur Anderson were actively

[15] Committee on the Financial Aspects of Corporate Governance, *Report of the Committee on the Financial Aspects of Corporate Governance (The Cadbury Report)*: 5.3b (London: Gee & Co, 1992).

[16] *Report of the Committee on the Financial Aspects of Corporate Governance (The Cadbury Report)*: 5.3c.

[17] For a discussion of the difference between formal and professional accountability, see M. Dubnick, "Sarbanes-Oxley and the Search for Accountable Corporate Governance" in J. O'Brien (ed), *Private Equity, Corporate Governance and the Dynamics of Capital Market Regulation* (London: Imperial College Press, 2007).

[18] J. Coffee, *Gatekeepers*, at 29.

discussing the prospects for Enron becoming a $100m client in 2001.[19] On this side of the Atlantic, with FTSE 100 firms paying British auditors "£3 for non-audit services for every £1 paid to them for audit fees" as of 2001,[20] it is no surprise that questions were raised in the wake of Enron's collapse regarding the regulatory balance required to ensure, "that the financial incentives to acquiesce to management pressure never outweigh the disincentives or deterrents to acquiesce."[21] While this practice may have peaked at the turn of the millennium, non-audit services still provide approximately two-thirds of business for the remaining four large audit firms that account for 85 per cent of audits carried out in the EU.[22] Within this context, any sense of accountability being driven by a private relationship between shareholders and directors, mediated by the auditor, is simply unwarranted.

Gatekeepers are of course businesses. They have an interest in revenue and profit and reward systems within the organisations are directed towards that end. The modern audit business is in a sense a constant trade-off between a conservative reputation-based accountability model and an aggressive revenue-generation model. Not only is it very difficult to strike an appropriate balance, if such a balance exists, but it does seem that, increasingly, other market players are not happy to accept that the balance has been struck, that accountability can be defined in terms of or reflected by the audit function. The rise in litigation must in part reflect this.

In this section I have pointed to the audit as imagined in the dominant theory of company law and the complex reality within which the audit works in financialised capitalism as it has formed. Identifying the discord between the two is crucial if we are to understand the context within which Irish corporate governance is formed and within which law and policy is to be made.

The next section sets out the background to the way that auditor liabilities to third parties are imagined in courts. This takes the argument on a step by setting out one important aspect of company law as it formulates the audit. It also shows how policy is formulated around concerns for the audit as a gatekeeping function as described above and the audit articulated as part of an industry that is subject to substantial and serious risks.

3. Auditor Liabilities and Company Law

Audit liabilities have to be defined very carefully if the viability of the audit function is to be maintained. Otherwise, the auditor risks being subject to unjust

19 J. Coffee, *Gatekeepers*, at 29.

20 The Auditing Practices Board, *APB Ethical Standards Consultation Paper: Draft Revised Ethical Standards for Auditors*: *3* (London: Auditing Practices Board, 2007).

21 D. Kershaw, "Waiting for Enron: The Unstable Equilibrium of Auditor Independence Regulation" (2006) *Journal of Law and Society* 33, 390.

22 J. Hughes and B. Masters, "Audit firms uneasy to be held to account" *Financial Times*, December 8, 2008.

costs and the audit will not be viable in anything like its present form. The primary principle by which courts have worked, in this light, is that the auditor is not expected to actively seek out error or fraud, although it should be noted that, should they come across evidence of wrongdoing, they ought to pursue a line of enquiry to establish what has happened.[23] In the words of Lopes J., the auditor is expected to be "a watch-dog, but not a bloodhound."[24] The auditor "is justified in believing tried servants of the company in whom confidence is placed by the company."[25] Given this, as Lord Denning has it in *Fomento v Selsdon*, the auditor's:

> "[V]ital task is to take care that errors are not made, be they errors of computation or of omission or commission, or downright untruths. To perform this task properly he must come to it with an inquiring mind—not suspicious of dishonesty, I agree—but suspecting that someone may have made a mistake somewhere and that a check must be made to ensure that there has been none."[26]

While the auditor owes duties in law to the body of shareholders, the liabilities arising from that duty have to be limited. Otherwise, as Cardozo J. famously put it in 1931, auditors would be exposed to "liability in an indeterminate amount, for an indeterminate time, to an indeterminate class", where aggrieved shareholders seek to hold the auditor responsible for every corporate failure.[27] For such an extensive liability to be introduced, as Lord Bridge put it in *Caparo v Dickman*, would entail "a legislative step which it would be for Parliament, not the courts, to take."[28] It is doubtful that the audit industry could survive in these circumstances.

The concern about the introduction of an "intolerable burden" has led courts to develop a very narrow perspective on proximity, through which they decide on whether an auditor does or does not owe duties to, say, a creditor or an individual shareholder (as opposed to the body of shareholders). In a dissenting judgment to *Candler v Crane*, on the question of whether an accountant could owe duties to parties with whom they did not have a contractual or fiduciary relationship, Lord Denning argued that auditors and others, namely those "whose profession and occupation it is to examine books, accounts, and other

[23] *Re Thomas Gerrard* [1967] 3 W.L.R. 84; On the *Thomas Gerrard* decision, see for instance R. Baxt, "The Modern Company Auditor. A Nineteenth-Century Watchdog?" (1970) *The Modern Law Review*, 33, 413–431.

[24] *In Re Kingston Cotton Mill Company* (No. 2) [1896] 2 Ch. 279 at 288.

[25] *In Re Kingston Cotton Mill Company* (No. 2) [1896] 2 Ch. 279 at 289.

[26] *Fomento (Sterling Area) Ltd. v Selsdon Fountain Pen Co. Ltd. and Others* [1958] 1 W.L.R. 45 at 61.

[27] *Ultramares Corp. v Touche* [1931] 174 N.E. 441 (1931). See also C. O'Leary, "Auditors' liability to third parties – the door remains open" (1998) *Managerial Auditing Journal*, 13, 521–524 at 521.

[28] *Caparo Industries plc v Dickman & Ors* [1990] 2 A.C. 605 at 623.

things, and to make reports on which other people—other than their clients—rely in the ordinary course of business",[29] owe a duty "to their employer or client; and also I think to any third person to whom they themselves show the accounts, or to whom they know their employer is going to show the accounts, so as to induce him to invest money or take some other action on them."[30] They do not owe duties to "strangers of whom they have heard nothing and to whom their employer without their knowledge may choose to show their accounts."[31] Finally, the duty of care extends "only to those transactions for which the accountants knew their accounts were required."[32] Denning's dissent has become the authoritative definition of the threshold past which a duty-creating relationship exists between auditors and third parties.

Arguments over auditor liabilities in the British financial sphere were played out across the 1980s, as a leveraged buy-out boom hit the UK and potential investors based their investment decisions on audited accounts.[33] Most notably, in *Caparo v Dickman*, the courts confirmed that close proximity or neighbourhood was required between plaintiff and defendant for a duty of care to be recognised.[34] The *Caparo* ruling followed Denning's argument from *Candler*, and sought to move slightly away from the more generous (to shareholders) *Anns* ruling by developing:

> "[N]ovel categories of negligence incrementally and by analogy with established categories, rather than by a massive extension of a prima facie duty of care restrained only by indefinable considerations which ought to negative, or to reduce or limit the scope of the duty or the class of person to whom it is owed."[35]

Auditors, as *Caparo* has it, only have duties towards third parties if they know the information they audit will be used by specific third parties in order to pursue some action or other and that the advice the auditor gives "must be relied upon for the purpose of the particular transaction for which it was known to the advisers that the advice was required."[36]

29 *Candler v Crane, Christmas & Co.* [1951] 2 K.B. 164 at 179.

30 *Candler v Crane, Christmas & Co.*, 181.

31 *Candler v Crane, Christmas & Co.*, 181.

32 *Candler v Crane, Christmas & Co.*, 182. The majority decision in *Candler* was overruled in *Hedley Byrne v Heller* and Denning's dissent was adopted into law. *Hedley Byrne & Co Ltd v Heller & Partners Ltd* [1963] UKHL 4.

33 See M. Percival, "After Caparo. Liability in Business Transactions Revisited" (1991) *The Modern Law Review* 54, 739–745.

34 *Caparo Industries plc v Dickman & Ors* [1990] 2 A.C. 605; *Hedley Byrne & Co Ltd v Heller & Partners Ltd* [1963] UKHL 4; See also K. Barker, "Wielding Occams Razor: Pruning Strategies for Economic Loss" (2006) *Oxford Journal of Legal Studies* 26, 289–302; K. Nicholson, "Third Party Reliance on Negligent Advice" (1991) *International Company Law Quarterly* 40, 551–582.

35 Brennan J. in *Sutherland Shire Council v Heyman* (1985) 60 A.L.R. 1, 43–44; *Caparo Industries plc v Dickman & Ors* [1990] 2 A.C. 605 at 618

36 *Caparo Industries plc v Dickman & Ors* [1990] 2 A.C. 605 at 617.

So, while auditors may have duties to the body of shareholders as a class, they certainly do not have obligations towards individual shareholders. Arguably, as Percival puts it:

> "[T]he House of Lords intended that a *caveat emptor* principle should always apply to transactions involving the acquisition of shares, irrespective of the type of document which had been relied upon ... the prudent would-be predator should conduct its own investigation into a target company rather than rely on information produced by the target company's advisers."[37]

By these lights, the information flow in the audit is of a very limited and formal character. In a sense, the audit is not a verification of truth—about accountability in terms of fidelity to truth—but is a formal device designed to generate bases for discussion in general meeting. *Caparo* imagines the audit as a process that ought strictly speaking not be relied upon for investment decisions, even by the company's individual shareholders.[38] Given this, while in some circumstances the trend in the courts towards restricting duties has not been entirely useful in restricting actual auditor liability,[39] shareholders' capacity to hold auditors to account for perceived or actual misdeeds has been substantially diminished.[40]

Auditors' duties to third parties in Ireland can be defined along similar lines to those developed in English courts. Auditors owe duties to the body of shareholders. Duties to individual third parties only arise where there is a direct and tangible arrangement by which the auditor's opinion is—with the auditor's knowledge—given with the aim of a specific third party using the opinion in order to make an investment decision or the like. So creditors or potential investors cannot assume that the auditor is liable to them for any opinion given on the state of a company's finances.[41]

While the various attempts to keep auditor liability in a narrow frame are borne from good motivations—the risks described in Cardozo's maxim, that a

[37] M. Percival, "After Caparo" (1991) *The Modern Law Review* 54 at 739.

[38] C. O'Leary, "Auditors' liability to third parties" (1998) *Managerial Auditing Journal* 13 at 522.

[39] Given the prevalence of tactics among powerful third parties, including "privity letters" between banks and auditors, which serve to act as "an acknowledgement by the auditors of the fact that the lender will rely on the audited accounts." M. Percival, "After Caparo" (1991) *The Modern Law Review* 54 at 744; See also D. McBarnet and C. Whelan, "The Elusive Spirit of the Law: Formalism and the Struggle for Legal Control" (1991) *The Modern Law Review* 54, 848–873. Moreover, auditors have agreed a range of out of court settlements with third parties in the last number of years. See G. McHugh and D. Rowe, "The Audit Gap" in G. McHugh and D. Rowe (eds), *Financial Reporting and Auditing: Bridging the expectations gap* (Dublin: Oak Tree Press, 1996), p.71.

[40] I. MacNeil, "Enforcement of Capital Markets Regulation: The United Kingdom and its International Markets" in J. O'Brien (ed), *Private Equity, Corporate Governance and the Dynamics of Capital Market Regulation* (London: Imperial College Press, 2007) at p.133.

[41] For some consideration of third party liability in the Irish courts, see *Ward v McMaster* [1988] IESC 3; *Glencar Exploration plc v Mayo County Council* [2001] IESC 64; and *Wildgust & anor. v The Governor and Company of the Bank of Ireland & anor.* [2006] IESC 19.

move towards unlimited liability would be a move towards unlimited litigation—the preservation of the narrow liability frame might mean that, without the disciplinary effects of litigation we run the risk that auditors might align themselves more with directorial power than with shareholder interests. That said, Irish auditors (as with elsewhere) have been made subject to a number of disclosure obligations over the last decade, designed to preserve the company from liability to the state by adding to auditor obligations. To take a number of instances, under s.1079 of the Taxes Consolidation Act 1997, if an auditor uncovers breaches of a company's statutory tax obligations, he is required to draw the attention of the company's officers to the offences. He must request that the company rectify the situation or notify the Revenue Commissioners within six months. If the company does nothing, the auditor must resign as auditor and must notify the company of the cause of their resignation and copy the notice to the Revenue Commissioners.[42] This whistleblowing obligation was introduced in s.172 of the Finance Act 1995, after the DIRT scandal, described below, unfolded.[43] Auditors also have reporting obligations under s.194 of the Companies Act 1990, updated by the Company Law Enforcement Act 2001,[44] where they are under an obligation to report a suspicion that books are being kept improperly or that other breaches of the Companies Acts 1963–2006 are taking place to the Director of Corporate Enforcement. Finally, the Companies (Auditing and Accounting) Act 2003 stipulated that auditors certify the ill-fated DCS, on which more below.[45]

Caparo went some way towards solving the perceived "litigation crisis" in the UK's regime.[46] Nevertheless, the audit industry has continued to press for

[42] Taxes Consolidation Act 1997, s.1079. As of the publication of *The Report of the Review Group on Auditing*, "no reports have been received by the Revenue Commissioners under obligations imposed on external auditors who have become aware of material tax offences. Yet the Revenue Commissioners discover irregularities in the affairs of companies the financial statements of which have been audited by an external auditor. This raises the question of whether there was wilful non-compliance with Section 1079 of the Taxes Consolidation Act 1997. No reports have been received by the Revenue Commissioners under obligations imposed on external auditors who have become aware of material tax offences. Yet the Revenue Commissioners discover irregularities in the affairs of companies the financial statements of which have been audited by an external auditor. This raises the question of whether there was wilful non-compliance with Section 1079 of the Taxes Consolidation Act 1997." The Revenue Commissioners, *Review Group on the Operation of The Auditing Profession: Submission by the Revenue Commissioners* (Dublin: Revenue Commissioners, 2000).

[43] Finance Act 1995; On whistleblowing in Ireland, see ICAI, *Blow the Whistle, Who, Why, When and Where? The 'Whistleblowing' Obligations of Accountants in the Republic of Ireland* (Dublin: The Institute of Chartered Accountants in Ireland, 2005); See also N. Brennan and J. Kelly, "A study of whistleblowing among trainee auditors" (2007) *The British Accounting Review*, 39, 61–87.

[44] Companies Act 1990 and Company Law Enforcement Act 2001.

[45] Companies (Auditing and Accounting) Act 2003, s.45.

[46] For an account of the "litigation crisis" see C. Pacini et al., "Commonwealth Convergence Toward a Narrower Scope of Auditor Liability to Third Parties for Negligent Misstatements" (2002) *Abacus* 38, 425–464.

reform. Despite recent high profile suits,[47] and presumably with many more to come,[48] it is difficult to know the extent either of increased litigation or increased litigation costs. For Cousins et al., writing before the Enron collapse, litigation was at that moment "virtually non-existent."[49] Enron and the subsequent Sarbanes-Oxley Act 2002 may, however, have changed the litigation environment worldwide. It has certainly a key part in the story of the diminishing reputation of audit's liability, a reputation that is surely not helped by the audit's narrow position in law. According to the London Economics report on audit liabilities to the European Commission, the number of claims is not rising in the EU, but the cost of claims is. Most importantly, averages are skewed by a few very costly liability claims against auditors.[50] This may confirm the big fear for European policymakers: rather than being entirely responsive to any perceptions about litigation volume, they may be motivated more by fear of another Anderson-style collapse in one of remaining the big four.[51]

In Britain, the Companies Act 2006 saw the introduction of limited liability agreements, whereby, through transparent agreements between companies and auditors, and subject to a range of provisions, potential liabilities could be capped.[52] The Institute for Chartered Accountants in Ireland have lobbied both for the incorporation of audit firms and for a statutory cap to be placed on liabilities.[53] A variety of initiatives at the EU level have produced shifts towards the capping and limiting of auditor liabilities. The Transparency (Directive 2004/109/EC) Regulations 2007 (S.I. No. 277 of 2007), as well as regulating disclosure through the production of a range of new company reports, allow auditors, the Central Bank and the Irish Auditing and Accounting Supervisory Authority (IAASA) to disclose and share information without creating liabilities for the auditors.[54] The Statutory Audit Directive 2006 (2006/43/EC) seeks harmonisation on ethical standards in European auditing. The Directive also invited the Commission to study the economic impact of unlimited auditor liability. This study pointed to liability risks as one of the issues preventing middle-tier audit firms from competing with the big

47 T. Thorniley, "Equitable Life to sue ex-auditor for £2.6bn" *Daily Telegraph*, April 15, 2002.

48 A. Jolis, "Madoff investors to sue UBS, HSBC, Medici and E&Y" *Reuters*, February 4, 2009.

49 J. Cousins, A. Mitchell, and P. Sikka, "Auditor Liability: the Other Side of the Debate" (1999) *Critical Perspectives on Accounting* 10, 285.

50 European Commission, London Economics, and R. Ewart, *Study on the Economic Impact of Auditors' Liability Regimes Final Report to EC-DG Internal Market and Services* (Brussels: London Economics, 2006), 82ff.

51 C. McCreevy, *Speech by the European Commissioner for Internal Market and Services to the JURI Committee of the European Parliament Presenting the Statutory Audit Package* (Brussels: European Parliament, 2007).

52 Companies Act 2006, ss.534–536. See also Financial Reporting Council, *Guidance on Auditor Liability Limitation Agreements* (London: Financial Reporting Council, 2008). The FRC regards agreements as very much desirable.

53 CLRG, *Report of the Company Law Review Group 2007* (Dublin: Company Law Review Group, 2007) p.47.

54 Iris Oifigiúil, *Transparency (Directive 2004/109/EC) Regulations 2007.*

four. It also pointed to the increasing risk of a catastrophic claim against one of the big four. The report recommended some limitation of liability across the Union that would protect auditors from:

> "'[D]eep pocket' syndrome, where, in joint and several liability regimes, plaintiffs view audit firms as having the largest resources" and therefore the audit firm becomes "the target of complaints irrespective of the contribution and responsibility of the firm to the event".[55]

The Commission's moves have been driven and matched by advocacy by audit firms in Ireland and in the rest of Europe. Irish audit firms point to the competitive disadvantage they are at, especially in the context of the limited liability agreements under the UK Companies Act 2006.[56] As such, they are seeking legislation placing caps on liability as soon as possible.[57] The Company Law Review Group (the "CLRG") is examining auditor liability in the context of Ireland's legal regime.[58] The Commission's recommendations for action were published in mid-2008.[59] At the same time, a debate has been taking place about establishing Irish audit firms as limited liability partnerships and a review is taking place.[60] On non-audit services, a debate is ongoing, with Irish auditors lobbying against.[61]

Again, the motivations behind the limitation of auditory liabilities are laudable. As Commissioner McCreevy has pointed out, the European market is characterised by a lack of competition and is exposed to the risk of a litigation-borne failure of one of the big-three audit firms in the Union.[62] At the same time, given the

55 European Commission, London Economics, and Ewart, *Study on the Economic Impact of Auditors' Liability Regimes*, 205ff.

56 Competitive disadvantage is also a major theme in the response to the Directors' Compliance Statement, as described in the next section.

57 Consultative Committee of Accountancy Bodies, *Remarks by the Consultative Committee of Accountancy Bodies – Ireland, on the proposed new EU Auditing Directive, to the Joint Oireachtas Committee on Enterprise and Small Business* (Dublin: Dáil Éireann, 2004); T. O'Rourke, *Remarks by Terence O'Rourke, Chairman of the Consultative Committee of Accountancy Bodies – Ireland, on the proposed new EU Auditing Directive, to the Joint Oireachtas Committee on Enterprise and Small Business* (Dublin: Dáil Éireann, 2004); S. Heaphy, "ICAI Welcomes McCreevy Remarks on Limiting Auditor Liability" (2007) *www.accountingnet.ie*.

58 Department of Enterprise, Trade and Employment, *Minister Michael Ahern refers current auditor liability regime to the Company Law Review Group (CLRG)* (Dublin: DETE, January 3, 2007).

59 Commission Recommendation *Concerning the Limitation of the Civil Liability of Statutory Auditors and Audit Firms Recommendation* (Brussels: European Commission, 2008); for some background, see "Commission plans to cap auditors' liability" (2007) *EurActiv.com* at *http://www.euractiv.com/en/financial-services/commission-plans-cap-auditors-liability/article-161024*.

60 For a good background piece on the pros and cons of the introduction of LLPs in Ireland, see CLRG, *Report 2007*, p.33 et seq.

61 Consultative Committee of Accountancy Bodies, *Remarks by the Consultative Committee*.

62 McCreevy, *Speech Presenting the Statutory Audit Package*; see also S. McGinley, "Charlie McCreevy on Auditor Liability and Other Issues for the Profession" (2005) *Accountancy Ireland* 37.

imbalances inherent in the various director-shareholder-gatekeeper relationships, the limitation of liability, especially through negotiation between company and auditor, risks widening to the gap between accountability as imagined in company law and actual fidelity to shareholder interests in the corporate body.

The environment within which the audit and regulation of the audit takes place is obviously going to undergo serious change in the next few years. The audit industry has been proactive in protecting the audit from liabilities, even if the problems are themselves somewhat overstated. Regulators seek to innovate towards not altogether compatible concerns. They sit between a fear for the audit industry and the detrimental effects of collapse and a fear for the audit function and the detrimental effects of the conflict between the audit business and the audit function, especially in the midst of the global financial crisis. The question of how these questions are resolved at a broad level will not primarily be answered by Irish policymakers, or at least not directly. Nevertheless, Ireland will still have to develop the details of policy through trade-offs between industry, global capital and the regulatory regime. As we see in the next section, we have some experience of how these trade-offs can occur in Ireland.

4. Gatekeeping and the Audit Industry

As the section above shows, the fact that auditors trade in reputation does not imply that they are spared the same market forces and pressures to innovate as other enterprises suffer.[63] Auditors are obviously subject to diverse and simultaneous expectations in terms of their role as gatekeepers and as businesses. Standards must compete with commercial gain. The challenge for Irish company law is to maintain a viable audit function *and* a viable audit industry. In markets characterised by diverse and diffuse shareholding bodies, there can be insufficient pressure to maintain independence from the directors to whom, after all, auditors are financially beholden.

One instance of mobilisation by the Irish audit industry was over the DCS, which constituted one major component of state's response to the DIRT scandal in the late 1990s.[64] When DIRT was introduced, fears were raised about the

[63] As McBarnet and Whelan note, pointing to one accountant saying "'Now a client will ask, "how can I capitalise my costs? How can I keep liabilities off the balance sheet?" If I don't tell him he'll go to a solicitor down the road who will.'" McBarnet and Whelan, "The Elusive Spirit of the Law" at 870; See also J. Coffee, *Gatekeepers*; the value of reputation can be seen most clearly where it fails. One knock-on effect of Enron's collapse, for instance, was the downgrading of the shares of other companies audited by Arthur Anderson. See P. Chaney and K. Philipich, "Shredded Reputation: The Cost of Audit Failure" (2002) *Journal of Accounting Research* 40, 1221–1245; See also K. Houghton and C. Jubb, "The Market for Financial Report Audits: Regulation of and Competition for Auditor Independence" (2003) *Law & Policy* 25, 299–321; S. Krishnamurthy, J. Zhou and N. Zhou, "Auditor Reputation, Auditor Independence, and the Stock-Market Impact of Andersen's Indictment on Its Client Firms" (2006) *Contemporary Accounting Research* 23, 465–490.

[64] On DIRT, see Committee of Public Accounts: Sub-committee on Certain Revenue Matters,

effect the tax would have on the deposits of non-residents (largely emigrants) who kept savings in Ireland. As a result, the tax was not levied on non-resident accounts. At the same time, people expressed concerns that examination of personal details of non-residents would discourage those non-residents from maintaining accounts in Ireland, so the Revenue Commissioners were instructed by government not to examine the documents supporting declarations of non-residency.[65] Unsurprisingly, the consequence of a complete lack of state oversight was that the evasion of the tax became an instrument for competition between banks. Evasion through "bogus non-resident" accounts developed into a massive scam.[66] In the case of the Allied Irish Bank (AIB), indications suggested that, in 1991, just short of 50 per cent of non-resident DIRT accounts were bogus.[67]

An investigation by Dáil Éireann's Public Accounts Committee (PAC) revealed not only widespread evasion, but apparent auditor acquiescence. The PAC of Dáil Éireann found in their 1999 report that:

> "[T]here were a number of serious defects and weaknesses in relation to the statutory external audit function, which contributed to the continuance of the bogus non-resident problem, and these require to be addressed urgently."[68]

The Committee asked:

> "[H]ow precisely were the financial accounts for the year just ended approved by the two relevant parties – the Directors and the External Auditors? How did they arrive at their separate decisions to provide for no liability for arrears of DIRT? Critically, did the External Auditors, as they were required, reach their conclusions independently?"[69]

The nub of the issue, as the Public Accounts Committee saw it, was the risk of an unhealthy alignment of interests between the auditors and the directors of AIB. This alignment of interests, as it turned out, was to the detriment of both the body of shareholders and the Revenue Commissioners. Auditors had relied

Parliamentary Inquiry into D.I.R.T. (First Report) (Dublin: Irish Oireachtas, 1999); for the ICAI's narrative, see J.P. Percy, *Report of Professor J P (Ian) Percy into the Sub Committee Inquiry into DIRT (the Percy Report)* (Dublin: ICAI, 2001); for a journalist's account, see L. Collins, *The Great Irish Bank Robbery: The Inside Story of Conflict, Betrayal and Corporate Greed in Irish Banking* (Dublin: Mentor, 2007).

65 Based on Superintending Inspector's Memorandum SIM 263. Committee of Public Accounts, *Parliamentary Inquiry into D.I.R.T,* 2.2; Indeed, Collins reports that one bogus non-resident account holder gave his address to the bank as "Main Street, New York, America." L. Collins, *The Great Irish Bank Robbery*, p.32.

66 Committee of Public Accounts *Parliamentary Inquiry into D.I.R.T.*

67 J.P. Percy, *Percy Report*, s.3.50.

68 Committee of Public Accounts *Parliamentary Inquiry into D.I.R.T.*, s.6.

69 Committee of Public Accounts *Parliamentary Inquiry into D.I.R.T.*, s.8.14.

on assurances from executives rather than on the reports of internal auditors or had even, in the case of ACC, withdrawn a report estimating huge tax liabilities after directors criticised it.[70]

The widespread and systematic evasion of DIRT, combined with other issues led to the Company Law Enforcement Act in 2001, which established the Director of Corporate Enforcement to regulate Company Law in the country. The DIRT scandal specifically led to the Companies (Auditing and Accounting) Act 2003, which established the Irish Auditing and Accounting Supervisory Authority and introduced the DCS.[71] This was itself a response to the recommendations of the Review Group on Auditing, established to develop solutions to the gatekeeping problems the Public Accounts Committee identified in the tax evasion. The review group published its report in 2000.[72] The Review Group was asked to assess whether the self-regulation of the audit industry was working effectively and consistently.[73] Other terms of reference (of a total 12) included "whether any new or revised structures and arrangements are necessary to improve public confidence, and if so, what form they should take."[74] The group was also asked to examine independence issues around non-audit services, auditor terms and the like.[75]

Of the 80 recommendations in the Review Group's report, the IAASA and the DCS were most notable.[76] The IAASA would be tasked with supervising the self-regulatory aspects of the professional bodies.[77] This "oversight board" would be responsible for recognising accountancy bodies, for approving each body's constitution and standards and for the bodies' supervising disciplinary procedures. Second, the Review Group recommended that company directors be compelled to:

> "[R]eport on an annual basis to the shareholders on the company's compliance with its obligations under company law, taxation law or other relevant statutory or regulatory requirements. The report should confirm that any instances of non-compliance have been reported to the relevant regulatory authority and that in all

70 Committee of Public Accounts *Parliamentary Inquiry into D.I.R.T.*, s.1.3.

71 Companies (Auditing and Accounting) Act 2003, ss.4–33 on the IAASA and s.45, amending the Companies Act 1990 through the introduction of new ss.205E and 205F on the Directors' Compliance Statement. Responses to other scandals had included the whistleblower provisions in the Taxes Consolidation Act 1997 mentioned above.

72 The Review Group on Auditing, *The Report of the Review Group on Auditing* (Dublin: Stationary Office, 2000).

73 The Review Group on Auditing, *The Report of the Review Group on Auditing*, p.18.

74 The Review Group on Auditing, *The Report of the Review Group on Auditing*, p.17.

75 The Review Group on Auditing, *The Report of the Review Group on Auditing*, pp.21–27.

76 Other recommendations acted fleshed out these two, or attended to the activities of audit committees, the relationships between auditors and client firms etc. Although all listed companies must have audit committees in order to comply with Irish Stock Exchange requirements, the requirement was introduced in law for non-listed companies in Companies (Auditing and Accounting) Act 2003, s.42, introducing s.205B to the Companies Act 1990.

77 The Review Group on Auditing, *The Report of the Review Group on Auditing*, p.129 et seq.

> other respects the company has complied with its obligations under company law, taxation law and other relevant statutory or regulatory requirements. The report should be appended to the annual financial statements."[78]

The review group argued that auditors ought to report on whether, in their opinion, the DCS is reasonable. Their report would address whether the directors have made an appropriate disclosure of any issues and, if they feel the directors have not made an appropriate disclosure, the auditors ought to include such information in their report.[79]

This proposal went quite a bit further than the ICAI would have preferred. The Report of the Commission of Inquiry into the Expectation of Users of Published Financial Statements (the Ryan Report), commissioned by the ICAI in 1992, recommended that a "responsibility statement" be introduced, where directors would acknowledge their responsibility for the maintenance of the company accounts.[80] The Ryan Report, it seems, focused on the expectations gap: that the primary problem with the audit was the inordinate expectations on people's parts that auditors would detect corporate wrongdoing.[81] The responsibility statement would help directors, shareholders and the general public see where responsibilities actually lie and expectations of auditors to detect fraud would revert to a more reasonable level.[82]

Given this, the reception by the professional accountancy bodies for the Review Group's report as a whole was somewhat mixed. The ACCA was relatively positive in its response for instance, citing the industry's interest in maintaining public confidence in the audit process. Roger Acton, the head of the ACCA, was quoted as saying:

> "[A]t last there is a willingness to tackle serious issues and create an appropriate platform for effective professional governance. Previous failures in regulation can now be overcome and a coherent—and efficient—system introduced. Proper professional governance is no longer a possible option, it is a requirement."[83]

78 The Review Group on Auditing, *The Report of the Review Group on Auditing*, p.218.

79 The Review Group on Auditing, *The Report of the Review Group on Auditing*, p.218.

80 Institute of Chartered Accountants in Ireland, *Report of the Commission of Inquiry into the Expectation of Users of Published Financial Statements (the Ryan Report)* (Dublin: ICAI, 1992).

81 For some different perspectives on the expectations gap, see D. Guy and J. Sullivan, "The Expectation Gap Auditing Standards" (1988) *Journal of Accountancy* 165, 36–46; C. Humphrey, P. Moizer, and S. Turley, "The audit expectations gap—plus ca change, plus c'est la meme chose?" (1992) *Critical Perspectives on Accounting* 3, 137–161; P. Sikka et al., "The Impossibility of Eliminating the Expectations Gap: Some Theory and Evidence" (1998) *Critical Perspectives on Accounting* 9, 299–330.

82 On the Ryan Report, see P. O'Connor, "Financial Reporting Reforms – An Irish Perspective" in McHugh and Rowe (eds), *Financial Reporting and Auditing*.

83 M. Canniffe, "ACCA Ireland welcomes accountancy regulation plan" *Irish Times*, July 13, 2000.

The ICAI, on the other hand, had proposed a body to supervise self-regulation in its submission to the Review Group on Auditing, and was not particularly sceptical about it, though it did lobby to have greater representation on the IAASA's board.

The DCS was not greeted with much enthusiasm at all.[84] Speaking in the Seanad, Michael Ahern, the Minister for State at the Department of Enterprise, Trade and Employment described the DCS's as being designed to require that "directors have to satisfy themselves that they know what their company's obligations are, have in place procedures designed to secure compliance and give their opinion regarding compliance with these obligations." These requirements, he said, "are entirely reasonable and should not create difficulties for directors who are committed to due diligence in the execution of their duties as directors, and this fact has been acknowledged in many quarters. It is neither the intention nor in my view, the effect, of these provisions to impose draconian requirements on company directors, as some would seek to suggest."[85] This view was not universally held, however, with one senator describing the proposed Statement as "impractical, unnecessary and unwieldy"[86] and the Minister acknowledged a great deal of correspondence and debate over the Statement. Certainly, the business and auditing communities lobbied hard to prevent it being enacted.

The accountancy bodies, notably the ICAI, expressed concern that the Compliance Statement as proposed would have required auditors to report every technical breach of the Companies Acts to the relevant authorities, obviously increasing their exposure to liabilities.[87] It would have required auditors to act as "judge and jury" despite their not being in the business of committing this level of surveillance on their clients.[88] It would also lead to a loss of international competitiveness for Irish industry.[89] American businesses, it was argued, would favour the UK's more light touch regime when making investment decisions. Moreover, there was a fear that the regime would be too costly for small and medium-sized enterprises.

Ceding to intensive industry lobbying, the Taoiseach referred the Compliance Statement[90] to the Company Law Review Group for a Regulatory Impact Analysis in April 2005.[91] The CLRG reported back that:

84 For another discussion of the Compliance Statement, see Conroy, "Revolutionising Irish Company Law" this volume, Ch.9, section 5(e).

85 Office of the Houses of the Oireachtas, *Dáil Debates Official Report*, October 16, 2003 at 1151–52.

86 Office of the Houses of the Oireachtas, *Dáil Debates Official Report*, October 16, 2003 at 1160.

87 B. Walsh, "Accountants argue in public interest" *Irish Times*, May 16, 2003.

88 B. Walsh, "Accountants argue in public interest" *Irish Times*, May 16, 2003.

89 D. Downes, "Companies (Auditing & Accounting) Bill: Boardroom Soundings" (2003) *Accountancy Ireland* 35; J. Smyth, "ICAI critical of audit review group recommendations".

90 That is, Companies (Auditing and Accounting) Act 2003, s.45.

91 For one report see Audit Committee Institute Ireland, "Compliance Statements to be Reviewed" (May 2–3, 2005) *Audit Committee Quarterly* 6.

> "A clear majority of the CLRG considered that it was simply not feasible to commence 45/2003 because of the additional unnecessary costs it causes for companies and the negative and disproportionate effect on national competitiveness and the likelihood of dysfunctional behaviour that would see companies registering outside of Ireland and so unaccountable to the Irish authorities."[92]

The CLRG concluded, based on estimates supplied by legal and accountancy firms and by the Irish Business and Employers Confederation (IBEC) that the DCS would have a one-off set-up cost for Irish businesses of between €90,000 and €1,000,000 and ongoing costs of between €40,000 and €600,000 per annum.[93] This would lead, the CLRG estimated, to a set-up cost to Irish business of €377m and ongoing costs of €202m per annum: a high price to pay for an enhanced international reputation for corporate governance.

In these circumstances and in the light of legislative innovations that placed obligations on directors to obey company law[94] and on auditors to report wrongdoing,[95] and given the regulatory activities of the Director of Corporate Enforcement, the CLRG recommended that the DCS be significantly reformed. In the CLRG's revised form, the Director's Compliance Statement would involve a statement of compliance with tax obligations and indictable offences under the Companies Acts 1963–2006 and an acknowledgement of responsibilities under the Acts. Company directors are obliged to adopt a compliance policy and make a statement about the policy, on a "comply or explain" basis.[96] The requirement for auditors to verify the statement is dropped.[97] These proposals were welcomed by industry,[98] though not entirely by international regulators.[99]

92 CLRG, *Report on the Directors' Compliance Statement* (Dublin: Company Law Review Group, 2005), 5. The Office of the Director of Corporate Enforcement's guidance on the Directors' Compliance Statement envisaged the DCS not being imposed on foreign-registered companies. As a result, the CLRG foresaw many firms incorporating outside Ireland in order to avoid the regulation.

93 The legal and accountancy bodies envisaged a set-up cost of between €90,000 and €750,000 with ongoing costs of between €40,000 and €210,000 per annum. IBEC envisaged a set-up cost of between €140,000 and €1,000,000 with ongoing costs of €50,000 and €600,000 per annum. CLRG, *Report on the Directors' Compliance Statement*, 59. The CLRG speculated that the higher costs reported by IBEC reflected the fact that IBEC represents large firms whereas the clients of legal and accountancy firms range in size from larger to smaller firms.

94 Company Law Enforcement Act 2001, s.100.

95 Company Law Enforcement Act 2001, s.74(e).

96 CLRG, *Report on the Directors' Compliance Statement*, at 130–2.

97 CLRG, *Report on the Directors' Compliance Statement*, at 132.

98 See for instance A. Lambe, "Directors' Compliance Statement – Section 45 – CLRG Shows Common Sense" (2006) *Accountancy Ireland* 38; KPMG and McCann Fitzgerald Solicitors, *Directors' Compliance Statements* (Dublin: KPMG/McCann Fitzgerald, 2006); John Greely, "Review group proposals welcomed" *Irish Times*, November 4, 2005.

99 OECD Directorate for Financial and Enterprise Affairs, *Ireland: Phase 2 – Report on the Application of the Convention on Combating Bribery of Foreign Public Officials in*

This revision of the DCS was not welcomed by the Irish Congress of Trade Unions, the Revenue Commissioners or the Office for the Director of Corporate Enforcement, each of whom attached dissenting appendices to the CLRG report. In his reservations, Paul Appleby, the Director for Corporate Enforcement wrote that the Compliance Statement was "a self-review framework for directors which adopts standard 'comply or explain' principles in seeking to engage them with their duty to ensure that their company fulfils its primary legal obligations"[100] and so did not present much of a departure from standard practice in the British model. Furthermore, the ODCE, as with the other two dissenters, suggested that the model for estimating the costs of the Compliance Statement was fundamentally flawed. No effort had been made to estimate how much of the costs cited by the ICAI and IBEC—the only two sources for costs—were a direct result of the incremental change represented by the Compliance Statement over an above costs associated with oversight under the Combined Code. Appleby also pointed out that the costs as cited represented less than 1 per cent of annual profit for set up and far less for ongoing costs. Furthermore, the study had neither estimated the opportunity costs of the Compliance Statement nor had it verified the accuracy of the ICAI's and IBEC's figures.[101]

Appleby pointed out that, moreover, that if the costs of the DCS were actually low, then the impact on global competitiveness would also be low. Apart from the fact that competitiveness is multifaceted, and so direct regulatory costs were only one factor:

> "In the absence of any analysis which would satisfactorily justify the indicated assumption that the present DCS would reduce the inflow of FDI by 10 per cent, it appears to the ODCE that 0.01 per cent is as valid a speculative assumption of likely impact as any other number."[102]

Nevertheless, the key driver of criticisms of the DCS was that Ireland is not in a position to pursue high regulatory standards if those standards have too high a price-tag attached. As Tom Courtney, head of the CLRG put it, the original introduction of the DCS had revealed:

> "[A] certain naivety in thinking that a country of our size could punch so much above its weight in raising the bar for corporate compliance without the result that FDI would vote with their dollars and exit. Ireland was going to be unique amongst developed countries in seeking to impose such a costly compliance

International Business Transactions and the 1997 Revised Recommendation on Combating Briberery in International Business Transactions: 73–74 (Paris: OECD, 2007).

100 CLRG, *Report on the Directors' Compliance Statement*, 141; for a discussion of the Office of the Director of Corporate Enforcement, see John Heneghan and David O'Donnell, "Governance, Compliance and Legal Enforcement: Evaluating a Recent Irish Initiative" (2007) *Corporate Governance International Journal of Business in Society* Vol.7, No. 1: 54–65.

101 CLRG, *Report on the Directors' Compliance Statement*, at 141.

102 CLRG, *Report on the Directors' Compliance Statement*, at 142.

> verification procedure; uniquely stringent is something to which I believe we should not aspire."[103]

The Irish state has a limited space for manoeuvre when it comes to regulation. Given all of this, Ireland finds itself between two great powers. The economy is imagined as relying on global, primarily American capital for its survival (a situation that has taken on a worrying tone at present). As a result governments and elites maintain a keen eye on Ireland's existence as a leader on price. At the same time, the United Kingdom looms large as a direct competitor on regulatory costs. The imperative for Ireland seems to be the maintenance of its historically British character—its "light touch" regulatory regime—in an effort to attract American capital that would otherwise cross over on its way to London.

As Conroy points out, the new statement as incorporated in s.7, Pt A5 of the Companies Consolidation Bill 2007, focuses on a compromise position with far less onerous reporting obligations.[104] The new statement seeks to strike a balance between business costs and oversight. It also reworks the balance between auditor exposure to liabilities, their obligations and their relationships with directors. How this pans out in the new consolidated act, of course, remains to be seen.

6. Conclusion

The lessons of the DIRT do not lie in wrongdoing, fraud or negligence on the part of directors or auditors. Rather, the important thing is to attempt to discover some of the underlying systematic issues that produced the problem in the first place. Furthermore, a question remains over whether the DCS and other innovations in the Irish regulatory regime have, or could have, resolved any structural problems in Irish capitalism that might have contributed to the problem. The Irish are in a difficult position given their limited freedom to manoeuvre and innovate in the context of their globalised economic model. While the 2007–08 crash in the global economy leaves major questions as to what the character of financialised capital will be in future years, the Irish will be faced with very similar questions to those they faced over the DCS: how to regulate but maintain an attractive regime. I do not argue that the DCS was or was not in fact too onerous for Irish capital. The important thing to note is that

[103] Daisy Downes, "In Conversation with Tom Courtney, CLRG" (2007), *http://www.accountancy ireland.ie/dsp_articles.cfm/goto/1376/page/In_Conversation_with_Tom_Courtney,_CLRG.htm.*

[104] See Conroy, this volume, Ch.9, section 5(e); Department of Enterprise, Trade and Employment, *Minister Michael Ahern Announces Reform of Directors' Compliance Statement* (*http://www.entemp.ie/press/2005/20051201b.htm*); See also Company Law Review Group, *Company Law Review Group Welcomes Proposed Reform of Directors* (*http://www.clrg.org/about/pressarticle.asp?NID=43&T=N*); Daisy Downes, "In Conversation with Tom Courtney, CLRG" (2007) 39 *Accountancy Ireland*; Department of Enterprise, Trade and Employment, *Regulatory Impact Analysis: The Company Law Consolidation and Reform Bill*; CLRG, *Report*

the question became the major fulcrum for debate, even among those who dissented from the CLRG's conclusions. It is unlikely that this sort of question will disappear in the future.

Part of the reason for this is that the new capitalism has allowed for the development of conflicts of interest to a greater degree than that imagined by company law or by law and economics theorists. These conflicts of interest ought not to be regarded as a simple externality associated with transaction costs. They reflect fundamental shifts in how one part of capitalism works: fundamental because the orientation of business has turned to such a degree towards the provision of financial and consultancy services. Auditors and other gatekeepers are to a greater degree than ever central to corporate financial management and financial planning in all layers of the relationships that form around corporations but they have been asked to oversee a range of products systems that, though articulated as alleviating risk, have actually been employed for speculative accumulations of risk. That this creates challenges for all parties to the relationship ought to come as no surprise. Neither ought it be a surprise that company law, with its relatively simple articulation or the quasi-partnership model corporate form, is ill-equipped to describe the challenges that capitalism faces.

So, what is to be done in the Irish context? The new Companies Bill has to be relatively conservative, given that its primary focus is on the private companies that make up the vast majority of the Irish corporate economy. Difficulties experienced in 2008 and 2009, primarily involving the near-collapse of the Irish banking sector, highlight the problems with auditors either helpless or unwilling to intervene in unorthodox practices. Moreover, very many of the practices that led to the slump of 2007–08 were verified by gatekeepers—ratings agencies in terms of American mortgage-backed securities and auditors in terms of Irish, British and other banks' exposures to the wholesale banking markets (and to the housing markets). The crash was not caused, in the main, by illegal activities. It was caused by a system where incentives pointed directly away from long-term corporate health and instead pushed people towards short-term share returns and fees-based accumulation. The Anglo-American legal and theoretical model for imagining business is no longer in step with the manner in which business is done. Despite its being provoked in immediate terms by a classical housing bust,[105] the crash was rooted in the Anglo-American corporate governance model. It is unclear, as of yet, if and how the model can be reconciled with the realities of contemporary capitalism.

In general, then, the Irish are at sea when it comes to major questions about the globalised financial model. How that model evolves is not a question that will be answered in Ireland, but the answer will be the primary driver of the Irish

on the General Scheme of Companies Consolidation and Reform Bill (Dublin: Company Law Review Group, 2007).

105 On boom and bust cycles over time, see C.P. Kindleberger and R.Z. Aliber, *Manias, Panics and Crashes: A History of Financial Crises*, 5th edn (Basingstoke: Palgrave Macmillan, 2005).

economy as time goes on. As we saw in the previous two sections, the audit function itself highlights the way in which gate-keeping in the current model for company law and regulation acts as a meeting-point for pressures over standards, industries and public and private interests. Shifts in the behaviour of gatekeepers are themselves one part of the transformation of corporate governance in recent years. The focus on corporate governance has, perhaps not accidentally, coincided with the financialisation of markets; the decline of the professions and of their insulation from commercial pressures; with the deregulation of government control and finally with technological changes leading to the commodification of complex financial information flows.[106] Perhaps the explicit turn to corporate governance is as much a reflection of the failures of legal and regulatory regimes as it is a reflection of discussions around good governance. In this sense, corporate governance, especially where its worth is conceptualised in the context of comparative measure of economic success,[107] leaves imagined accountability in the corporation so distant from the relationships, structures and processes that produce wrongdoing as to be more or less meaningless. As such, we are faced with a serious lag between the corporate economy and the legal and regulatory architecture under which it functions. The excesses of global financial capital are not reconcilable through reinforcing company law: company law was simply not written with these processes in mind.

[106] There are a vast number of studies on each of these issues. Some interesting perspectives include J. Froud et al., *Financialization and Strategy: Narrative and Numbers* (London: Routledge, 2006); J. Froud, A. Leaver, and K. Williams, "New Actors in a Financialised Economy and the Remaking of Capitalism" (2007) *New Political Economy* 12, 339–347; K. Williams, "From shareholder value to present-day capitalism" (2000) *Economy and Society* 29, 1; I. Erturk, J. Froud, and K. Williams, "Corporate Governance and Disappointment" (2004) *Review of International Political Economy* 11, 677–713; J. Froud and S. Johal, "'Questioning Finance': A Special Issue of Competition Change" (2008) *Competition and Change* 12, 107–109; for an early report, see Committee on the Global Financial System, *Recent Innovations in International Banking (The Cross Report),* CGFS Publications (Geneva: Bank for International Settlements, 1986); see also Committee on the Global Financial System, *Ratings in Structured Finance: What Went Wrong and What can be Done to Address Shortcomings?* CGFS Publications (Geneva: Bank for International Settlements, 2008); E. Hüpkes, M. Quintyn, and M. Taylor, *The Accountability of Financial Sector Supervisors: Principles and Practice* Working Paper (Washington, D.C.: International Monetary Fund, 2005).

[107] See for instance H. Hansmann and R.H. Kraakman, "The End Of History For Corporate Law" (2001) *Georgetown Law Journal* 89, 439–468.

CHAPTER 6

TRUSTEESHIP IN IRISH OCCUPATIONAL PENSIONS

Orla Ormsby, Trainee Solicitor, Arthur Cox

1. INTRODUCTION

The Maxwell scandal put pensions at the forefront of public attention, culminating in greater scrutiny and a raft of pensions legislation both here and in the United Kingdom. Pension regulation had begun in earnest. For a long period, employers made the primary decisions regarding their employees' pensions and trustees kept a low profile. Pension trusts have traditionally been passive investors. In recent years, trusts have become more active by purchasing or controlling companies that are not related to the sponsor of the trust. Trustees had shied away from this type of ownership or control in the past due to a reluctance to take on such increased responsibility. Today, however, large pension trusts have begun to take a more active role in the companies in which they own shares.[1]

There have been several recent high profile pension cases in the context of takeovers that have received considerable media attention. These include the takeovers at Aer Lingus (attempted), W.H. Smith and Marks & Spencer. These takeover situations focused attention on the powers of trustees which the corporate parties involved could not ignore. The trustees' powers enabled them to block proposed takeovers by demanding commitments to the pension schemes that meant the deals were no longer commercially viable. These events showed trustees as key actors in commercial events. What were traditionally relatively tame powers had evolved and adapted to changing contexts. Pension trustees thus become highly significant players in unanticipated circumstances. These instances underlined the power of pension trustees and, thus, also of the governance issues associated with them.

This article explores these governance issues. It begins with a brief outline of the current occupational pension regulatory scheme in Ireland as well as exploring material from other common law jurisdictions with a trust law history similar to our own. It goes on to examine trustee training, the role and responsibilities of trustees, accountability of trustees and competence of trustees before drawing a number of conclusions. One such conclusion is that, despite the continued support for a trust based system of pension scheme governance in

[1] Vitucci, "Trusts as Active Investors" (1992) *The CPA Journal*, Vol.62 No.9, 80.

Ireland, greater emphasis must be placed on trustee education and understanding in order to improve monitoring standards and plan performance in today's changing market climate.

2. The Regulation of Pensions: An Overview

(a) The development of the regulatory framework in Ireland

The regulatory environment on which the Irish pension scheme rests has frequently changed in response to developments both external and internal to the schemes themselves. Trustees have huge financial responsibilities and further duties to act in the best interests of their schemes' members. At the end of the calendar year 2007 there were 99,802 occupational pension schemes registered in Ireland with the Pensions Board, comprising 800,398 members. There were over 130,000 PRSAs and total pension assets of €80 billion.[2] These schemes are clearly very significant for Irish society.

Much of pensions trust law has been a consolidation of case law. The provisions of the Trustee Act 1893 and Trustee (Authorised Investments) Act 1958 concern the appointment and removal of trustees, the protection of trustees from liability in certain circumstances and the permitting of investment in certain authorised securities. Trust rules are often decided by the employer before the appointment of trustees and sometimes in consultation with employee representatives.

The Taxes Consolidation Act 1997 provides that occupational pension schemes are established under an irrevocable trust. An occupational pension scheme is a good example of a trust. The property held in the trust fund is the assets of the scheme. Although the assets are held in the name of the trustees, they do not belong to them. The trust serves three functions: it is the primary source of payment of pension entitlements; it is a security for payment; and it is a vehicle for the collective protection and enforcement of the rights of individual scheme members. The first scheme to adopt this legal vehicle was that of Colmans, the mustard manufacturer, in 1900.[3]

The trust deed could be drawn up in virtually any way that suited the employer, and the employer could ensure effective control of the fund through his appointment of the trustees. A trust is a means of attaching to assets the interests of a wide class of beneficiaries. Further, establishing a pension fund as a trust qualifies it for certain tax exemptions.

The Pensions Act 1990 (as amended) sets out the framework for statutory regulation of occupational pension funds and Personal Retirement Savings

[2] The Pensions Board, *Annual Report and Accounts 2007*, June 2008.

[3] Blake, "UK Pensions System: Key Issues" (2003) *Pensions: An International Journal*, Vol.8 No.4, p.330.

Accounts.[4] It ensures the preservation of benefits and sets out disclosure requirements and trustees' statutory duties. The Pensions Act 1990 collated and outlined the duties and responsibilities of pension scheme trustees. There is a high degree of overlap between trustees' duties under the general principles of trust law and their duties as prescribed in the Pensions Act 1990.

In setting out the duties of pension scheme trustees the 2007 "So You're a Pension Scheme Trustee?" Handbook highlights the following duties and responsibilities of trustees:

> "To carry out the trust in accordance with the law and the terms of the trust deed and rules, act in the best interests of beneficiaries, act fairly between beneficiaries, act prudently and diligently, exercise care and utmost good faith in carrying out your duties, seek professional advice as necessary, supervise those to whom functions have been properly delegated, not profit from the trust, be aware of possible conflicts of interest.
>
> A trustee who is negligent, does not act in good faith or does something which is contrary to the rules of the trust, can be sued by the beneficiaries. In this case the trustee can be held to be personally liable for the whole of the amount of any loss which occurs. No matter who appoints the trustees, they must act in accordance with the scheme rules, and not as a representative of the employer or the members."[5]

The Pension (Amendment) Act 1996 introduced whistleblowing with regard to fraudulent activities. Where a trustee has reason to believe that material misappropriation or fraudulent conversion of a scheme's resources has occurred/is occurring, or is to be attempted, the trustee must report in writing to the Pensions Board of the particulars of the misappropriation or conversion as the case may be. The duty to report is absolute and a penalty of a fine and/or imprisonment applies to anyone convicted of failure to comply.[6]

The Pensions (Amendment) Act 2002 introduced Private Retirement Savings Accounts and established the office of the Pensions Ombudsman. The Pensions Ombudsman may investigate and determine complaints made in writing by or on behalf of an actual or potential beneficiary of an occupational pension scheme, who alleges that he or she has suffered financial loss as a result of maladministration on the part of those responsible for the management of the scheme. The Ombudsman is also empowered to investigate and decide any dispute of fact or law which arises in respect of an act or omission by those responsible for a scheme and which is referred to him by an actual or potential beneficiary. The Pensions Ombudsman

4 Hereafter PRSAs.

5 The Pensions Board, "So You're a Pension Scheme Trustee? A Brief Guide to Your Duties and Responsibilities" (2007).

6 "So You're a Pension Scheme Trustee? A Brief Guide to Your Duties and Responsibilities" (2007), p.18.

Regulations provide that the trustees of every occupational pension scheme must establish Internal Dispute Resolution (IDR) procedures.[7]

The Social Welfare and Pensions Act 2005 transposed the IORPs[8] Directive of 2003; as part of its remit new requirements were imposed on trustees including a duty to produce a statement of investment principles and requirements on experience and qualifications of trustees.

(b) The current situation

Ireland operates a Three Tier Pension system:

Tier 1: State pensions under the Social Welfare system since 1909
The State provides these pensions from public finances and operates this system on a pay-as-you-go basis. Following the creation of the National Pension Reserve Fund in 2001 the government appears to be moving towards a funded scheme approach.

Tier 2: Occupational or Supplementary Pensions
These are linked to an individual's employment. McNally and Stewart[9] define occupational pensions as privately managed pension schemes offered by an employer to some or all employees as part of an overall remuneration package. Often facilitated by tax concessions and regulated by governments their objective is to provide a targeted level of income on retirement, in most cases complementing social security.[10]

With regard to Defined Benefit schemes, the investment performance of the fund's assets are of no direct relevance to the scheme member, since the pension depends on the final salary and years of service only and not on investment performance—the sponsor bears the risk. This is one of several reasons why many employers are closing such schemes to new entrants in favour of an employee risk-borne Defined Contribution scheme.[11] From an employee's

[7] Note that it is the trustees who are responsible for establishing procedures in respect of occupational pension schemes.

[8] European Union Pensions Directive affecting trustees, 2003/41/EC.

[9] McNally and Stewart, "Occupational Pension Schemes in Ireland – A Review of Risk and Investment Strategies" (NUI Maynooth, Department of Economics, Working Paper, October 2003), p.5.

[10] *Green Paper on Pensions 2007*, p.13: "The number of occupational pension schemes in existence creates particular regulatory challenges. Information on pensions is essential to heighten pension awareness, safeguard the rights of scheme members and to ensure that people have sufficient information to make appropriate financial decisions. The overall approach to pension regulation continues to evolve to address, proactively, challenges of a changing environment. In order to address these challenges, the Pensions Board is undertaking an operational review, with the intention of moving towards a risk-based approach. This will ensure that the Board is structured and skilled to ensure confidence and stability in the occupational pension system as far as possible." See also the IAPF response to Green Paper on Pensions, May 2008.

[11] *Green Paper on Pensions 2007*, Executive Summary, p.9: "Defined Benefit scheme members outweigh Defined Contribution scheme members by a ratio of 2:1."

perspective the investment risk associated with the scheme is now borne by the employee, there is no guarantee of retirement income, the risk to the employer is reduced.[12] It is arguable that there must be some worth in certainty and assurance that the plan, by defining benefit level, is not subjected to volatile market conditions.

Tier 3: Private Pensions

Personal Retirement Savings Accounts, established on foot of the Pensions (Amendment) Act 2002 are very significant in this context. CSO data[13] shows over half the Irish workforce has supplemental pension cover. This figure is far below the 70 per cent recommended by the Pensions Board in 1998 National Pension Policy Initiative. PRSAs were introduced as an attempt to increase this figure.

(c) The 2006 Report on pension governance

A Report on Trusteeship for the Minister of Social and Family Affairs[14] was written by the Pensions Board in November 2006 and published in February 2007. Its aims were to evaluate the trust model of pension scheme governance, identify potential regulatory and governance improvements that can be made to enable the trust model to perform more effectively, and examine the supports in place for trustees.[15] Several of the recommendations in this report have been included in the recent Social Welfare and Pensions Act 2008 which is discussed in more detail below.

Two notables issues were discussed in this report:

(a) the competence of trustees, and
(b) the continued use of trust law to regulate pension scheme governance.

(i) Competence of trustees

The 2006 Report, like the Pension Board's previous Report of 1988,[16] devoted considerable attention to this question of trustee competence. As the OECD noted in 2001,[17] the significance of a pension fund to the members of the scheme cannot be underestimated. Despite this, however, many pension schemes have

12 "Implications for the shift from defined benefit to defined contributions for pensions", Dublin Economic Workshop 2002, p.60.

13 "Quarterly National Households Pensions Update: Quarter 1" (Dublin: Central Statistics Office, 2006) p.20.

14 *Report of the Pensions Board to the Minister for Social and Family Affairs on Trusteeship* (Dublin: Pensions Board, November 2006).

15 *Report of the Pensions Board to the Minister for Social and Family Affairs on Trusteeship* (Dublin: Pensions Board, November 2006).

16 Report of the National Pensions Board to the Minister for Social Welfare, June 1988.

17 Organisation for Economic Co-operation and Development, "Regulatory Reform in Ireland", (Paris, 2001).

substantial pension deficits. In 2005, for example, this was the situation for the schemes of Waterford Wedgwood,[18] Allied Irish Bank and the Electricity Supply Board. This clearly raised questions about the competence of some trustees to manage the funds under their control.

In drawing up their November 2006 Report on Trusteeship to the Minister of Social and Family Affairs, the Irish Pensions Board referred extensively to Lawler's qualitative analysis of the contribution made by trusteeship to pension scheme governance in Ireland.[19] The Report concluded however, that efforts ought to be made to ensure that governance standards were raised[20]—via compulsory training, use of modern technology, addressing gaps in the regulatory framework, better guidance and support and a revised Pensions Board handbook.[21]

(ii) Use of trust law to regulate governance

The Report concluded that the advantages of trust law for pension scheme regulation and governance centred around flexibility in the potential for trustee discretionary decision-making and the ability of trust law to adapt to changing circumstances. (This is a controversial area and will be discussed later below). Other advantages identified included the separation of assets; the ability of third party beneficiaries to enforce rights; and familiarity with, and general understanding of the trust concept among trustees and pension practitioners.

Disadvantages regarding the internal governance of trust-based pension schemes included: bureaucracy, cost and time involved in administering trust-based schemes (particularly for employers); potential for conflicts of interests among trustees, particularly for employer-nominated trustees of defined benefit schemes; regulatory burden on trustees.

Pension provision is one of the most important investment decisions undertaken by or on behalf of an individual. It is paramount that members'

[18] The recent collapse of the Waterford Wedgwood group followed debts of €500 million and a pension deficit of €110 million. Current workers at the plant will rank in lowest priority, at best their pensions drastically reduced if the trustees decide to wind up the pension scheme. Even if buyers are interested in an asset sale, they would be unlikely to take on the liability associated with the pension fund. If the trustees opt to continue with the scheme, it will need buoyant market conditions to redress some of its losses—if the scheme were to be wound up it would mark the first occupational scheme to collapse since the Pensions Board was established as industry regulator and although their British colleagues are covered by a Pension Protection Fund it is unclear to what extent, if any, this may cover its Irish workers.

[19] Lawler, "Does Trusteeship Contribute Positively to Pension Scheme Governance in Ireland? A Qualitative Analysis" (Dublin: Institute of Public Administration, 2006). Lawler's research was based on interviews with pension industry professionals, lawyers, members of the Pensions Board, member nominated, elected and professional trustees and close examination of trusteeship and pension literature.

[20] Lawler, "Does Trusteeship Contribute Positively to Pension Scheme Governance in Ireland? A Qualitative Analysis" (Dublin: Institute of Public Administration, 2006).

[21] Pensions Boards, "So You're a Pension Scheme Trustee? A Brief Guide to Your Duties and Responsibilities" (2007).

interests are protected. Riddal[22] notes that in light of the Maxwell affair, a trust does not always guarantee security but he suggests that any loss is more to do with the failure of those with responsibilities in the pension sphere to draw awareness for the need for better regulation of pensions funds. Reports on cumulative developments in pension regulation highlight a lack of investment experience on the part of trustees.

In examining trust law's contribution to pension scheme governance we must bear in mind its interaction with rules established under primary legislation. The continued establishment of pensions under trusts cannot simply be attributed to its being the most suitable arrangement; rather it remains a Revenue requirement that they be so established in order to become tax exempt.

(d) Liability of pension trustees

According to the Handbook,[23] a trustee who is negligent, does not act in good faith or does something which is contrary to the rules of the trust can be sued by the beneficiaries. It is useful to consider the United States Supreme Court decision in *Harris Trust and Savings Bank v Salomon Smith Barney*[24]: ERISA[25] bars a fiduciary of an employee benefit plan from causing a plan to engage in certain transactions with a party in interest. A participant or beneficiary can seek to obtain "appropriate relief". It would be difficult to confidently say that reduced returns due to ineffective monitoring do not represent a breach of duty although the Harris Trust decision also highlights that trust law imposes limits on restitution against defendants other than the principal wrongdoer.

The Myner's Report itself suggested that trustees might be sued for poor investment decisions.[26] This suggestion may have been aimed at increasing and encouraging trustee investment training. For trustees uncomfortable with the investment process, a "Manager of Managers'" approach exists. As one experienced consultant put it: "There is a popular misconception that one can just wash one's hands of any monitoring responsibilities by handing a fund over to a Manager of Managers. One cannot and you still need to monitor who is managing your money to see they are still doing a good job, rather than thinking this is one way to get rid of the issue."[27]

Fiduciaries such as pension trustees must thus act prudently in the interest of their beneficiaries, particularly in the context of market timing. But what does prudently mean in this context? Reish, Faucher and Davis[28] give excellent

22 Riddal, *The Law of Trusts* (London: Butterworths, 1996) p.3.
23 "So You're a Pension Scheme Trustee? A Brief Guide to Your Duties and Responsibilities" (2007).
24 U.S. 120 S. Ct. 2180, L.Ed. 2d. 2000 U.S. Lexis 3962.
25 The Employee Retirement Income Security Act 1974 (US).
26 Rowley, "Management of managers: Leaving Investment up to the 'experts'", *Employee Benefits*, October 6, 2003, p.10.
27 Steven Vale, senior investment consultant at Hewitt Bacon & Woodrow.
28 Reish, Faucher and Davis, "401(k) Investment: Responing Prudently to the Mutual Fund

examples of this need to respond prudently in the context of market timing scandals which have blighted the United States asset pension industry. ERISA s.404 (a) requires fiduciaries to act in the best interests of participants and in a prudent manner.[29] Fiduciaries need to evaluate both whether the funds in their plans continue to be appropriate for their participants, and whether there are participants in their plans who are market timing to the detriment of other participants.

The United States courts objectively assess compliance with prudent man standards in light of ERISA. The Pensions Board commenting on the Law Reform Commission's Report on Trustees[30] endorsed both this assessment and the more subjective assessment contained in the comparative UK legislation.[31]

There may be a fiduciary duty to investigate the activities of members and prevent them from harming other participants.[32] Defined contribution plan participants may sue to recover losses for alleged breaches of fiduciary duty, even if not all participants lost money, according to a ruling by the 3rd US Circuit Court of Appeals in Philadelphia.[33]

Scheme members in the United Kingdom can sue for compensation if they suffer loss as a result of negligence by trustees under the Trustee Act 1925. Further, the Pensions Act 1995 requires trustees to prepare and maintain a Statement of Investment Principles.[34]

(e) The rule in *Hastings Bass*

Apart from issues of liability, trustees are constrained by the rule in *Hastings Bass*.[35] This is the principle that a court will hold a trustee's bona fide exercise

Scandal" (2004) *Journal of Pension Benefits*, Vol.11 No.3, p.39. Permitting market timing (excessive short-term trading in order to exploit inefficiencies in mutual fund pricing) is contrary to the interest of a fund's long term investors.

29 Subsection IB states that "a fiduciary shall discharge his duties with respect to a plan solely in the interest of the participants and beneficiaries and with the care skill and prudence and diligence under the circumstances then prevailing that a prudent man acting in a like capacity and familiar with such matters would use in the conduct of an enterprise of a like character and with like aims ..."

30 Consultation Paper on Trust Law – General Proposals (LRC CP 35–05).

31 *Bussian v RJR Nabisco* 223 F.3d 286 (5th Cir. 2000)—fiduciaries are entitled to rely on the advice they receive from independent experts but they may not rely blindly on that advice. Plan fiduciaries should have more communication with fund management in order to meet their requirements under ERISA.

32 Reish, Faucher and Davis, "401(K) Investment Responding Prudently to the Mutual Fund Scandal" fn.82—the author is are unaware of any case law on this point.

33 *Jingdong Zhu v Schering Plough Corp* 04–3073, United States Court of Appeals for the Third Circuit, on appeal from the United States District Court of New Jersey 2005.

34 See 2006 Pensions Regulations in Ireland, the Act also introduced whistleblowing provisions similar to those contained in the 1990 Pensions Act: where a trustee has reason to believe that material misappropriation or fraudulent conversion of a scheme's resources has occurred, is occurring, or is to be attempted, he or she must report in writing to the Pensions Board of the particulars of the misappropriation or conversion as the case may be. The duty to report is absolute and a penalty of a fine and/or imprisonment applies to anyone convicted of failure to comply.

35 *Re Hastings Bass (deceased), Hastings and ors. v Commissioners of the Inland Revenue* [1974] 2 All E.R. 193.

of discretion to be void if it is clear that he would not have acted as he did: (a) had he not taken into account considerations which he ought not to have taken into account or (b) had he not failed to take into account considerations which he ought to have taken into account.

The application of the rule needs to be in the minds of trustees when any exercise of their discretion is made. It may affect ways in which trustees' discretion can be challenged, to undo an undesired consequence, and it may need to be considered by trustees in their decision-making. The rule should be at the forefront of trustees' minds in corporate acquisitions.[36]

This rule in *Hastings Bass* should be part of the armoury of lawyers considering the validity of a trustee decision. Colacicchi and Hickey[37] have questioned how far this goes. The authors query if it means that when trustees make a mistake with disastrous consequences could they simply turn back the clock and get themselves off the hook. Will it allow third party rights to be litigated and vindicated? In *AMP (UK) Plc v Barker,*[38] Collins J. held that the case law suggested that the application of the rule leads to the act being void rather than voidable.

Trustee discretion, while viewed as problematic in certain circumstances, is a crucial component of prudent decision making.[39] Many trustees are covered by indemnity insurance. Section 61 of the United Kingdom's Trustee Act 1925 provides an indemnity for trustees who "acted honestly and ought fairly to be excused ...". This is, however, at the courts' discretion. A similar provision had been proposed in the Law Reform Commission's 2005 paper[40] "involving a statutory duty of care, and prohibiting reliance on indemnity clauses for certain 'irreducible core functions'". It is submitted that these irreducible core functions should be outlined clearly in trustee training sessions and materials.

(f) Standards of administration

The Pensions Board has recently recognised that in order to assess standards, there needs to be a benchmark against which such standards can be measured and assessed. In relation to trustee duties, it has been suggested that, in order to raise standards among those to whom trustees delegate, service level agreements (between trustees and their delegates) should be considered as a compulsory requirement. This may achieve higher standards, while maintaining trustee responsibility to fulfil their statutory functions and increase awareness among

[36] Colacicchi and Hickey, "The developing rule in Hastings Bass" (2004) *Pensions: An International Journal*, Vol.9 No.3, p.203.

[37] Colacicchi and Hickey, "The developing rule in Hastings Bass" (2004) *Pensions: An International Journal*, Vol.9 No.3, p.203.

[38] [2001] O.P.L.R. 197.

[39] Lawler, "Does Trusteeship Contribute Positively to Pension Scheme Governance In Ireland? A Qualitative Analysis" (Dublin: Institute of Public Administration, 2006), p.53.

[40] Consultation paper on Charitable Trust Law – General Proposals, 2005 (LRC CP 36–05).

trustees of their core responsibilities.[41] The Board's "Codes of Practice for Trustees" already states that trustees should "put a service level agreement in place when delegating any of their functions to any person or organisation".[42]

It recommended that trustees make administration of their schemes a primary priority. An approach requiring compulsory service level agreements between trustees and administrators, combined with auditing and disciplinary powers attached to the Board, is viewed as the most appropriate response. Richards notes that best model statements would include the identity of who is taking decisions and why this structure has been selected, the fund's investment objective, the fund's planned asset allocation strategy, including projected investment returns on each asset class, the mandates given to all advisors and managers.[43]

(g) Considerations of trustees—to whom are these responsibilities owed?

It has been suggested that the size of the scheme tends to dictate and influence trustees' awareness of their duties and responsibilities.[44] In a UK case, *Edge v Pensions Ombudsman*,[45] which considered the distribution of a pension fund surplus, a broad view was taken that the interests of the employer should be considered part of the trustees' fiduciary role.

A narrower view was taken in *Hagen v ICI Chemicals*[46] which dealt with wind-up issues. The ruling stated that trustees' fiduciary obligations were to the members of the scheme, although extreme circumstances (such as the employer being in a particularly unhealthy financial situation) may necessitate the employers' interests being taken into account. In the absence of sufficient Irish case law, it may be appropriate that trustees be provided with guidance outlining the importance of communicating with sponsoring employers, considering their interests, when making key decisions at the trustee board. Such guidance would need to emphasise, however, that the ultimate driver behind trustee decision-making is the best interests of beneficiaries. The Pensions Board decided that such guidance should be included in trustee training.[47] In the US case of *Varity Corp v Howe*[48] the court stated the duty of loyalty requires an ERISA fiduciary to communicate any material facts which could adversely affect plan members' interests.[49]

41 Consultation paper on Charitable Trust Law – General Proposals, 2005 at 5.4.10.

42 Pensions Board, "Codes of Practice for Trustees" (2005), p.18.

43 Richards, "Evolving Role of Pension Fund Trustees: Institutional Investment in the United Kingdom – a Review" (2002) *Pensions: An International Journal*, Vol.8 No.1, p.17.

44 Lawler, "Does Trusteeship Contribute Positively to Pension Scheme Governance In Ireland? A Qualitative Analysis" (Dublin: Institute of Public Administration, 2006) p.74.

45 [1999] 4 All E.R. 546 (CA) at 566.

46 [2002] I.R.L.R. 31.

47 Pensions Board, "Report of the Pensions Board to the Minister for Social and Family Affairs on Trusteeship" (November 2006) at 7.3.6.

48 36 F.3d 746, 754.

49 For example, possible lay-offs etc. See also United States Department of Labour regulations

3. A Corporate Governance Analysis of Issues in Pension Regulation

Many of the arguments about pension scheme governance canvassed above follow previously rehearsed debates in corporate governance. The implications of some of these for the specific area of pension regulation are considered in this section.

(a) Role and responsibility of trustees

Trustees are bound by the overall objective of the pension scheme. Mahon[50] questions whether trustees fully understand their duties and whether or not trustees should receive payment for the work and duties undertaken by them. The results were mixed. Only 38 per cent of his respondents agreed that trustees fully understand their duties and responsibilities. 35 per cent of respondents were neutral as to the issue, and 27 per cent were of the opinion that trustees did not understand their duties and responsibilities.

The Pensions Board "Trustee Handbook" (2007) stresses that pension scheme trustees have duties under trust law which include inter alia: to carry out the trust in accordance with the law and the terms of the trust deed and rules, act in the best interests of beneficiaries, act fairly between beneficiaries, act prudently and diligently, exercise care and utmost good faith in carrying out your duties, seek professional advice as necessary, supervise those to whom functions have been properly delegated, not profit from the trust, and be aware of possible conflicts of interest.

An analogy can be drawn between trustees and managers, and members and beneficiaries and shareholders.[51] The corporate governance literature gives us a solid background for the debate on pension fund governance. At the heart of the corporate governance literature is the separation of ownership and control, and the principal-agent problem that may create tensions between shareholders and management.

Myners[52] took the view that it would be better if trustees would treat their responsibilities very much like the job of running a company, noting the similarity between non-executive directors and independent trustees. Cadbury

which indicate that fiduciaries must give appropriate consideration to those facts and circumstances that the fiduciary knows or should have known are relevant to the particular investment. 29 CFR 2509.94–2.

50 Mahon, "Irish Occupational Pensions: An Overview and Analysis of Scale Economies" *http://eprints.wit.ie/426/1/presentation2,1364,en.pdf* (last accessed April 16, 2009). Mahon sent out detailed questionnaires to trustees and spoke to several of them in interviews concerning their duties and responsibilities. The results of this research were used as a basis of the Pensions Board Report on Trusteeship.

51 Lawler, "Does Trusteeship Contribute Positively to Pension Scheme Governance in Ireland? A Qualitative Analysis" (Dublin: Institute of Public Administration, 2006).

52 Paul Myners, "Institutional Investment in the United Kingdom, a review" (London: HM Treasury, 2001) p.16.

also addressed the issues[53] and noted that non-executive directors should bring independent judgment to bear on issues of strategy, performance, resources etc. The report could easily be speaking of trustees here.

(b) Use of trust law to regulate pensions

The 1993 Goode Report[54] was the first time detailed analysis of the law and regulatory structure of occupational pension schemes was undertaken. It resulted in the 1995 Pensions Act in the UK. The report noted that there were distinct advantages to trusts as a basis for pensions schemes:

> "[N]ot only as a means of segregating assets to protect beneficiaries, it also provides a mechanism for collective representation and protection of members of a group linked by a common interest."[55]

At the time of the Goode Report in 1992, the Pensions Act 1990 and the Pensions Board were already in place and so these deficiencies had already been addressed in this jurisdiction. Several themes of the first report of the National Pensions Board in 1988 were echoed in the Goode Report.

It could be argued that contract law could also be used as a vehicle for the prudent person rule so closely associated with trusteeship. Galer[56] and Pickering[57] have noted the increasing contractualisation of pension commitments. One difficulty with this is that privity of contract would operate to defeat a claim to contractual rights by or against those who are strangers to the contract.[58] The flexibility of trust law is vital in the pensions context. The rapid speed of development in the pension industry has left the question as to the appropriate model of pension fund regulation a more pressing issue.

53 Cabdury, "Report of the Committee on the Financial Aspects of Corporate Governance" (Financial Reporting Council, London Stock Exchange, 1992).

54 Goode, "Pension Law Reform – The Report of the Pension Law Review Committee", (London: HMSO, 1993).

55 Goode, "Pension Law Reform – The Report of the Pension Law Review Committee", p.187.

56 Galer, "'Prudent Person Rule' for the Investment of Pension Fund Assets" (2002) Financial Market Trends No.32, OECD, p.46. Suggests that there is nothing inherently sacred about the trust forum, arguing that contract law can also be used as a vehicle for the prudent person rule that is soclosely associated with trusteeship.

57 Pickering, "A Simpler Way to Better Pensions" (United Kingdom Department for Work and Pensions, 2004), points towards the increasing contractualisation of pension commitments and asks whether the employer/trustee/employee relationship offers any more security or value for money than a bilateral arrangement between the employer and the employee. This is an interesting topic, worthy of discussion further but falls outside the bounds of this particular essay.

58 Lawler, "Does Trusteeship Contribute Positively to Pension Scheme Governance in Ireland? A Qualitative Analysis" (Dublin: Institute of Public Administration, 2006).

Meanwhile, the National Association of Pension Funds[59] in the UK has emphasised that the trust system will no longer apply to increasing numbers of pension scheme members. It is important to note that they are not promoting the removal of trust law for existing occupational pension schemes. This does suggest, however, that there may be merit in the adoption of a voluntary code of governance for trustees. Clarke[60] advocates a type of governance through contract which maintains the fiduciary responsibility of the trust model. It would allow for greater cost efficiency and consistency of decision-making and provide a benchmark for performance evaluation.

(c) Expertise and competence of trustees

The corporate governance literature on the role of non-executive directors is particularly relevant to this issue. As the passage below indicates, similar themes are discussed in relation to non-executive directors as have arisen in the debate about the competence of pension trustees

> "The quality of non executive directors seems to be improving and non executive directors are increasingly being recruited for their skills in financial, governance and business matters and for their ability to offer an outside perspective on the company's activities rather than for reasons of business or social connections … at the same time factors such as lack of training and lack of understanding of the role inhibit non executive directors' effectiveness."[61]

This mirrors one of the key problems in the context of pensions governance—the lack of expertise on the part of trustees. Pension fund trustees, the very centre of the system are being asked to take crucial investment decisions, yet many lack resources and expertise. They rely heavily on a narrow group of investment consulting firms for advice. Their performance is not usually assessed or measured. Where trustees elect to take investment decisions, they must have sufficient expertise to be able to evaluate critically any advice they take. Intervention in companies, where it is in shareholders' (beneficiaries') interests, should be a duty for fund managers. The US Department of Labour Interpretative Bulletin 94–2 on Activism[62] may be of some assistance is assessing when to act and considering the extent of that action:

59 "Pension Scheme Governance, fit for the 21st Century" (London: National Association of Pension Funds, 2005).

60 Clarke, "Pension Fund Governance: Expertise and Organisational form" (Working Paper, Oxford School of Geography and Environment, 2004), p.24.

61 Fraser and Henry, "The Future of Corporate Governance: Insights from the UK" (Institute of Chartered Accountants of Scotland, 2003), p.158.

62 29 CFR 2509.94–2.

> "Active monitoring and communication may include such matters as consideration of the appropriateness of executive compensation, the corporation's policy regarding mergers and acquisitions, the extent of debt financing and capitalisation, the nature of long-term business plans, the corporation's investment in training to develop its workforce. The fiduciary obligations of prudence and loyalty to plan participants and to beneficiaries requires the responsible fiduciary to vote proxy on issues that may affect the value of the plan's investments."

Myners's report[63] focussed mainly on investment issues and an examination of trusteeship was not specifically undertaken. Myners advocated less prescription and regulation and a more flexible approach to governance of occupational pension schemes, stating: "The principles may seem little more than common sense. In a way they are—yet they certainly do not describe the status quo. Following them would require substantial change in decision-making behaviour and structures."[64]

The lack of investment understanding among trustees was flagged as a serious problem, and Myners took the view that this led to poor decision-making in the investment context. Trust law was "not designed to introduce the expertise likely to be required in the management of substantial pools of pension assets."[65] Trustees, according to Myners, should become prudent experts, in line with the approach taken in United States legislation such as the ERISA.[66] They should delegate investment decisions to a person or body who they believe has the requisite level of skill and care. The figures contained in the report showed 62 per cent of trustees had no investment qualifications, 26 per cent had less than one day's training and that 49 per cent spent less than three hours preparing for investment matters before a board meeting.

The Pensions Board's 2003 research figures[67] show that 75 per cent of trustees completed a training course within 12 months of their appointment. 65 per cent had no additional or specialised training. 71 per cent had no "refresher" courses. Despite these deficiencies in training, 84 per cent felt adequately informed to carry out trustee duties effectively and accordance with their legal obligations. This is alarming in light of the assertion by the OECD that the central figure in governance of pension funds is the governing body responsible for its management, i.e. the trustee board.[68]

On the other hand, Segars[69] has noted that, in an environment where trustees are voluntary appointments, it could be argued that compulsory training may

63 Myners, "Institutional Investment in the United Kingdom: a Review" (London: HM Treasury, 2001).

64 Myners, "Institutional Investment in the United Kingdom: a Review" (London: HM Treasury, 2001).

65 Myners, "Institutional Investment in the United Kingdom: a Review" (London: HM Treasury, 2001).

66 The Employee Retirement Income Security Act 1974 (US).

67 Pensions Board, "Trustee Training Survey 2002: The Results" (2003). Cited in Mahon, "Irish Occupational Pensions: An Overview and Analysis of Scale Economies" (MBS, WIT, 2005).

68 "Guidelines for Pension Fund Governance" (Paris: Organisation for Economic Co-operation and Development, 2005), p.2.

69 Segars, "Keeping a Tight Ship" (2005) *Pensions World*, Vol.34, No.9, p.21.

have a deterrent effect on those persons considering becoming trustees. This is less likely to be a problem if trustees are given adequate time off to attend training sessions and if they were fairly recompensed for expenses incurred in their capacity as a trustee.

It is true that in principal-agent relationships there may be information asymmetries whereby the members and beneficiaries cannot know at all times whether the trustees are acting in their best interests. In particular, it has been argued that the presence of "insiders" on the trustee board creates agency problems whereby employer-nominated trustees favour the shareholders of the company over the pension plan beneficiaries.[70] As against this, Punter Southall's report[71] suggests that 59 per cent of respondents believed that "employer nominated trustees bring essential pension and financial experience to a pension scheme."

In this jurisdiction, the Occupational Pension Schemes (Trustee) Regulations 2006[72] require that trustees who do not enter into an arrangement with an investment manager to provide an investment service in respect of the investment of the resources of the scheme, must satisfy the Board that they possess qualifications and experience appropriate and relevant to investment of the resources of the scheme or have entered into arrangements with advisers possessing the necessary qualifications and experience.[73]

However, the Myners Report seems sceptical as to whether the existing legislation regarding trustees' duties to seek advice can be an adequate substitute for trustees raising the level of their expertise.

Rubber stamping of such advice is undesirable. In practice, even if most trustees were sufficiently professional and knowledgeable to meet the prudent expert test, they would likely feel exposed if they were to take professional advice and then not follow it in the absence of very compelling reasons. However, the duty may require trustees to be more proactive and to seek further advice if they consider that the initial advice is incorrect or insufficient.

As a consequence of the higher standard of care, trustees may turn to the employer to appoint trustees to the board with the requisite skills and experience to assist in the formulation of investment policy.[74] It is probable that such skills would be found more on the employer side than on the membership side. But the

70 Cocco and Volpin, "The Corporate Governance of Defined Benefit Pension Plans: Evidence form the United Kingdom" (Discussion Paper, Centre for Economic Policy Research, 2005).

71 Punter Southall and Co, "Survey presents a different picture of insider trustees to recent study by London Business School" (2005) Press release, March 1, 2005. Cited in Lawler, "Does Trusteeship Contribute Positively to Pension Scheme Governance in Ireland? A Qualitative Analysis" (Dublin: Institute of Public Adminstration, 2006).

72 S.I. No. 293 of 2006.

73 Pensions Board, "Report of the Pensions Board to the Minister for Social and Family Affairs on Trusteeship" (November 2006), 3.3.2.

74 Richards, "Evolving Role of Pension Fund Trustees: Institutional Investment in the United Kingdom – a Review" (2002) *Pensions: An International Journal*, Vol.8 No.1, p.17. Mahon's research suggests that in at least 68 per cent of appointments and selections the employer is the ultimate decision maker.

question remains if the trustees as a whole will be judged by the raised duty of care even though their investments decisions were delegated to an investment sub-committee.[75] Does the new raised duty apply individually or collectively? Is there any reason to think that the members would be in a better position?

4. The Situation in Ireland: Present and Future?

(a) Trustee responsibilities

It must be acknowledged that there is not a sufficient body of pension case law to determine clear pension trustee responsibilities and standards of competence in this jurisdiction. The Pensions Board supports the introduction of a statutory duty of care along the lines of the Trustee Act 2000 (UK) as has been suggested by the Law Reform Commission.[76] The Board notes the duty is to exercise such care and skill as is reasonable in the circumstances, having regard in particular:

(a) to any special knowledge or experience an individual trustee has or holds himself out as having, and
(b) if the individual acts as trustee in the course of a business or profession, to any special knowledge or experience that it is reasonable to expect of a person acting in the course of that kind of business or profession.

If trustee duties were prescribed in stone they could create too great a burden for trustees to bear. It could also lead to inconsistencies in decisions of the courts.[77] Mahon's examination of the pension industry indicated that the role and responsibilities of trustees and 3rd-party advisors had been clearly defined to 84 per cent of respondents; 7 per cent noted the issue was under consideration and 9 per cent noted that their roles and responsibilities had not been clearly defined—lack of knowledge of trust law may lead to inefficient trusteeship and decision making. Trustees rarely have a deep understanding of trust law and related issues—lack of knowledge of trust law may lead to inefficient trusteeship and decision-making. Trustees relied heavily upon advice from third party professionals.

Cohen[78] contends that the distinct difference in the competence of trustees lies with their work experience and notes that if seniority governs the appointment of a fiduciary, often only luck will ensure that the individual in question has

75 See also Myners Report, para.24.

76 Law Reform Commission, "Consultation paper on Charitable Trust Law – General Proposals" (LRC CP 36–05) Ch.3.

77 Lawler, "Does Trusteeship Contribute Positively to Pension Scheme Governance in Ireland? A Qualitative Analysis" (Dublin: Institute of Public Adminstration, 2006) p.60. Lawler's thesis was based on results of interviews carried out with trustees and pension professionals in 2006. His work was relied upon by the Pensions Board in compiling its November 2006 *Report on Trusteeship*.

78 Cohen, "Question of Duty" (2001) *Benefits Canada*, Vol.25 No.4, p.102.

some financial background. If this theory is accepted, it makes it very difficult to see how the effectiveness of the decision-making can be ensured. Given the general lack of trustee education,[79] pension management and oversight is just too complex to leave to amateurs no matter how efficiently they manage their own financial affairs.

Canadian pensions groups have created a corporate governance guide for the industry and a self-assessment questionnaire for every corporation with a pension plan.[80] But both of these are voluntary programmes and so they are of little use in ascertaining the competency of trustees to actually oversee their schemes. This situation is far from ideal.

(b) Employer as sole trustee

Where an employer acts as sole trustee, the potential for conflict of interest rises significantly. While the Pensions Board agreed, in principle, that an arrangement whereby the employer acts as sole trustee is far from satisfactory, the ability to find suitable, practical alternative options proved difficult. The Board considered that the introduction and regulation of administrators and improvements to the training regime, in tandem with existing provisions requiring whistleblowing where non-remittance of contributions occurs, may provide the additional protections necessary to overcome some of the difficulties associated with this arrangement. Accordingly, the Board decided to keep the issue under review, but this writer finds it difficult to envision a better method of dealing with the problems posed by employers as sole trustees.

(c) Network communication

The Irish Association of Pension Funds provides a much needed mentoring facility to pension trustees. Trustees need back up advice and guidance, databases, access to court cases where the facts and principles applying are set out, and to cases that come before the Pensions Board (though the parties' identities are withheld) for training purposes. This suggests the possibility of a pensions network in which peer communication and review fosters higher standards.

However, not all trustees interviewed were aware of the Irish Association of Pension Funds Trustee Forum—a facility whereby trustees can share knowledge and experiences. The IAPF has recently introduced two courses for trustees entitled *Trustee Essentials* and *Trustee Investment*. It might be best for the

[79] Apart from the Regulatory code of practice No. 7 "Trustee Knowledge and Understanding", The Pensions Regulator (UK) 2006.

[80] Apart from the Regulatory code of practice No. 7 "Trustee Knowledge and Understanding", The Pensions Regulator (UK) 2006.

Pensions Board and IAPF to proactively seek out trustees or to distribute the presentations and papers. Arguably this may lead to issues regarding trustees' constructive knowledge and implied acceptance of standards of care. In relation to sourcing of suitable trustees, a first scenario is that the Board draw upon a register where independent trustees can be called upon to act in cases where trustees cannot be found.[81] Again, discretion would need to be exercised in such cases, recognising the potential drain that trustee fees might place on the fund.

(d) Professional trustees v Member trustees

It has been questioned whether non-professional trustees can continue to contribute positively to pension scheme governance in an era of increasing investment complexity and uncertainty, the challenge of funding requirements, and continuous regulatory change.[82]

Member trustees, where they existed, were valued for the unique contribution they made to pension scheme governance, including acting as a conduit for providing information to members. Defined Contribution scheme members who should know more given the risks appear to know less about their pension than Defined Benefit Scheme members. However, it may be the case that a structured education process allowing an elevated contribution would be advisable. Employer-nominated trustees were relied upon for expertise in certain areas, particularly finance. Professionals will often have broader experience than trustees and one might ask whether the new increased duty of care requires them to be more proactive?

Appointment of member trustees in particular was seen as resulting from a sense of obligation rather than based on any empirical measure of their competence or decision-making ability.

Outside trustees are often experts who can potentially exercise very effective vigilance, but since they have no direct stake in the pension scheme they are motivated by external factors. In contrast, inside trustees have less investment expertise but a greater intrinsic commitment to the beneficiaries. Whelan notes that, "the competent but career orientated trustee may be a useful way of capturing the professional type of pension fund trustee." Whelan goes on to say:

> "It may be posited that an outside trustee performs better than an insider when strong career concerns are provided by the market and the link between vigilance and return is direct."[83]

[81] Pensions Board, "Report of the Pensions Board to the Minister for Social and Family Affairs on Trusteeship" (November 2006), 5.8.2.

[82] Pensions Board, "Report of the Pensions Board to the Minister for Social and Family Affairs on Trusteeship" (November 2006), 3.2.2.

[83] Whelan, "Pension Provision in Ireland in 21st Century" (2005) (A Report for the Irish Association of Pension Funds to help further the debate on our national pensions policy), p.19

(e) Trustee training

The current focus on trusteeship has stemmed from various corporate and accounting scandals and the reports and recommendations that followed e.g. Enron and Sarbanes-Oxley Act 2002 in the US and the Combined Code on Corporate Governance, together with new accountancy regulation in the United Kingdom, OECD guidelines for Pension Fund Governance and the EU Pensions Directive.

It has been suggested that, "the competent but career orientated trustee may be a useful way of capturing the professional type of pension fund trustee that was suggested by the Myners report."[84] Whelan goes on to make a convincing observation that, " … in reality, some insiders have great technical competence while some outsiders can feel a strong sense of duty to the fund beneficiaries … this distinction reflects an important trade off that may arise in the selection of trustees."

The Trustee Handbook 2007[85] stresses that pension scheme trustees have duties under trust law which include the following: to act in the best interests of beneficiaries, act prudently and diligently, and exercise care and utmost good faith in carrying out one's duties. A trustee who is negligent, does not act in good faith or does something which is contrary to the rules of the trust can be sued by the beneficiaries. In this case, the trustee can be held to be personally liable for the whole of the amount of any loss which occurs. Trustees nominally act on behalf of trustees but the plan sponsor/employer has considerable influence on the nomination process and on the decision-making process of trustees. Employers do influence asset allocation.[86]

In the American context, breaches of ERISA violations can be costly. Trustees involved in a breach of duties, permitting a plan to engage in a prohibited transaction, or engaging in a prohibited transaction themselves can be forced to restore all losses to the plan and account for any profits they may have earned. A court can also grant any other equitable relief that it finds appropriate. With some limited exceptions, fiduciaries are also liable for the breaches of other fiduciaries.[87] It is therefore vital that trustees are trained to recognise and respond prudently to situations which may attract such liability.

If one examines the Canadian Pensions climate, positive outcomes have been achieved by clearly defining responsibilities and accountabilities.[88] The Canadian

[84] Whelan, "Pension Provision in Ireland in 21st Century" (2005). It may be posited that an outside trustee performs better than an insider when strong career concerns are provided by the market and the link between vigilance and return is direct.

[85] "So You're a Pension Scheme Trustee? A Brief Guide to your Duties and Responsibilities" (Pensions Board, 2007).

[86] Mitchell and Utkus, "Company Stock Retirement Plan Diversification" (March 2002) The Pensions Institute, report that over five million American employees have a DC plan in which 60 per cent of funds are invested in their employers' stock.

[87] Fiduciaries are people and entities who have authority and control over the plan's assets, provide investment advice or a fee, or have discretionary authority in the administration of the plan.

Pension Plan Investment Board advocated annual reporting outlining rates of return and the market value of assets—their motto seems to be disclose, disclose, disclose! Our own National Pensions Reserve Fund Act 2000 provides for similar transparency and disclosure.[89] At the end of the day trustees carry the can, they risk personal liability for making imprudent or negligent decisions affecting plan beneficiaries—training is paramount.

It had been advocated that a compulsory system of training should be introduced on a phased basis via a combination of general and scheme specific training. The phased approach would be targeted at new trustees only, since it has been acknowledged throughout the course of the interviews that experience as a trustee greatly helps in the development of trustee knowledge.[90] Lawler further suggested that a model code of governance should be included in the Trustee Handbook, outlining corporate governance developments in best practice and allowing schemes to examine ways in which their management structure could be improved.

The merits of these suggestions were recognised by the Pensions Board in their Report on Trusteeship.[91] It suggested that trustees should have access to a centralised database of educational information similar to the E-learning Trustee Toolkit in United Kingdom. The Pensions Board Annual Report and Accounts for 2007 states that the Board is currently developing web-based training tools for trustees and is liaising with the Department of Social and Family Affairs about the commencement of the trustee training legislation.[92]

Trustees are also obliged to familiarise themselves with Trustee Knowledge and Understanding requirements.[93] A similar approach could be taken in this jurisdiction by amending the Occupational Pensions Schemes (Disclosure of Information) Regulations 2005 to require similar reporting standards in annual reports.

It appears that generally, trustees are satisfied with the contribution of the Pensions Board towards education but it is recognised among industry participants that ultimate responsibility would rest with the Board in the wake of a pensions scandal.

Improvement of regulatory supports and increased standards of trusteeship are likely to contribute to greater public confidence and pensions generally and

[88] See further: Anne Maher (CEO, Pensions Board), "It all begins and ends with good corporate governance", Presentation before European Institute Sovereign Funds Roundtable, May 16, 2006.

[89] Reporting of Information to Minister—Each report must include: Information on investment strategy, report on investment return, valuation of net assets and detailed list of assets, information about investment management and custodianship.

[90] C. Lawler, "Does Trusteeship Contribute Positively to Pension Scheme Governance In Ireland? A Qualitative Analysis." (Dublin: Institute of Public Administration, 2006), pp.78, 100.

[91] Report of the Pensions Board to the Minister for Social and Family Affairs on Trusteeship, Pensions Board, November 2006.

[92] Pensions Board, "Annual Report and Accounts 2007" (June 2008), p.8.

[93] Regulatory code of practice No. 7 "Trustee Knowledge and Understanding" (The Pensions Regulator UK, 2006).

assist in achieving pension policy goals. There is a need for compulsory trustee training. The Irish Association of Pension Funds' training seminars should be well advertised and materials circulated to all trustees registered on a central database maintained by either the IAPF or the Pensions Board.

Trustees deserve to have their roles and responsibilities defined. They may benefit from a centrally accessible database of anonymous common law decisions regarding trustees and pensions[94] so as to be aware of the standards of conduct expected of them and of what actions in certain situations may amount to breach of duty or negligence and may lead to personal liability along ERISA standards. This is particularly important given the development of the rule in *Hastings Bass* and the fallout from the Aer Lingus-Ryanair takeover and collapse of Waterford Wedgwood.

The Pensions Board noted in its recent *Trusteeship Report*[95] that training in this jurisdiction is, at present, unstructured and sporadic.[96] Further, the lack of ability has impacted negatively on the administration and investment performance of pension schemes. One option to increase standards is the introduction of mandatory training. An alternative, or parallel, option is to extend the IORPs trustee requirements.[97] But if a mandatory approach to training was adopted, for example, the need for extending the IORPs requirements would not be necessary.

Unlike the Irish requirements on investment, Trustee Knowledge and Understanding[98] requires such knowledge and understanding from each trustee. In 1993, the UK's Pension Law Review Committee[99] devoted little attention to the area of trustee knowledge and training eight years later, the Myners Review[100] (2001), while concentrating on investment issues, saw trustee skill levels as crucial for effective performance:

Employer-nominated trustees are generally satisfied with the training they received upon taking up the trustee role but the majority did not attend any further courses or training sessions.[101] Member trustees attached great value to training but gaining access to courses was an issue for some. Lawler concluded that mandatory training be introduced for, at the very least, all new trustees. Such

[94] Lawler, "Does Trusteeship Contribute Positively to Pension Scheme Governance in Ireland? A Qualitative Analysis" (Dublin: Institute of Public Administration, 2006).

[95] Report of the Pensions Board to the Minister for Social and Family Affairs on Trusteeship (Pensions Board, 2006).

[96] The Pensions Board has recently drawn up a list of approved trustee training courses, details of which are available on their website: *www.pensionsboard.ie*.

[97] IORPS – 2003/41/EC on the activities and supervision of institutions for occupational retirement provision.

[98] Regulatory Code of Practice No. 7, "Trustee Knowledge and Understanding" (The Pensions Regulator).

[99] Goode, "Pension Law Reform – The Report of the Pension Law Review Committee" (London: HMSO, 1993).

[100] Myners, "Institutional Investment in the United Kingdom: A Review" (London: HM Treasury, 2001).

[101] Lawler, "Does Trusteeship Contribute Positively to Pension Scheme Governance in Ireland? A Qualitative Analysis" (Dublin: Institute of Public Administration, 2006).

an approach would be supported by an e-learning system, similar to that adopted in the UK, and compulsory reporting on the level and type of training received would be included in the trustee annual report. He suggested that such an approach would not introduce a disincentive effect on take-up of trustee positions. Lawler's recommendations were endorsed by the Board who felt an e-learning system similar to that in operation in the United Kingdom would be an appropriate mechanism for basic training, overcoming geographical, time and financial constraints.

Section 28 of the Social Welfare and Pensions Act 2008 provides for amendments to the Pensions Act in relation to trustee training as recommended by the *Report of The Pensions Board to The Minister for Social and Family Affairs on Trusteeship*.[102] As a result of the amendments, employers are required to arrange trustee training for each trustee within six months of their appointment and at least every two years thereafter. Where a person is already a trustee at the time the legislation commences, there is no requirement on the trustee to undertake training within six months. The ongoing two-year training requirement does, however apply. Where an employer breaches the obligation to provide regular training it may be prosecuted. Employers are not under an obligation to provide training to professional trustees and pension trustees. It is expected that such trustees will undertake regular training to keep their skills current.

Where a trustee fails to undertake the required training, s.3A has been amended to allow the Board to apply an on-the-spot-fine.

Trustees are required as a result of an amendment to s.54(1) to confirm in the Annual Report that they have undertaken the required training and to confirm that they have access to the latest edition of the Board's Trustee Handbook. The training undertaken must cover the Pensions Act and regulations, duties and responsibilities of trustees both under the Act and at common law and effective management of a scheme.

The Occupational Pension Schemes (Disclosure of Information) Regulations 2006 require that the annual report includes a statement as to whether trustees have access to appropriate training on their duties and responsibilities. The Board considered this provision to be inadequate and decided that it should be replaced by a requirement that the annual report should include a statement by the trustees on what training has actually been arranged and received. To support this provision, the Board decided that legislation should be introduced so that employers are obliged to arrange trustee training for each individual trustees within six months of their appointment and at least every two years thereafter—which is reflected in the Social Welfare and Pensions Act 2008. The course offered by the Irish Institute of Pension Managers—the Trustee Certificate of Essential Pensions Knowledge—offers trustees the opportunity to receive a formal qualification as part of their training regime. Training courses should be kept up to date, reflecting any relevant changes in legislation or trustee duties

[102] Pensions Board 2006.

and the Board should maintain its role of monitoring the quality of trainers and training content (including, for example, trustee ethical behaviour, service level agreements).[103] The Board was also of the opinion that a "trustee checklist" should be appended to the next edition of the Handbook to assist trustees in meeting their obligations.[104] However, a self-assessment of trustees' procedures is ill-advised given its subjectivity and the possibility of merely ticking boxes to indicate compliance.

(f) Provision of reasons for decisions

Traditionally, the position was that trustees were advised not to disclose reasons for their decision making, for fear of exposing themselves to personal liability. Since 2003 in the UK, the Pension Ombudsman has upset that tradition. This is a move which may be followed by our own pensions regulatory bodies.

Case law suggests that trustees should now give reasons for their decisions as a matter of good administrative practice. *Schmidt v Rosewood*[105] is authority for the suggestion that there may be an entitlement to disclosure of documents showing whether breaches of fiduciary duty had reduced the amount available for distribution.[106] It is possible that in the future, the Irish courts will be more likely to class pension scheme trustees alongside public bodies as opposed to similar to family trustees, who benefit from total confidentiality.[107] Given the lack of case law on point in this jurisdiction, such indications are based only on

[103] Social Welfare and Pensions Act 2008 inserts a new subs.(1A) to provide that for the purposes of preparing an annual report, the trustees of a scheme must appoint a registered administrator. It should be noted that a trustee may itself apply to the Board to be appointed as the registered administrator for a scheme. Section 64C states that the Board shall establish a Register of Administrators with the names and addresses of all registered administrators. It is proposed that the Register shall be available online for inspection by the public.

[104] Pensions Board, "Annual Report and Accounts 2007" (June 2008), p.8, states that both an Employer and Trustee Checklist are to be introduced.

[105] [2003] 3 All E.R. 76.

[106] See J. Reilly in *Sunday Independent*, July 1, 2007:

> "Aer Lingus pensioners and employees have paid a heavy price for the controversial decision to invest in their own company when it was faced with a takeover by Ryanair … facing a loss of 5 million euro on their investment … the investment was the subject of a warning letter from the Irish Pensions Board to the pension fund trustees reminding them of the need to invest wisely … reiterating their responsibilities and with due regard to the potential return … all pension schemes in Ireland should proceed on the 'prudent person principle'."

The prudent person test focuses on processes of decision making. Courts determine this issue by looking at what the trustees knew at the time the investment decision was made and then deciding whether that was the decision of a prudent person e.g. to "vigorously and independently investigate the wisdom of a contemplated investment, it matters not that the investment succeeds or fails"—*Donovan v Walton* 609 F.Supp. 1221, 1238.

[107] In administrative law, public bodies are often obliged to give reasons for their decisions. It is possible that in future the court will be more likely to class pension scheme trustees alongside public bodies as opposed to similar to family trustees, who benefit from total confidentiality.

the dicta of English decisions regarding trusts and pensions. However, the persuasive authority of these decisions should not be ignored given the sharp similarities in our overall pension governance.

There are, however, some arguments against a requirement to give reasons. Traditionally, trustees of occupational pension schemes did not have a general duty to give reasons for the exercise of their discretion. As noted above, *Schmidt v Rosewood Trust*[108] casts doubt on the traditional approach that trustees of occupational pension schemes do not have a general duty to give reasons for decisions made. However, it has been argued that the decision of itself does not reverse the traditional stance[109] and that it would be unfortunate if the law developed in such a way as to impose a duty to give reasons.

This issue is important in light of the rule in *Hastings Bass*[110] discussed earlier. This specifies that the trustees must ask themselves the "correct questions", they must direct themselves correctly in law, they must adopt a correct construction of the pension fund rules, they must not arrive at a perverse decision and they must take into account all relevant but no irrelevant factors. It would be difficult to bring a challenge on the basis of the factors considered unless the trustees have to give reasons for their answers. This has been a factor in the courts' consideration of the existence of a duty to give reasons in the context of administrative bodies which are susceptible to judicial review.

Administrative law cases such as *R v Higher Education Funding Council, ex p Institute of Dental Surgery* [1994] 1 All E.R. 651; *Doody v Secretary of State for the Home Department* [1993] 3 All E.R. 92; *R v Civil Service Appeal Board ex p Cunningham* [1991] 4 All E.R. 310 and *The Millennium Commission v The Asha Foundation* [2003] All E.R. 81. See Evans's discussion of this (text to n.8):

> "The traditional position of the courts has been that there is no general duty under public law to give reasons … it has been suggested that the Court of Appeal's decision in the recent *Asha Foundation* case may have been a significant development in the law … The judgement is notable for a statement that 'in the case of a decision of a sort that the Millennium Commission (arguably in a similar position to a trustee board when considering the granting of funds) was making, as a matter of good administration and fairness the body concerned should give such reasons as are appropriate and reasonable in the circumstances.' The main focus of the Court was on the content of the reasons to be given rather than on whether reasons were required in the first place. However, to suggest that this will become the norm in future public law (or pensions) cases seems to overlook an important fact – the Commission had promised potential applicants that reasons would be given … So in the absence of a promise, the Court – would have accepted that no reasons- or at least no meaningful reasons would have to be given not withstanding the effort invested by Asha in the application process. Indeed even in the light of the promise the Court felt that the obligation on the Commission was very limited, it was required to give reasons appropriate in the circumstances, which it was deemed to have done."

Cf. Cox, "Should trustees give reasons for decisions? The argument for" (2003) *Pensions: An International Journal*, Vol.9, No.2, p.118.

108 [2003] 3 All E.R. 76.

109 Evans, "Are trustees required to give reasons? The argument against" (2003) *Pensions: An International Journal*, Vol.9, No.2, p.124.

110 *Re Hastings Bass (deceased), Hastings and ors. v Commissioners of the Inland Revenue* [1974] 2 All E.R. 193.

In *Re Londonderry's Settlement*,[111] Harman L.J. in the Court of Appeal, noted two competing trust law principles. The first was that "trustees exercising discretionary power are not bound to disclose the reasons actuating them in coming to a decision." The second was that:

> "... [T]he relevant documents had come into existence for the purpose of the trust, were in the possession of the trustees and therefore were trust documents. As such they were the property of the beneficiaries and open to the beneficiaries to inspect."[112]

Ratee J. drew out a more interesting point, that in the absence of evidence to the contrary, a trustee was presumed to have exercised his discretion properly, i.e. there was no reason not to apply the well-established principle that reasons did not have to be given.

Lord Walker noted that the better approach would be to recognise the right to seek disclosure of documents as one aspect of the court's jurisdiction to supervise and to intervene in the administration of trusts. He approved an Australian case *Hartigan Nominees v Rydge*,[113] which suggested that any right of a beneficiary to see documents was based not on a proprietary interest but on the trustees' fiduciary duty to keep the beneficiary informed and to render accounts.

The Privy Council noted that the plaintiff would have a strong claim as to documents showing whether breaches of fiduciary duty had reduced the amount available for distribution.

The common law may be entering new and very uncertain waters here.[114] Lord Walker (giving leading judgment in *Schmidt*) wrote a paper in 1996[115] discussing *Londonderry* in which he stressed that the decision was made in the light of family settlements of a discretionary nature and that pension schemes differed.

There were strong arguments that trustees should be ready to justify their decisions. He noted that in administrative law the "tide is running towards a general duty to give reasons for the decisions." The parallels between trustees and official bodies have been noted in several subsequent cases, indeed to could be remarked that the *Hastings Bass* rule is "virtually identical" to the *Wednesbury* principles to which the decisions of official bodies are subject.[116]

111 [1996] O.P.L.R. 129.

112 [1996] O.P.L.R. 129.

113 (1992) 29 N.S.W.L.R. 405, [1999] 43 P.B.L.R. 107 The right to seek intervention applied not just to beneficiaries but also to potential beneficiaries and objects of powers, who could not be said to have a proprietary right. The claimant was also deemed to have a strong claim as to documents showing whether breaches of fiduciary duty had reduced the amount available for distribution.

114 Evans, "Are trustees required to give reasons? The argument against'" (2003) *Pensions: An International Journal*, Vol.9 No.2, p.124.

115 Walker, "Some Trust principles in the Pensions Context" [1996] P.L.R. 107.

116 Walker, "Some Trust Principles in the Pensions Context" [1996] P.L.R. 107.

Disclosure of reasons can lead to animosity between the members and employer, and members and trustees. It appears the courts view confidentiality not as an absolute right but merely a factor to be considered. If this is so, it would mark a radical and regrettable reversal of the prior principle that unless there is evidence to the contrary, a trustee is presumed to have exercised his discretion properly.

Despite the concerns raised about these new developments, the United Kingdom Pensions Ombudsman has departed from the traditional approach in several cases. Repeatedly, the Ombudsman has made clear that trustees should give reasons for their decisions.

In *Allen v TKM*,[117] for example, the Ombudsman directed that the trustees should provide Mr Allen with a copy of the material placed before them as part of their considerations in rejecting his claim for an unreduced early retirement pension, and that reasons should be given for that decision. The Ombudsman also noted that there is no legal duty on the trustee to make copies of their minutes available to Mr Allen. Thus, Mr Allen could not as a matter of law seek some order from the courts to obtain the minutes. It would be wrong, however, to assume that the absence of a breach of law means there is no act of maladministration. Maladministration is in some ways a wider concept than a breach of law and respondents may sometimes be judged to have maladministered in circumstances where they would not be regarded as acting unlawfully.

> "As a matter of good administrative practice trustees should provide reasons for their decisions to those legitimately interested in the matter and subject to the need to preserve right to privacy of individual members, should also make the minutes of their meeting available to scheme members … failure to have done this is maladministration."[118]

It appears, that maladministration covers more than simple breach of duty but it is hard to see that exercising a legal right (not to give reasons) can be maladministration. Neither does it follow from a duty to give reasons that the trustees should also disclose their minutes.

It would be difficult to argue against the reasonableness of requiring pension trustees to give appropriate reasons for decisions that significantly affect the financial stability of the scheme members.

(g) External expertise?

It has been suggested by the Board that schemes would benefit from the experience of a "registered administrator", registered with the Board. Any such regulation, however, would need to be balanced in ensuring that trustees uphold

[117] [2002] P.L.R. 333.

[118] *www.pension-ombudsman.org.uk/determinations/docs/2002/apr/100370.doc*, para.30.

their trust law duty to monitor the activities of those to whom they delegate functions, assisted through service level agreements.[119]

Concern about pension plan governance has arisen in light of increased litigation, global competition, attention to shareholder value and institutional shareholder activism. The Canadian *Dey Report*[120] raises the possibility of a new governance responsibility for pension plans; as institutional investors are they in any way responsible for improving the corporate governance of the companies they invest in?

The National Association of Pension Funds suggests that trustees should engage in self-assessment procedures, peer appraisal etc. and arrange for formal assessments of their own procedures and decision-making (including delegated decision-making) But the Irish Pensions Board determined in their recent *Trusteeship Report* that such an approach was ill-advised and suffered from being too subjective.[121] It seems, therefore, that trustees remain unaccountable for the decisions they make and the reasoning behind their decision-making until a formal complaint is made by a beneficiary or scheme member under the Pension Act 1990 (as amended). It is unclear at the time of writing whether such action will be taken by Aer Lingus pension scheme members on foot of potential financial loss suffered by them and the warning letters received from the Pensions Board on foot of the trustees' investment decisions. It is possible that this decision may amount to a breach of prudent expert standards espoused in legislation or at least a breach of good faith.[122]

Employees almost inevitably specialise their capital in their employer firm, exposing each employee to even further firm-specific risk. To the extent that beneficiaries can control the management of funds and can assess their risk exposure, they would probably oppose activism. To the extent that beneficiary control cannot serve this purpose, trustees ought to require that beneficiaries be protected from this risk.

5. Conclusion

Close examination of the Irish occupational pension system and the role of trustees therein has highlighted the need for improvement of regulatory supports. This in turn will lead to increased standards of trusteeship which are likely to

[119] In June 2008, Mary Hanafin TD, Minister for Social and Family Affairs launched the Pensions Board's *Annual Report 2007*. The Chief Executive of the Board Brendan Kennedy welcomed the initiative that will require all administrators to be registered with the Pensions Board from November 1, 2008. This will result in more effective and efficient supervision of pension schemes.

[120] "Where were the Directors? Guidelines for Improved Corporate Governance in Canada" (Toronto: Toronto Street Exchange, 1994).

[121] Report of the Pensions Board to the Minister for Social and Family Affairs on Trusteeship (Pensions Board, 2006).

[122] See T-411/07 and T-411/07R – Order of President of Court of First Instance where Aer

contribute to greater public confidence in pensions generally and assist in achieving pension policy goals.

The most pressing issue facing pension scheme trustees is the lack of uniform understanding and training. There is a need for compulsory trustee training along the lines of the Trustee Toolkit adopted in Britain. This development would be warmly welcomed by the Pensions Board. Further, in the opinion of this writer, the Irish Association of Pension Funds' training seminars should be more widely and accessibly advertised and materials circulated to all trustees who should be registered on a central database maintained by either the Irish Association of Pension Funds or the Pensions Board. The importance of training, and allowing trustees to develop the requisite supervisory skill set is outlined well by Whelan:

> "Saving for a distant pension is like steering a large ship towards a distant port. If it goes off course after only a few miles than only a small change in its course is necessary to home in on its distant target again. As the port is approached the bearing is checked more frequently to ensure no large swerve is needed. However, at retirement, the pensioner having provided for their own pension is exposed to investment and longevity risk: they are completely adrift."[123]

At present, the outlines of trusteeship are murky at best. Trustees deserve to have their role and responsibilities defined They may benefit from a centrally accessible database of anonymous common law decisions regarding trustees and pensions so as to be aware of the standards of conduct expected of them. They must also be aware of what actions in certain situations may amount to breach of duty or negligence and may lead to personal liability along ERISA standards. This is particularly important given the development of the rule in *Hastings Bass*.

At present there seems to be no measure of accountability for trustees' actions and decisions other than certain grievances being specifically aired in court or before the Pensions Ombudsman. Self assessment of trustees' procedures is ill advisable given its subjectivity and the possibility of merely ticking boxes to indicate compliance. A more rigorous "certification" process is suggested to overcome these shortcomings. This fact was recognised by Lawler and acknowledged by the Pensions Board in its 2006 Trusteeship Report, however no specific course of action has been seized upon and the situation will be monitored by the Board in the coming years.

Lingus's request for interim measures to prevent Ryanair from exercising voting rights was rejected. See further "EU Court rejects Aerlingus bid to stop Ryanair voting rights" March 25, 2008, *www.eubusiness.com/news-eu/1205927221.18*.

123 Whelan, "Pension Provision in Ireland in 21st Century" (A report prepared for the Irish Association of Pension Funds to help further the debate on our national pensions policy, 2005), p.22.

Recent Irish research[124] has revealed that, despite its shortcomings there are distinct advantages to the trust model, particularly in relation to separating the scheme assets from the employer, the flexibility associated with trustee discretion and trust law, the ability of third parties (e.g. a member's dependants) to enforce their rights under the trust and the fact that it is a tried and tested model with which pension practitioners are comfortable and familiar. Indeed, a more appropriate model has not been cited in that research. However, some commentators have pointed to the increasing contractualisation of pension schemes and so it may be argued that a hybrid trust law/contract model may become appropriate in time, but further research into this area is needed.

Despite many flaws, the trust model still remains the most appropriate mechanism for implementing and supervising pensions law in Ireland. The fiduciary responsibility on trustees to act in the best interests of beneficiaries is a particularly strong point. Member trusteeship, in particular, provides a form of democratic representation to pension scheme members and a further layer of protection of their interests.[125]

Disadvantages of the trust model focused on internal scheme governance, particularly the ability of trustees to manage large financial entities in an increasingly complex environment. The bureaucracy and cost (e.g. time spent on trusteeship activities) associated with operating pension scheme trusts and the potential for conflicts of interest continue to be flagged as areas needing attention by the regulatory bodies. It is suggested that implementing a scheme such as the Trustee Toolkit and adopting mechanisms such as the United Kingdom's Trustee Knowledge and Understanding requirements, make it possible to overcome some or all of these difficulties in comprehensive accessible trustee training.

Trust law requires trustees to act with the best interests of the beneficiaries in mind, while adapting to changing circumstances. If a more rigid approach was introduced in place of trust law, it would likely present major difficulties to for trustees in that the flexible framework provided by trust law would no longer be available to plug loopholes or gaps that, potentially, could be created through reliance on prescriptive primary legislation alone. A dynamic and adaptive governance model incorporating similar trustee training elements to those in Britain, coupled with more specific and defined roles and responsibilities along American lines (both in case law and legislation) and a consideration of administrative law's accountability requirements may help to ensure greater trustee vigilance and understanding in order to increase monitoring standards and plan performance in today's changing market climate.

124 Lawler,"Does Trusteeship Contribute Positively to Pension Scheme Governance In Ireland? A Qualitative Analysis" (Dublin: Institute of Public Administration, 2006).

125 Pensions Board, "Report of the Pensions Board to the Minister for Social and Family Affairs on Trusteeship" (November 2006), 5.1.2.

Part III

Current Regulatory Issues

CHAPTER 7

FINANCIAL FRAGILITY AND CORPORATE GOVERNANCE IN IRELAND

*Stephen Kinsella, Department of Economics, Kemmy Business School, University of Limerick**

This article advances a financial fragility hypothesis[1] to explain many of the determinants of the 2009/2010 Irish recessionary period. This article gives the context in terms of governance for the poor performance of the Irish economy to date, suggests one theory to explain the changes we have witnessed in Irish economic conditions in 2008 and 2009, and advances an "emergent" theory of corporate governance for the 21st century to better protect the Irish economy from the inevitable excesses of the financial sector.

1. INTRODUCTION

Governance concerns the exercise of power through policies enacted by self-interested agents working within institutions. These policies necessarily affect different agents in different ways. The Irish finance industry, together with the Irish government and its attendant regulatory bodies, have seen spectacular successes and failures from 1990 to 2009. The regulatory climate they helped create allowed a housing bubble to develop, which has now burst, with unpleasant consequences for the Irish economy.[2]

In addition to the economy-wide effects of a collapse in an industry which employed one in five Irish males up to late 2007, the decline of the Irish economy has come at a time of an international crisis, as the contagion of bad debt began, by the sub-prime mortgage crisis in the USA, to spread to banks and financial intermediaries around the world in a matter of months. The Irish economy, because of its location, geography and size, is dependent on trade,

* Stephen.kinsella@ul.ie, *www.stephenkinsella.net*. Written for a collection of essays on governance in an Irish context edited by Dr Ailbhe O'Neill, and the Honorable Mr Justice Ronan Keane whom I sincerely thank for the invitation to contribute. All errors and omissions are my own.

1 Advanced by the late Hyman Minsky in his *Stabilising and Unstable Economy* (New York: McGraw-Hill, 1986).

2 At a time when the international economy is recording its worst period of cumulative economic growth since the Great Depression of the 1930s.

which means that to enrich itself, Ireland's exports must be cheaper and better, on average, than their competitors. This is no longer the case.

Much of the housing bubble from 2003 to 2008 was fueled by rising real wages,[3] which increased private consumption of houses and other large, durable goods, as well as services. Buoyed by increased levels of private domestic investment, this increase in wages fueled the boom, even as it eroded our competitiveness in export markets.[4]

This article surveys the evolution of the Irish financial industry in the context of an evolving set of codes of practice, market structures, and macroeconomic conditions. We will see that, through its negligence, the financial regulator allowed the Irish finance industry to sow the seeds of its own destruction in a boom/bust "credit cycle", which we will be at pains to explain.

The stakes could not be higher. The costs of financial crises are enormous. Honohan[5] estimates that just the public sector costs of resolving banking crises in developing countries between 1980 and 1995 amounted to US$250 billion.[6] A prescriptive model of financial fragility, and its relationship to financial governance is urgently needed. This article makes an initial foray in that direction.

Section 2 will set the scene. Section 3 will give the macroeconomic justification for a "financial fragility" hypothesis. Section 4 will discuss the role of governance in the protection of society from the excesses of the markets. Section 5 will conclude with some observations on what an "emergent" theory of financial regulation might look like, and offers some recommendations for changes at the policy level in 2009.

2. Financial Governance and Financial Fragility in Ireland

Governance is important to the operation of the Irish financial system.[7] Governance concerns the basic structural and operational relationships between firms, whose stated objectives are both to maximise profit (and therefore shareholder value) and regulatory authorities, whose objective is to minimise non-compliance with legal and regulatory strictures concerning those firms.

3 Real wages are nominal wages divided by a measure of changes in the price level, normally called inflation. When averaged across sectors, average real wages measure the purchasing power of workers in the economy in terms of the goods they may consume in a given period.

4 National Competitiveness Council, *Annual Competitiveness Report 2008, Vol. 1: Benchmarking Ireland's Performance* (Dublin: Stationary Office, 2008), pp.6–8.

5 Patrick Honohan, "Banking System Failures in Developing and Transition Countries: Diagnosis and Prediction" (1997) Bank for International Settlements Working Paper No. 39.

6 This language might seem overblown, were it not for the fact that, given the severity of the market corrections of the Irish Stock Exchange, ISEQ since late 2007, some Irish banking stocks have lost 98 per cent of their peak value.

7 In the same way governance is important to the operational success of other public enterprises and to the profitability and effectiveness of private corporations.

Whether those stated objectives map readily onto the reality of modern firm behaviour is an open question.[8]

The essence of financial governance, itself a proper subset of corporate governance, for this article at least, can be summed up in the twofold question: "Who *does* and who *should* regulate banks and financial intermediaries?"

(a) The international context: crises have happened before, and will happen again

The international economy has been characterised by periods of financial instability since at least the 16th century.[9] Since the early 20th century, however, the frequency and severity of these boom and bust cycles have increased, each cycle taking a toll on economic activity, proxied (poorly) by Gross Domestic Product (GDP).[10] A "boom" period can be viewed as an increase in the rate of GDP growth above trend, where the trend can be imagined as an "equilibrium" usage of the economy's resources of capital, land, and labour for the given period, about 3 per cent in most developed countries. So, when Ireland grows at 6–10 per cent a year as it did over the period from 1992–2000, we can call this a boom.

When the economy contracts by 2.5 per cent in one year, as it will almost certainly do in 2009,[11] we can, with some certainty, call this period the beginnings of a bust. Figure 1 below shows the rate of change of real GDP, which is GDP-adjusted for changes in the price level, over the period 1971 to 2008/9. We can clearly see the cycles of boom and bust in the Irish economy, from the oil crises of 1973 and 1979, to the "basket case" economy of the mid-1980s, to the Celtic Tiger of the early 1990s, and to our present, rather sorry state, where a precipitous fall in output guarantees the Irish economy will contract in size, with all the attendent economic and social difficulties in investment, consumption, government expenditure, and real wage contractions that will cause.

Figure 1 traces out the story of the Irish economy over the last 30 years, showing the relative[12] percentage change in real GDP over the 30-year period. Values for 2008 and 2008 are estimated from government sources. The story Figure 1 tells is clearly one of boom and bust, boom and bust, boom and bust. Ireland's experience, from 1990, say, to the present day, stands out as a period qualitatively different from previous economic eras. The Irish are not alone in experiencing business cycles.

8 Indeed, the fundamental issue concerning governance by shareholders today seems to be how to regulate large or active shareholders so as to obtain the right balance between managerial discretion and small shareholder protection.

9 Charles P. Kindleberger, *Manias, Panics, and Crashes: A History of Financial Crisis* (New York: John Wiley and Sons, 2005), in particular, Chs 1 and 2.

10 Gross Domestic Product is the value of all final goods and services produced in a given year. The Gross Domestic Product of Ireland in 2007 was an estimated €258 billion, and in 2008 was an estimated €285 billion.

11 A conservative forecast by Alan Barrett, Ide Kearney and Jean Goggin, Q. Ec. Commentary (Dublin: ESRI, Winter 2008), p.4.

12 i.e. logged percentage change.

Figure 1: Changes in real GDP for Ireland, 1971–2008.

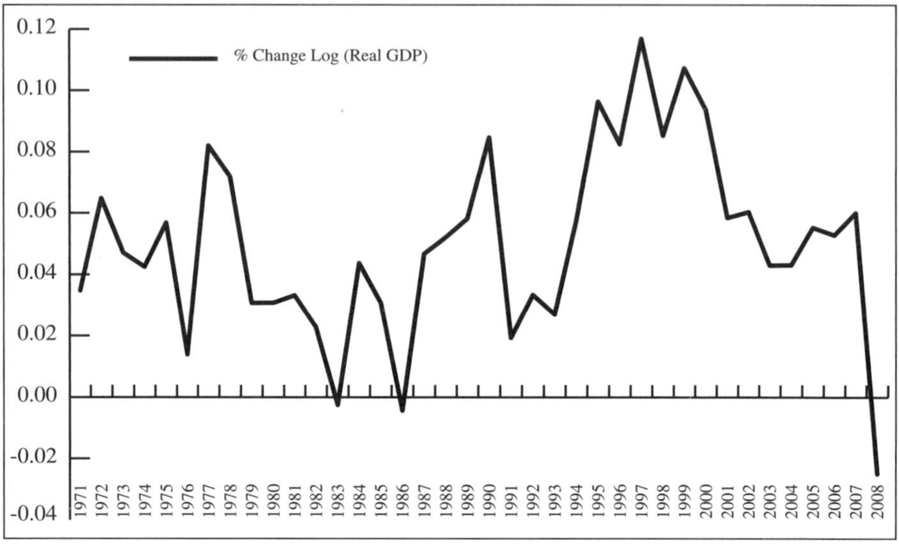

Source: Central Statistics Office, Economic and Social Research Institute, and author's calculations. Note: 2007 and 2008 are estimates.

Just focusing on the more recent busts, a non-exhaustive list for the international economy over the same period as Figure 1, 1980–2008, would contain the Latin American debt crisis of the 1980s, the US stock market crash of 1987, the Japanese real estate and stock market crisis (and ensuing liquidity trap) in the 1990s, the UK housing crash in 1991 and 1992, the Mexican Peso crisis of 1994, the long-running Russian crisis of the mid-90s, the East-Asian crisis of 1997/8, the bursting of the "dot com" bubble in the US in 2000, the worldwide recession following the terrorist attacks of 9/11 in 2001, the Argentinian currency crisis in 2002, the sub-prime crisis which began in the US in August 2007, which led to an international currency and liquidity crisis, and whose ramifications are still being felt in the Irish and international economy more widely. Again, quoting Honohan,[13] recovering from each of these busts costs the public sector US $250 billion. Given that the current downturn is the most severe in terms of drops in consumer spending, increases in unemployment, and the collapse of confidence in Irish banking, the cost of returning "Ireland Inc." to profitability may be substantially higher than Honohan's estimate.

Behind most of those boom-bust cycles stands the instability of credit.[14] When financial markets collapse and, perforce, credit dries up, real economic

[13] Alan Barrett, Ide Kearney and Jean Goggin, *Quarterly Economic Commentary* (Dublin: ESRI, Winter 2008) p.6.

[14] As Charles P. Kindleberger has termed it in *Manias, Panics, and Crashes: A History of Financial Crisis* (Hoboken, New Jersey: John Wiley & Sons, 2005).

activity tends to decline, bringing large output losses in agriculture, services, and manufacturing, with the widespread effects of unemployment, business collapse, retrenched investment, and increases in debt defaults. The macroeconomic pain is felt especially by low income households and small businesses because respectively, they spend a larger proportion of earned income on necessities, and require access to credit lines more often. Downturns are not only painful for the entire economy, but affect the weaker in society more acutely. That business cycle amplitudes should be damped by any means necessary is taken as a given in this article, purely on grounds of economic equity, if not efficiency.

Before discussing Ireland's current financial fragility in detail however, we should digress and focus for a time on the business of modern banking, and what it is Irish banks think they are doing in the financial system.

(b) The business of banks

Banks and financial intermediaries like credit unions, stock broking houses, insurers and reinsurers, and so on, are legally created entities, licensed in Ireland by the Financial Services Regulatory Authority (the "FSAI"). The remit of the FSAI since its inception in May 2003 has been to license, liaise with, and monitor the activities of licensed agents in the financial services sector, to ensure they act in the public interest according to legal strictures. The FSAI is the actualisation of the Irish government's role in financial governance. Previously the Central Bank was charged with that role.

The business of banks in Ireland has historically been to take money on deposit from households and firms, pay the account holder a small interest for the use of their money, and lend out a large proportion of the cash on deposit (up to some predefined limit, called the reserve ratio, now about 7 per cent), charging a higher rate of interest as it does so, and making its profit on the difference. The business of banks, therefore, has been to transmit liquidity from those who save to those who wish to borrow and invest in productive capacity. Recently, however, the role of the bank as systemically important liquidity facilitator has undergone a rapid revision.

Banks engage in contracted activities of financing, because financing for investment (other than out of retained earnings or savings) requires contracts denominated in money. Banks are the institutional architectures we create around the activity of financing businesses and households.

In the modern Irish economy, private banks concern themselves with the process of creating and controlling capital assets, such as houses and factories. Money in this framework is not simply a token which reduces the costs of a transaction, as some economists[15] assume, it is a sort of bond which exists between banks and those they borrow from and lend to, which allows different agents in the economy to take different positions in capital and financial assets

[15] For example, Robert Barro, *Macroeconomics* (London: Cengage Press, 2007).

with respect to some time in the future. As a side effect of this contracting process, money is created via fractional reserve banking, as bankers go about their business of arranging the finance for a trade, the financing of an investment, or taking positions in a financial asset. The inevitable increase in the quantity of money, which society can measure, through bank lending to businesses and households is what transforms the desire for investment or capital assets into an effective demand: the creation of money is actually a part of the mechanism by which the surplus product of society is allocated to the production of particular investment projects, and their eventual productive outputs. Anyone can create money. The difficulty is to have it accepted by others. Only licensed financial agents may do so, and when they create money via fractional reserve banking for the purpose of loan creation (and their own profit), they start the credit cycle, explained in detail in Section 3.

Once money is created via the double-entry accounting system, the borrower enters directly into a contractual commitment to repay the lendor at some series of points in the future. The ability of the business or household to actually make that series of repayments depends critically on the proceeds earned in the use of the capital resource, as it is used in production of a good or service. The normal functioning of the economy rests on the income generation of a profitable subset of productive elements, which services loans, which leads to more investment, and via the mechanism just described, to more profits.

This is, of course, a simplification, but it does yield an important insight: lending by banks, for the most part, should be for *productive, profit-making* activities. In the Irish case, it is not clear that the practice of lending for investment in property, based on an expectation of ever-higher price increases in the value of that property, could be considered a productive activity. It was, instead, a *redistributive* activity, where the future incomes of borrowers were transferred to the present to finance loans for mortgages on residential and commercial properties.

Why all the borrowing? Individuals were willing to borrow because their real wages were rising dramatically over the period 2002–2008. Since the second quarter of 2000, labour costs, a proxy for real wages, in all sectors of the Irish economy have increased by more than the Eurozone average, meaning the real cost of hiring a worker in Ireland was going up more than the European average. Irish wage inflation grew by more than *double* the Eurozone average in construction and communications between the second quarter of 2004 and the second quarter of 2008.[16]

Changes in the quantity of money in the Irish economy are a sign that interactions between economics agents desirous of spending in excess of their current income are increasing. Recent statistical evidence on the growth of the level of money in the Irish economy confirm this fact.[17] The essential spending

[16] National Competitiveness Council, *Annual Competitiveness Report, Vol. 1: Benchmarking Ireland's Performance* (Dublin: Stationary Office, 2008), p.59.

[17] Central Bank of Ireland, *Monthly Statistics to December 2008* (Central Bank and Financial Services Authority of Ireland, January 2008), at p.2.

in excess of income, or deficit financing, is done by business for investment and the purchase of capital assets. The viability of debts due to household behaviour depends on the levels of employment and money wages. We have seen that wage inflation in Ireland over the period 2002–2008 was more than double the European average. What about employment? Employment in manufacturing decreased by 34,000 over the same period, while employment in financial services, construction, and retail tripled in size.[18]

Employment in the public sector has also seen large rises. Average weekly earnings in the public sector (excluding the health sector, itself, an employer of 110,000 individuals) rose by 2.9 per cent in the year to September 2008. The index of average earnings, which excludes some effects of changes in employment composition, rose by 3.6 per cent for the same period. Figure 2 below maps out this change.

Figure 2: Right axis: average weekly earnings, 2007–2008. Left axis: change in numbers employed in the public sector. Statistics exclude the health sector.

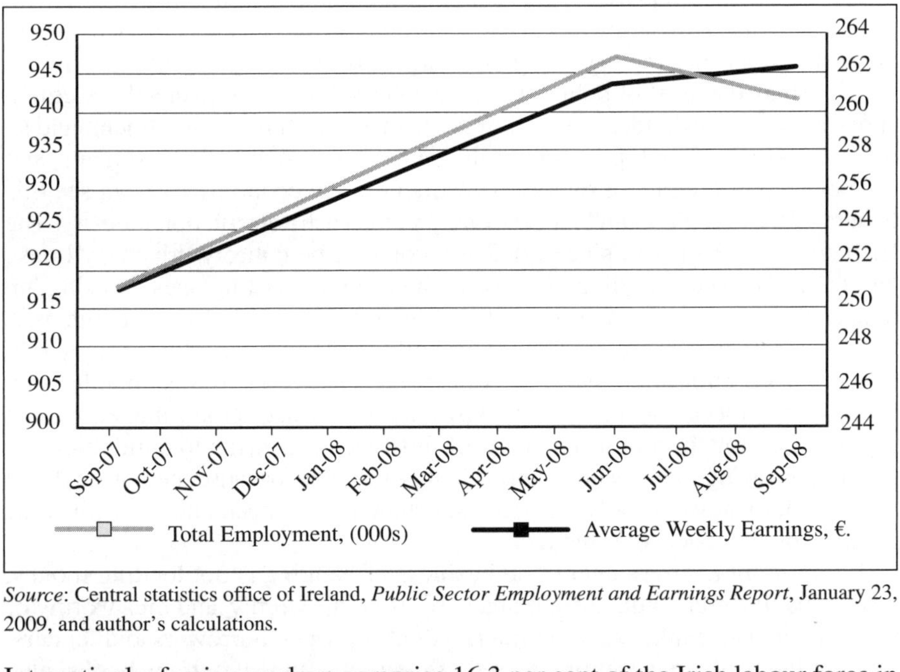

Source: Central statistics office of Ireland, *Public Sector Employment and Earnings Report*, January 23, 2009, and author's calculations.

Interestingly, foreign workers comprise 16.3 per cent of the Irish labour force in the second quarter of 2008, compared to 3.7 per cent in 2000. Unemployment rates are now on the rise after a steep fall in the demand for construction labour, with high labour costs, as well as deteriorating international economic

[18] National Competitiveness Council, *Annual Competitiveness Report, Vol 1: Benchmarking Ireland's Performance* (Dublin: Stationary Office, 2008), p.93.

conditions, leading major multinationals like Dell, Kostal and Microsoft to reconsider Ireland as a manufacturing hub for their European operations.

Investment in Ireland in 2009 and 2010 will be conducted at low levels, because the demand for investment changes as views about the future change. Current (January 2009) estimates for cumulative world growth from 2009 to 2011 are, on average, 2.5 per cent. The last time the world grew so slowly was 1946–1949. Conditions for investment are not ideal[19] and investor confidence is low. However, even if investor confidence was high, the demand for future investment depends on the excess of the capitalised value of future expected profits over the supply price of investment, given these straightened financing conditions, so even if the price of investment goods went up, making an investment a more attractive option, the demand price for investment will not rise unless financing is forthcoming. Simply put, you cannot invest in a project if you cannot get a loan.

(i) Finance matters

There is a certain circularity to this simple description of what it is banks do. We can see that investment growth above a certain threshold is necessary to assure other investors that the economy is doing well, which spurs them to invest, which brings the level of belief about the robustness of the financial system up above another threshold, accelerating the demand for further investment, and so on, in a process of multiplication of the gains from individual investments, and acceleration of the rate of overall investment in the economy. We can see this feature of the "credit boom" most strongly in the Irish construction industry. The Irish economy's growth since 2002 has come to be entirely driven by house building.[20] Between building new houses and selling existing ones, housing, up to late 2007, generated almost one-fifth of Ireland's national income. Large parts of the Irish economy are now based on building houses for all the people that have got jobs building houses. This property bubble was unsustainable, and, because the process is well described by a multiplier/accelerator model, we can say that the growth from investments of this type (borrowing to build, building to sell, borrowing to buy, and so on) is highly unstable, because there is no direct value creation at work: only investor expectations have been altered, with value addition taking place after the fact.

It important to stress again: the business of banking is not lending money. Rather, banks offer a guarantee that a party is credit-worthy, and thus worthy of investment. The bank acts as an intermediary between borrowers and lenders, yes, but the bank, by accepting a credit or debt instrument onto its books, also agrees to make some form of payment to the creditor if the debtor cannot. This is why loans are both assets and liabilities on banks' balance sheets.

19 Putting the case mildly.

20 Morgan Kelly, "On the likely extent of falls in Irish house prices" (2007) *Quarterly Economic Commentary*, Special Articles, (2) Summer, pp.42–54.

The bank's loan becomes, in effect, an endorsed note which other banks can accept as an object of value. The transactions of these endorsed notes is called the commercial paper market. Abstract investment products can be created, using the tools of modern mathematical finance, to exploit the rather imprecise relationship between the probability of a loan on an asset achieving maturity through a constant stream of payments, and the probability of that loan's default.

Commercial paper markets are excellent examples of how financial institutions' unsecured promises to pay affect the level of investment in the normal economy. It is commonplace for an issuer of commercial paper, such as a corporation, to keep unsued lines of credit open which match or exceed the amount of outstanding unsecured paper, as an insurance against anything going wrong. Both the borrower and the lender can be confident that, in a normal business climate, when, for some reason a refinancing is required, there is credit available to meet the demand for it.

All of these unused lines of credit are, of course, purely notional, and exist only as potential income streams unless actualised by a default or some other miscarriage in the market. When everyone defaults, or when confidence in the ability of the institution to repay a debt evaporates,[21] these extra lines of credit disappear, as has happened in the international credit crunch.

One little understood facet of the international monetary system is how much of it is based upon one bank vouching for the credit-worthiness of another, so that a single bank need not have uncommitted assets on hand at any time. In lieu of actual secured assets, the bank can access funds from international markets as needed. The modern Irish bank holds assets which are negotiable in markets, and hold credit lines at other banks. Because most of these connections are *potential* rather than *actual,* they do not appear on banks' balance sheets. These commitments to finance are actually financial products in and of themselves, actualised in good faith when the need arises.

(c) Governance and corporate remuneration policies

Bebchuck and Fried[22] argue persuasively that the received wisdom on the principal agent problem which bank executives represent relative to their shareholders and the public at large is simply wrong. Rather, executives have been able to effectively set their own pay through capture of boards of management and remuneration committees. In addition to the basic salary afforded the executive, they may also enjoy inflated pension plans, insurance policies, and golden parachutes.

Bebchuk and Fried write that:

21 Or, when further lines of credit are advanced to these institutions become eroded, because the credit extending counterparty is *also* in some financial distress.

22 L. Bebchuk and J. Fried, *Pay without Performance: The Unfulfilled Promise of Executive Compensation* (Boston: Harvard University Press, 2004), p.ix.

> "... [T]he wave of corporate scandals that began in late 2001 shook confidence in the performance of public company boards and drew attention to potential flaws in their executurive compensation packages. There is now recognition that many boards have employed compensation arragnements that do not servce shareholders' interests. But there is still substantial disagreement about the scope of such problems and, not surprisingly, how to address them."

This view[23] has been expanded upon and modeled extensively and intensively for economies experiencing house-price collapses.[24] The role of excecutive compensation in Ireland over the 2002–2008 period has yet to be addressed but it can be assumed that, as share prices appreciated, so did the salaries, bonuses, and other remunerations of Ireland's banking elite. Whether this salary appreciation caused an incentive imbalance with regard to the capital gearing of these banks is still an open question, and I highlight it here so that a reader might think about attempting an answer.[25]

(d) Lessons from the subprime crisis

The packaging of loans of different qualities seems like an arcane art of mathematical trickery. It is not. The rules of financial governance apply to the packaging of these products, and, in particular, to their "risk weights".

The Federal Deposit Insurance Corporation (the "FDIC") produces standardised guidelines on the operational risk and disclosure standards. The FDIC also issues guidelines on the "risk weights" of different bank assets.[26] The higher the weight, the more capital the bank has to hold against that asset. In the US in 2007, one way to package potentially bad debt was to originate a loan with a down payment of 20 to 40 per cent, the risk weight of which would be 35. But then, by adding a AA-rated security, the risk weight would drop to only 20. So

[23] Marco Brecht, Patrick Bolton and Ailsa Röell, "Corporate Law and Governance" in A. Mitchell Polinsky and Steven Shavell (eds.), *Volume 2, Handbook of Law and Economics* (Netherlands: Elsevier BV, 2007) pp.901–904; Patrick Bolton, José Scheinkman and Wei Xiong, "Pay for Short-Term Performance: Executive Compensation in Speculative Markets" (2003) 30(4) J. Corp. Law, p.721, especially.

[24] See Steven Kaplan, "Top executive rewards and firm performance: a comparison of Japan and the U.S." (1994) J. Pol. Econ. 102(3), pp.510–546, for an example of this approach.

[25] What matters in corporate governance is oversight, to balance the needs of the market's participants with the needs of society. Clearly, CEO compensation and the composition of CEO pay in the US and Ireland is a factor in the incentive structures of large corporations. Some examples of CEO salaries in the USA in 2006 may give some context: Bear Stearns: $34 million for CEO James Cayne; Lehman Brothers: $27 million for CEO Richard Fuld; Citigroup: $25 million for CEO Charles Prince; Countrywide Financial: $43 million for CEO Angelo Mozilo.

[26] FDIC PR-64–2007, Joint Release, "Banking Agencies Reach Agreement on Basel II Implementation" July 20, 2007, and FDIC Financial Institution Letters (69–2008), "Key Aspects of the Proposed Rule on Risk-Based Capital Standards: Standardized Framework", particularly, tables 2 and 3; pp.6–7.

a junk mortgage originator, say, could pool loans with down payments of less than 5 per cent, carve them into tranches, and get a rating agency to rate some of the tranches as AA or higher, thus making those investment vehicles more attractive to a bank than originating a relatively safe loan. This is why "securitisation" dominated the US mortgage market. The innovation of bending bad loans into reputable investment product shapes, playing strictly by the rules, is an example of regulatory arbitrage[27] and perforce, poor governance.

How did sub-prime loans in the US actually work, and what lessons can we learn and apply to the Irish case in terms of changing governance structure?

Until relatively recently, the origination of mortgages and issuance of mortgage-backed securities (MBS) was dominated by loans to prime borrowers conforming to underwriting standards set by Government Sponsored Agencies (GSAs). Outside of conforming loans are non-agency asset classes that include Jumbo, Alt-A, and Subprime. The Jumbo asset class includes loans to prime borrowers with an original principal balance larger than the conforming limits imposed on the agencies by Congress; the Alt-A asset class involves loans to borrowers with good credit but include more aggressive underwriting than the conforming or Jumbo classes (i.e. no documentation of income, high leverage); and the Subprime asset class involves loans to borrowers with poor (and very poor) credit history.

Figure 3 below traces out the development of the sub-prime market in the USA by looking at the origination of sub-prime loans to their extant creditors.[28] In 2001, banks originated $1.433 trillion in conforming mortgage loans and issued $1.087 trillion in mortgage-backed securities secured by those mortgages. In contrast, the non-agency sector originated $680 billion ($190 billion subprime + $60 billion Alt-A + $430 billion jumbo) and issued $240 billion ($87.1 billion subprime + $11.4 billion Alt-A + $142.2 billion jumbo), and most of these were in the Jumbo sector. The Alt-A and Subprime sectors were relatively small, together comprising $250 billion of $2.1 trillion (12 per cent) in total origination during 2001.

27 See Adam B. Ashcraft and Til Schuermann, "Understanding the securitization of subprime mortgage credit" (2008) Staff Reports 318, Federal Reserve Bank of New York, for more details on regulatory arbitrage during the subprime crisis.

28 Inside Mortgage Finance, The 2008 Mortgage Market Statistical Annual (2008) Inside Mortgage Finance, INC. *www.imfspubs.org*.

Figure 3: Origination of Subprime Loans, 2001–2006. Fraction of loans of the subprime category soared after the interest rate cuts of 2003.

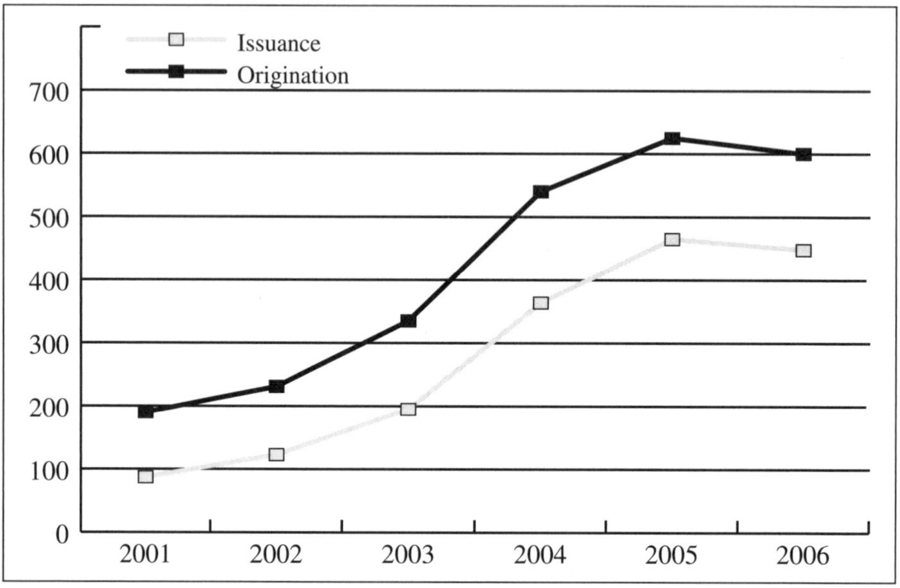

Source: Inside Mortgage Finance, 2007, Tables 3 & 4 and author's calculations.

Jump to 2006/7, and the story is entirely different. Now the increase in Subprime and Alt-A origination was associated with a significant *increase* in the ratio of issuance to origination, which is a reasonable proxy for the fraction of loans sold.

In particular, the ratio of subprime MBS issuance to subprime mortgage origination was close to 75 per cent in both 2005 and 2006. While there is typically a one-quarter lag between origination and issuance, the data document that a large and increasing fraction of both subprime and Alt-A loans are sold to investors, and very little is retained on the balance sheets of the institutions who originate them. The process through which loans are removed from the institutions which originate them is the process of securitization. Securitization, as monitored by the FDIC, was a cause for concern after the explosive growth of the CDO markets after 2003. The problem announced itself through the near exponential growth in these markets, and the lack of oversight and regulation associated with these new and mathematically complex debt instruments.
It is clear that poorly supervised agencies lending products they knew to be highly risky damaged public confidence in the banking system, once the extent of the exposure of the international financial system to the risk of poorly priced subprime mortgage default was known.

The FDIC, which is an implicit investor in commercial banks through the provision of deposit insurance, prevents insured banks from investing in speculative-grade securities or enforces risk-based capital requirements that use credit ratings to assess risk-weights. An actively managed collateralized debt obligation (CDO) imposes covenants on the weighted average rating of securities in an actively-managed portfolio as well as the fraction of securities with a low credit rating. Figure 4 below shows clearly that, in line with the increase in subprime mortgages from agencies from 2003–2007, the issuance of securitised CDOs grew in proportion. It is instructive to note that CDO issuance grew faster than any other type of financial product from 1996–2006.[29] By the fourth quarter of 2007, almost $4.8 trillion had been issued as CDOs, approximately four times the GDP of the US that year.

A system which ignores risky investments based on even riskier tranches of unsecured debt, which still manages to play by the rules as set down by the governing authorities of the day, is a system with too little financial governance. The lesson from the subprime crisis for Ireland is to ensure that complex debt instruments, as well as rating agencies themselves, are bound to disclose their holdings more fully, and in a more strigent manner. The risk-return profile for these highly risky investments should be made as transparent as possible via the

Figure 4: Global Collateralized Debt Obligation Market Issuance, 2004–2007. The CDO market's growth outstripped any other type of bond during this period. Growth proxy is a 2 period moving average, the solid line above.

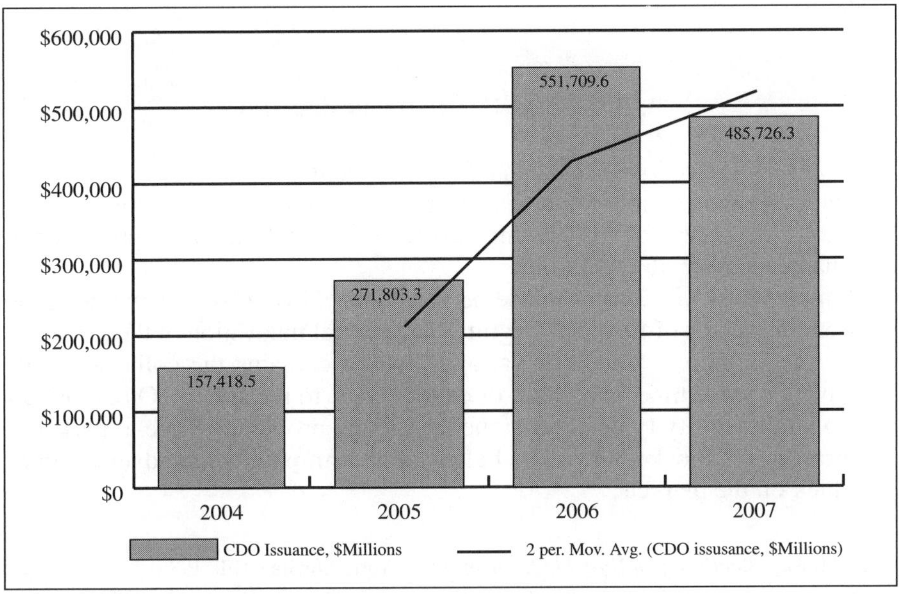

Source: SIFMA report on global CDO issuance, 2008, Table 1, and author's calculations.

29 Securities industry and financial markets association (2008) SIFMA, Global CDO Market Issuance Data.

inclusion of "sand in the gear" clauses, where the transferral of such products from issuer to lender and so on into the system is accompanied first by a highly leveraged guarantee of unused lines of credit, say, 8:1, and also subject to a 1 per cent levy on all transactions in this market place. Effectively limiting the spread of these types of products is key to reforming our banking system, and scrubbing the uncertainty which clings to Irish banks in 2009. The Irish government should consider legislation and regulations to this effect as a matter of priority.

A final word on rating agencies. As investment mandates typically involve credit ratings, it should be obvious that credit rating agencies play an important role in the securitization process. By presenting an opinion on the riskiness of offered securities, the rating agencies help resolve the information frictions which, perforce, exist between the investor and the portfolio manager. Credit ratings are intended to capture the expectations about the long-run or through-the-cycle performance of a debt security. A credit rating is fundamentally a statement about the suitability of an instrument to be included in a risk class, but importantly, it is an opinion only about credit risk. It follows that the opinion of credit rating agencies is a crucial part of securitization, because in the end the rating is the means through which much of the funding by investors finds its way into the deal. The regulatory arbitrage shown above could not have taken place to the same extent in a more stringent regulatory environment and for that, the regulatory authorities should be held accountable.

Is there a model to explain the diverse set of occurences documented in this section?

3. Financial Fragility in Ireland

We have seen in Sections 1 and 2 that financial fragility was a feature of the Irish and international economy in recent years. The challenge for economists is to build the correct type of model which explains the "stylised facts" presented in this chapter's preceeding sections.

Hyman Minsky,[30] Charles Kindelberger,[31] and Edward Nell[32] are among the pioneers of models of financial fragility. The central innovation of these models is that the economic "fact", or variable, which explains the collapse of the system after some time, is built in, or endogenous, to the system. Other models of financial fragility typically assume an agency problem, where a market in equilibrium is "shocked" from its balanced growth path by an adverse run of poor luck on the markets.[33]

30 H. Minsky, *Stabilizing an Unstable Economy* (New York: McGraw Hill, 1986).

31 As Charles P. Kindleberger, *Manias, Panics, and Crashes: A History of Financial Crisis* (Hoboken, New Jersey: John Wiley and Sons, 2005).

32 Edward J. Nell, *The General Theory of Transformational Growth* (Cambridge: Cambridge University Press, 1998).

33 Representative articles from this approach are Gary Gorton, "Banking Panics and Business

Putting such approaches aside for the rest of this article, let us discuss a model of financial fragility, where the economy cycles around a trend, where boom and bust cycles follow one another in irregular and unpredictable fashion.

Financial markets no longer constrain economic activity in Ireland. The individual agents within the economy—firms, households, the government—face competing incentives and pressures. For the firm, when the economy's progress is uncertain, the firm finds itself carrying excess capacity, excess inventory, and it sees the cost of its fixed costs (rent, utilities, etc.) rising slowly. When an upswing of economic activity is particularly severe, as in Ireland from 1990 to 2008, the upswing favours the workers in households, leading to increases in real wages for workers above the rate of inflation. This increase in wages does two things. First, it squeezes profits, which, although growing as well during the upswing, will return to trend as the upswing fades, leaving the second problem—higher costs of production—there for the employer to deal with. It has been the case that Ireland's real wage appreciation was more than double the Eurozone average cumulatively since 2003.[34]

The interaction between the real and financial parts of the economy tend to produce financial innovations, such as the 100 per cent mortgage,[35] the CDO or CDO^2. The CDO^2 prices the probability of the derivative of a derivative failing. Quite a financial innovation. We do see evolution of financial institutions and regulatory mechanisms in the upswings, but the regulatory mechanisms, perforce, evolve more slowly than their profit-driven counterparts in the markets. During upswings, we do see evidence for new types of firm size and firm organisation, as experimental firm designs are attempted. Most fail.

To pull the economy back from the excesses of the market during a boom, fiscal policy, Minsky, Keynes, and Nell argue, should be countercyclical. The government spends more during the downturn, and taxes more during the upturn. One damps the other in a reinforcing spiral. By allowing this dampening to happen, the market is ceding some of its power to the government, which regulates, we presume, in the public interest.

The firm is the central actor in this story. We allow the firm some capital, and encourage it to spend that capital in profit-making activities. Businesses make decisions about prices and investment levels in each period, determining the level of investment in the economy. The firm's current output and employment

Cycles" (1988) Ox. Ec. Pap. 40(4), pp.751–781; Rafael La Porta, Florencio Lopez-De-Silanes and Andrei Shleifer, "Government Ownership of Banks" (2002) J. Finance 57(1), pp.265–301; Ben Bernanke and Mark Gertler, "Agency Costs, Net Worth, and Business Fluctuations" (1989) Am. Ec. Rev. 79(1), pp.14–31.

34 National Competitiveness Council, *Annual Competitiveness Report, Vol. 1: Benchmarking Ireland's Performance* (Dublin: Stationary Office, 2008), p.40. Most of this wage increase came from increases in the retail, services, and construction sectors of the Irish economy.

35 The 100 per cent mortgage is not an innovation but a *reinvention*, a financial instrument rolled out when the cost of borrowing becomes relatively cheap. That 100 per cent mortgages can lead easily to negative equity is never discussed in the boom period, and obsesses the public in the bust period.

decisions will determine the level of remuneration for the average worker. This gives us the wage bill, and from there we can fix consumption levels, since we know households will spend a proportion of their income out of current income. Households will also spend a proportion of their income from the past on consumption of goods and services produced in the economy, giving us the total level consumed in a given period. We can see immediately that when wages go up, consumption will rise, but that when wages are too high and profits become squeezed, firms can fail and unemployment will be the result. We can value the cost of capital at its supply price—essentially the cost of producing the finance for a given capital project.

Profits are generated first from productive processes ongoing in the economy, and second from realised investment opportunities, at a lag. These second types of profit-generating activities are subject to high levels of uncertainty, as well as measurable risk. The firm, when it commits to an investment project, must gamble on the risks, and can do little but pray about the uncertainty they face. What matters here is the *expected* profit rate, which determines the capital asset valuation ratio.[36] When confidence is high and expectations of the future seem solid, the investment community ratifies its own views by increasing its estimates of corporate wealth. The net worth of firms rises, as the capital asset ratio rises, all buoyed by loan and equity markets. Because asset prices are rising, demand for loans goes up, driving up the interest rate and making banks wealthier. The increase in the interest rate only holds for a short while though because the supply of loans is increasing as well, which bids down the loanable amount of interest. The rise and rise of investor confidence (and hence behaviour) can only last so long. Once the bubble bursts, and they always burst quickly, then the cycle can start again.

Minsky and Nell, as we shall see, put great store in the ability of the central bank (the "big bank") to damp this cycle. Interventions by the "big bank" allow for the possibility of moral hazard, where people hold riskier portfolios because they assume the government is implicitly underwriting the decisions of the banks in this regard.

(a) Minsky's model of the credit cycle for Ireland

There are five stages in Minsky's model of the credit cycle: displacement, boom, euphoria, profit taking, and panic. We are at stage five at the time of writing. A displacement occurs when investors get excited about an event—an invention, such as the internet, or a war, or an abrupt change of economic policy—something which favours an upswing in investment.

The current cycle can be dated from 2003, with the decision of US monetary authorities to reduce short-term interest rates to one per cent, and an unexpected

[36] Known in the literature as "Tobins' q", which is calculated as: (Equity Market Value + Liabilities Book Value)/(Equity Book Value + Liabilities Book Value).

influx of foreign money, particularly Chinese money, into US Treasury bonds. With the cost of borrowing—mortgage rates, in particular—at historic lows, a speculative real-estate boom quickly developed, which was much bigger, in terms of over-all valuation, than the previous bubble in technology stocks which had burst in 2000.

Ireland was caught in the same perfect storm of cheap credit, buoyant domestic demand for new housing, an increasing population (many brought to Ireland by the promise of building these houses), rising real wages, and property price appreciation. Displacement, boom, and euphoria can be dated from 2003 to 2007.

As a boom leads to euphoria, banks and other commercial lenders extend credit to ever more dubious borrowers, often creating new financial instruments to do the job. During the 1980s, junk bonds played that role. More recently, it was the securitization of mortgages, which enabled banks to provide home loans and create unsecured debt instruments, such as CDOs. At the top of the market (in this case, mid-2006), some smart traders start to cash in their profits.

The onset of panic is usually heralded by a dramatic effect, as we can see from monthly figures released by the Central Bank of Ireland in December 2008, the percentage of private credit on issue in Ireland from 2005 to 2008 has fallen from a growth rate of 30 per cent in 2005 to a rate of 3 per cent by the end of 2008.[37] Mortgage lending has practically disappeared, and new house starts are at a 15-year low.

To sum up, Minsky and, later, Nell write of the instability of the economy as a reflection of the instability of the financial institutions which are embedded within the economy. We have seen in this article how banks and other financial intermediaries in Ireland and abroad have taken on large liabilities with respect to residential and commercial developments, which, it turns out after the boom has passed its peak, turn out to be excessively risky. Because the market for the previously appreciating security on the loan—the property—has disappeared, the banks are faced with assets which are significantly lower in value than their initial valuations. The large debts held by the banks are either converted into bad debts and sold off and perhaps the bank is allowed to fail as a going concern, or the bank and its debts are nationalised. The reaction of the government at each stage has been entirely rational, from the point of view of a self interested political elite. From a public policy and governance perspective, there are several turns of the wheel yet to run in this crisis.

Section 4 sketches a theory of emergent governance, where a regulatory may be simultaneously reactive and proactive with regard to financial innovations.

[37] Central Bank of Ireland, Monthly Statistics to December 2008 (Central Bank and Financial Services Authority of Ireland, January 2008), p.4.

4. Emergent Structures in Financial Governance

Emergence is a tricky concept, but for our purposes let us define it as the pattern which arises from simple interactions between agents in ways that are sometimes surprising and counter-intuitive. An anthill is an emergent structure: thousands of ants pile grains of sand together, and produce an anthill. The economy is an emergent process, where complex interactions between individuals, companies, and the government create the economic reality we perceive.

Financial governance can be roughly described as "the rules of the game", but when the game is changing, how do the rules keep up? We have seen in Section 2 that FDIC compliant companies were able to create well-rated debt instruments from subprime mortgages, a sure sign of regulatory arbitrage, as well as a signal that the rules were not adequate to the pricing of the risk inherent in the debt instruments.

The outline of the theory runs like this: assume banks, financial intermediaries and agents (let's simply call them "banks", for short), *hate* their customers, and want to maximize profits at all costs. The quickest way to maximize short run profits is to create finance by changing the leveraging ratios within the banks' books. By hate, I mean the banks do not care if their customers' interests are damaged within a transaction, and in the cause of maximizing profits, the customers' welfares are simply ignored if not actively militated against. I take this radical position for a purpose. Say the regulator *hates* the banks and financial intermediaries, in that the officials who work within the regulatory system are tasked and encouraged to work *against* the banks' attempts to innovate. Impose a non-trivial cost on financial product innovation, and strict guidelines and lead-in time for the development of this product. Emulate the strictures imposed on the prescription drug industry for the development of potentially life-enhancing (or threatening) drugs.

Now allow the regulator and the banks to interact. The banks will naturally continue to try to innovate, though at a slower rate than before, and the job of the regulator will become much more onerous, as banks' attempts to adjust to prevailing macroeconomic conditions (low interest rates and easy credit, a credit crunch, primary hedge financing, etc.) become more difficult. To guard against uncertainty, the banks will have to hold larger amounts of capital and other assets for surety.

What will banks do? Their job is to make the most money they can, while working against their customer's interests if need be. They will innovate around the regulatory strictures by creating asset classes, debt instruments, and finance vehicles not covered by the rules already in place. We have seen such practices in the move from junk bonds in the 1980s to CDO and other debt issuances in the present day.

An emergent governance theory assumes such an innovation path by banks as natural, given the objectives of the industry. The regulator, therefore, must innovate in a similar fashion, by exposing the banks to ever-changing regulations regarding the creation of new products, the repackaging of old products, and the extension of existing products.

What will "emerge" from a hyper-efficient regulator actively working towards a reduction in banks' profits? A larger, more bureaucratic governance structure, with slower times to market for new products, and greater emphasis on *systematic* leveraging, where the risk-return composition of banks' portfolios is included in the oversight required for financial licensing. Liquidity requirements that constrain the composition of assets should complement traditional capital requirements. The imposition of a maximum leverage ratio for banks should also be considered. This would provide the upper bound beyond which no further lending could take place, throwing yet more sand into the gears. The rationale for a leverage ratio derives not from the traditional view that capital is a buffer against loss on the assets, but rather from the stability of liabilities in an interrelated financial system.

Such a view should be typical of financial regulators around the world, who should be tasked to work together to ensure adherence to an international standard far beyond Basel II. Financial stability is best viewed from a system perspective, rather than from the point of view of each individual financial institution. In an influential article, Andrew Crockett[38] has argued for a distinction between the micro-prudential aspects of financial stability from the macro-prudential one. Elements of this theory have been sketched out before.[39] The micro-prudential dimension has to do with the soundness of individual institutions. The macro-prudential aspect should deal with the stability of the system as a whole.

So, an emergent theory of governance would increase public information about banks' activities, ensure macro stability by aggressively resisting the introduction of new financial vehicles until after extremely stringent tests are passed, include measures of overall financial stability of a firm in the granting of permission to issue a new product, reduce idiosyncratic risk,[40] normalize risk-return portfolios, and leave the real economy less exposed to the explosive character of financial markets in boom periods, while mitigating their significant losses once the bust period comes. The overall effect would dampen the credit cycle via prudential financial regulation, itself the hallmark of good governance.

5. Recommendations for Reforms of Governance in the Irish Economy in 2009 and Beyond

This article gives the national and international context for Ireland's recent boom-bust cycle from 2002–2008, arguing that the increase in personal wealth

[38] Andrew Crockett, "Marrying the Micro- and Macro-Prudential Dimensions of Financial Stability" (Bank for International Settlements, September 21, 2000).

[39] Mathias Dewatripont and Jean Tirole, *The Prudential Regulation of Banks* (Cambridge, MA: MIT Press, 1993), and Charles Goodhart, "Liquidity and Risk Management" (Banque de France: Financial Stability Review, 2008), pp.29–38.

[40] Idiosyncratic risk applies to the individual financial institution. It is the risk arising from high expected margins, based on cheap sources of funding for extremely leveraged speculative or "Ponzi" positions, often compounded by lack of adequate internal risk assessment in the financial institution itself, and lack of diversification where all parties in an industry follow the same strategies.

came from real wage appreciation backed by high levels of private and public investment predicated on low interest rates, and a booming construction sector. As the construction bubble burst in late 2007 and early 2008, Ireland has been left a high-cost, high-spend economy, dependent on construction and related sectors to spur its economic growth. Ireland has lost 34,000 manufacturing jobs since 2000, while it created jobs in retail, finance, and construction. Structural change is happening in the Irish economy. As we develop, we are moving from a light manufacturing regional distribution centre for foreign-owned multinationals to a high value, precision manufacturing and service economy, where value creation rather than addition is the norm.

It does not feel that way now. As this article is written in January 2009, 5,000 people a week sign onto the Live Register, and the nationalization of two of Ireland's largest banks (AIB and Bank of Ireland) are being mooted. Consumer and investor confidence have collapsed, residential and commercial lending by banks is low, and Ireland's exports are suffering, as our export partners prosecute a strategy increasing their export competitiveness by devaluing their exchange rates via open market operations and credit easing. As part of the Euro zone, Ireland does not have the option of a targeted deflation in the value of its currency, and, even if it did, the Irish economy is too small to effect global exchange markets in the desired direction.[41] Due to our high export multiplier, a direct government stimulus plan will only enrich our export partners, ensuring more taxpayer's money is lost. The only option open to the government is coordinated real wage contraction, combined with emigration, and focused policies to increase capital expenditure in certain areas of the country.

Ireland's economy is in the midst of a shaky macroeconomic period caused by financial, rather than real, instability. The problem is twofold, as the construction bubble is domestic in nature, while the global slowdown is affecting all of Ireland's exporting sectors, of which there are many. Both facets of the problem have negative consequences for Ireland's growth in the medium term and both are symptoms of financial fragility.

Financial fragility refers to the instability of the credit cycle, where investor confidence creates real investments, which achieve positive returns in a low interest rate climate, thus confirming the expectations of other investors, who enter the markets, bidding up the price of each investment, and the profits forthcoming from them, creating a cycle where ever higher profits justify ever higher investments, with attendant increases in real wages, inflation, and decreases in competitiveness—the ratio of the cost of our export goods to our competitors' goods in international markets.

The credit cycle views banks and financial intermediaries as self-interested, profit-maximising agents, fueling the rise in overpriced investments through novel, highly leveraged debt instruments because the banks' profits depend on increases in business the new products provide, and top managers' salaries are

[41] Anthony Leddin and Patrick Honohan, "Ireland in EMU – More Shocks, Less Insulation?" (2006) *Economic and Social Review* 37(2), pp.263–294.

directly tied to the performance, year on year, of their company's shares on the open market. The role of governance, therefore, is to temper the natural inclinations of other macroeconomic actors like households, firms, banks, financial intermediaries, and indeed the government. The Irish government should, as a matter of priority, increase oversight of and regulation for, new financial products and existing debt instruments. This may seem like closing the gate once the horse has bolted, but remember the title of Section 2(a): all this has happened before, and will happen again. Along with a more fully fleshed out version of the emergent theory of regulation and financial governance I set out in Section 4 above, some concrete suggestions for constructive solutions to the present crisis follow.

(a) Speed up structural change

Encouraging former middle managers, engineers, and technicians to create indigenous Irish businesses should be a priority for Irish policy makers. Little outlay is required. The expertise now exists in the form of successful entrepreneurs, who have blossomed over the last 15 years in Ireland in certain sectors of the Irish economy. The economic need now exists for those individuals, in the form of mass layoffs and the movement of multinational-sponsored light manufacturing to low cost bases in Eastern Europe and Asia. A national restructuring programme should be enacted, where small businesses can access grants effectively and quickly, while retaining expertise and mentoring services as they grow. Cheap credit should be provided to these new firms, and acceptance of their inevitable failure should be countenanced. Over 80 per cent of new firms dissolve in less than five years. This is less failure, and more feedback. The market will bear new entrants, and those firms, which make it through the first five years, some of which will take place in an unprecedented national and international economic downturn, should be well positioned to reap super normal profits.

Ireland's future lies in small, agile service-driven companies and medium to large size precision manufacturing companies. Regional development is possible in places like Limerick to sponsor on the ground structural change, if the policy mix is correct.

(b) Sponsor-focused job creation programmes

The European Central Bank is the lender of last resort in the European economy. It follows that the Irish economy should become the employer of last resort for those individuals hurt by the restructuring of Irish industry detailed above. Job creation programmes and public works schemes, when well designed, serve the public good and rectify the excesses of the market, while keeping individuals working, paying taxes, productive, and stopping them from emigrating. Ireland's level of human capital has never been higher. To lose the experience and expertise of a generation to the flows of international finance would be a social evil.

(c) Nationalise wayward Irish banks

Buy banks' bad and toxic assets from them. The government has already essentially guaranteed the liabilities of the banking system (and no one can risk a Lehman re-run), bank assets at market value must be massively lower than liabilities, and a severe global recession may yet turn into the Greatest Depression.

Nationalization would simplify enormously the job of cleaning up the balance sheets of the banking system, without which no amount of recapitalization can make sense. An asset management company would be constructed for each nationalized bank, and loans and securities could be clearly divided into "definitely good" and "everything else". The arbitrariness of this procedure is not a worry when it all belongs to the government in any case.

The good loans would go into a newly recapitalized bank, where the taxpayer not only holds all the risk (as now) but also gets all the upside. Careful disposal of the bad assets would yield lower losses than feared, although the final net addition to government debt would no doubt be in the standard range for major banking fiascos: between 10 per cent and 20 per cent of GDP.

(d) Foster less procyclical leveraging

Leverage is procyclical in the sense that leverage is high when balance sheets are large, while leverage is low when balance sheets are small, a corollary of Tobin's *q*.[42] This is exactly the opposite finding compared to small Irish households, whose leverage is high when balance sheets are small, thus exposing Irish households and businesses to significant downside risk in the event of a large correction in the price of durable assets, such as commercial and residential properties. If a household owns a house that is financed by a mortgage, leverage falls when the house price increases, since the equity of the household is increasing at a faster rate than assets.

(e) Transparency

The risk-return profile for highly risky investments should be made as transparent as possible via the inclusion of "sand in the gear" clauses, where the transferral of such products from issuer to lender and so on into the system is accompanied first by a highly leveraged guarantee of unused lines of credit, say, 8:1, and also subject to a 1 per cent levy on all transactions in this market place. Effectively limiting the spread of these types of products is key to reforming our banking system, and scrubbing the uncertainty which clings to Irish banks in 2009. The Irish government should consider legislation and regulations to this effect as a matter of priority.

[42] Tobias Adrian and Hyun Song Shin in "Financial Intermediary Leverage and Value at Risk" (2008) Working paper No.338 (Federal Reserve Bank of New York and Princeton University), describe the pro-cyclical nature of the leveraging process in great detail.

Chapter 8

INSIDER DEALING AFTER *FYFFES* AND THE MARKET ABUSE REGULATIONS

Stephen Dowling, B.L. and Conor Feeney, B.L.

1. Introduction

The case of *Fyffes v D.C.C.*[1] involved the first civil claim of insider dealing in this jurisdiction.[2] Ironically, the Superior Courts' first opportunity to review the legislation on insider dealing came at a time when that legislation was being replaced by a new regime. The claim in *Fyffes* was brought under s.108(1) of Pt V of the Companies Act 1990 (the "1990 Act"), which provided as follows:

> "It shall not be lawful for a person who is, or at any time in the preceding 6 months has been, connected with a company to deal in any securities of that company if by reason of his so being, or having been, connected with that company he is in possession of information that is not generally available, but, if it were, would be likely materially to affect the price of those securities."

Part V of the 1990 Act has been repealed by s.31 of the Investment Funds, Companies and Miscellaneous Provisions Act 2005 (the "2005 Act"). Further, pursuant to s.30 of the 2005 Act, the Market Abuse (Directive 2003/6/EC) Regulations 2005 (S.I. No. 342 of 2005) (the "Market Abuse Regulations") have replaced the old regime with the harmonised EU regime on market abuse, including insider dealing.

Regulation 5(1) of the Market Abuse Regulations provides:

> "... [A] person to whom this paragraph applies who possesses inside information shall not use that information by acquiring or disposing of, or by trying to acquire or dispose of, for the person's own account or for the account of a third party, directly or indirectly, financial instruments to which that information relates."

1 *Fyffes plc v DCC plc, S. & L. Investments Ltd., James Flavin and Lotus Green Ltd.*, unreported, High Court, Laffoy J., December 21, 2005; unreported, Supreme Court, July 27, 2007. To be reported in an upcoming volume of the Irish Reports. Paragraph numbers below refer to the numbering in the Irish Reports.

2 There was a criminal prosecution for insider dealing in 2002, in which the defendant, Philip Byrne, was found not guilty in the Circuit Criminal Court.

This article analyses the constituent parts of the test for insider dealing provided in reg.5(1) and compares the test with the old test, as interpreted in the High Court and the Supreme Court in *Fyffes*.

2. The Test for Price Sensitivity

Regulation 5(1) of the Market Abuse Regulations prohibits certain persons who possess "inside information" from using that information to deal in financial instruments to which the information relates. The meaning of "inside information" is set out in reg.2, in the following two definitions:

> "'inside information' means -
> (a) information of a precise nature relating directly or indirectly to one or more issuers of financial instruments or to one or more financial instruments which has not been made public and which, if it were made public, *would be likely to have a significant effect on the price of those financial instruments* or on the price of related derivative financial instruments ..."
> "'information which, if it were made public, would be likely to have a significant effect on the prices of financial instruments or related derivative financial instruments' means *information that a reasonable investor would be likely to use as part of the basis of the investor's investment decisions*, and includes cognate expressions". (emphasis added)

(a) The statutory hypothesis

The test for price sensitivity of information in both the 1990 Act and the Market Abuse Regulations is based on a statutory hypothesis. For an application to be successful under s.108(1) the claimant was required to show that the insider possessed "information that is not generally available, but, if it were, would be likely materially to affect the price of those securities". Similarly, reg.5(1) requires proof of "inside information" which is defined in reg.2 as "information which, if it were made public, would be likely to have a significant effect on the prices of financial instruments or related derivative financial instruments".

It is submitted that the minor difference in the wording of these hypotheses has no real effect and that the two provisions are based on the same core test. This contention finds support in the following passage from the judgment of Denham J. in *Fyffes*:

> "The word 'materially' is also not defined in the Act of 1990. It is a word in common usage, not dissimilar to 'significantly'. Thus the phrase 'likely materially', refers to a situation where information would probably significantly affect the price of shares, if it were generally available."[3]

[3] Paragraph 75. See also the comments of the District Court in Singapore in *Public Prosecutor v Allan Ng Poh Meng* [1990] 1 M.L.J. v, p.x, in this regard.

Denham J. also agreed with the conclusion of Fennelly J. that s.108 had to be interpreted in the light of the Directive which it had implemented,[4] which employed the word "significant" rather than "materially".

(b) Measuring whether effect would be significant

Laffoy J. in the High Court in *Fyffes* held that there was no absolute measurement of a substantial or significant movement in share price. These terms were relative and the assessment must be made having regard to all the factors which have a bearing on the value of the company's shares at the date of dealing.[5] But to what degree of certainty must it be shown that the information would have a significant or substantial effect? Given the wording of s.108(1), Laffoy J. concluded that this was on the balance of probabilities. In particular, she rejected the suggestion that the test be one of "substantial likelihood", as applied in *T.S.C. Industries Inc. v Northway Inc.*[6]

If the information itself is a prediction of a future event, how should that be assessed? In this regard, Laffoy J. said that the probability test should be applied in the way suggested in *Securities and Exchange Commission v Texas Gulf Sulpher Company.*[7] This is the seminal decision on insider trading in the United States where Waterman J. held that:

> "... [W]hether facts are material ... when the facts relate to a particular event ... will depend at any given time upon a balancing of both the indicated probability that the event will occur and the anticipated magnitude of the event in light of the totality of the company activity."[8]

This last point is to some extent reflected in the test for price sensitivity in the Market Abuse Regulations. Regulation 2 confirms that the information must be "of a precise nature" before it can be deemed price-sensitive. This is in turn defined as "information that ... indicates ... a set of circumstances which exists or may reasonably be expected to come into existence, or ... an event which has occurred or may be reasonably expected to occur". Regulation 2 further clarifies that the information must be "specific enough to enable a conclusion to be drawn as to the possible effect of that set of circumstances or event ... on the prices of" the financial instruments in question.

4 Council Directive 89/592/EEC of November 13, 1989.
5 Paragraph 397.
6 (1976) 426 U.S. 438.
7 (1968) 401 F.2d 833.
8 At p.849.

LIBRARY
INSTITUTE OF TECHNOLOGY
CARLOW

(c) Objectivity and the reasonable investor

In the High Court, Laffoy J. interpreted the phrase "would be likely materially to affect the price of those securities", in s.108(1), as setting down an objective test. Laffoy J. further found that this test was to be approached from the viewpoint of the "reasonable investor". She found support for this approach in United States jurisprudence dealing with legislation she found to be informed by the same legislative purpose as Pt V of the 1990 Act.[9]

Laffoy J. also found support for the reasonable investor test in the Singapore case of *Public Prosecutor v Allan Ng Poh Meng*.[10] The provision at issue in that case was almost identical to s.108(1), requiring that the information "if generally available would be likely materially to affect the price of securities". Laffoy J. referred to the following passage from the judgment of Foenander S.D.J.:

> "… [T]he standard by which materiality is to be judged is whether the information on the particular share is such as would influence the ordinary reasonable investor in deciding whether or not to buy or whether or not to sell that share. A movement in price which would not influence such an investor, may be termed immaterial. Price is, after all, to a large extent determined by what investors do. If generally available, it is the impact of the information on the ordinary reasonable investor, and thus on price, which has to be judged in an insider dealing case … The test is an objective one."[11]

On the basis of these persuasive authorities, Laffoy J. favoured utilising the reasonable investor test and gave it the following formulation, within the factual matrix of the case:

> "… [T]he hypothetical test is whether on 3rd February, 2000, 8th February, 2000 and 14th February, 2000, had it been available to him, the information contained in the November and December Trading Reports, viewed by him against the "total mix" of information about Fyffes' trading and earnings available on those dates, would have impacted on the judgment of the reasonable investor in relation to an investment decision about Fyffes' shares to the extent that he would have concluded that the information probably would have a substantial effect on Fyffes' shares."[12]

In terms of the profile of the reasonable investor, Laffoy J. was of the view that, in general terms, it was not necessary to profile the reasonable investor any more than it was necessary to profile the reasonable man in applying the principles of

9 See para.362. Laffoy J. relied in particular on the judgment of Marshall J. in *T.S.C. Industries Inc. v Northway Inc.* (1976) 426 U.S. 438.

10 [1990] 1 M.L.J. v.

11 [1990] 1 M.L.J. v at p.x.

12 Paragraph 397.

the tort of negligence. However, she did provide that the reasonable investor had to "represent the type of investor who was typically found in the market at the time". Thus, if, on the evidence before the court, the typical investor at the time of the share sales at issue in the case was "one who was anxious to own internet stocks or stocks with an internet element", that was a relevant factor in the profile of the reasonable investor.

The Supreme Court, while agreeing that s.108(1) set down an objective test, rejected the use by the High Court of the reasonable investor approach and found that the jurisprudence relied upon in the High Court was not of assistance in interpreting the section. The court found that the reasonable investor approach was not expressly or impliedly required by the section and that, in any event, it was not an appropriate or useful legal tool. Addressing what he found to be inherent problems in the approach, Finnegan J. stated:

> "The difficulty in using the reasonable investor as a test, and not just to categorise the test as objective, is compounded in that it is, to my mind, impossible to profile the reasonable investor. There are innumerable categories of investor from the small private investor who will check the value of his shares but now and then to the institutional investor who is in touch with the market throughout the trading day. Is it the dealer who trades within the account or the trustee whose shareholding dates back decades? One investor may concentrate on return, another on capital gain. An investor may be cautious or adventurous and to a greater or lesser degree."[13]

Similarly, Denham J. stated:

> "… [T]here is a myriad of factors and investors in a market, and to choose some or either as representative of a reasonable investor appears subjective and arbitrary. The issue is the effect on the share price in the market of the information if the information were generally available."[14]

The Supreme Court favoured an objective test based on the wording of the section. Finnegan J. set out this test as follows:

> "The court's function it appears to me is as follows:—
> 1. first to determine the generality or '*total mix*' of information generally available;
> 2. to determine the information not generally available but available to the dealer;
> 3. to determine whether that information, if it were generally available, would be likely to materially affect the price of the shares having regard to the total mix of information available in the market. The

[13] Paragraph 295.
[14] Paragraph 51.

> evidence which would normally be available to the court, and which was available in this case, is the evidence of experts and the evidence of actual market movements upon some or all of the not generally available information becoming available."[15]

(d) The reasonable investor under the Market Abuse Regulations

Significantly, the Market Abuse Regulations expand on the statutory hypothesis and expressly require the use of the reasonable investor test in assessing whether information, if made public, would be likely to have a significant effect on share price. This results from reg.2 which requires the information to be "information that a reasonable investor would be likely to use as part of the basis of the investor's investment decisions".

This definition does not appear in Directive 2003/6/EC[16] (the "Market Abuse Directive"), to which the Market Abuse Regulations give effect. However, it is provided by art.2(1) of Commission Directive 2003/124/EC[17] (the "Implementing Directive"), the first of three level 2 implementing Directives for the Market Abuse Directive.[18] While the State was required to transpose the provisions of the Implementing Directive into national law, there are question marks over whether the expanded definition reflected in reg.2 above replaced the basic test for price sensitivity laid down by the Market Abuse Directive (that the information, if made public, "would be likely to have a significant effect" on price) with a reasonable investor test. Indeed, none other than the Committee of European Securities Regulators (CESR), in its second set of level 3 implementing guidance on the Market Abuse Directive, has pointed out that art.17(2) of the Market Abuse Directive provides that the implementing measures provided in the implementing Directives shall not modify the provisions of the Market Abuse Directive.[19]

One could foresee an argument being made on the basis of art.17(2) that, despite the wording adopted by the State, the court can interpret the Market Abuse Regulations in line with the wording of the Market Abuse Directive and apply the statutory hypothesis simpliciter, without resorting to the reasonable investor. There would seem to be support in this from the comment of the CESR that the reasonable investor test merely "assists in determining the type of information to be taken into account for the purposes of the 'significant price effect' criterion".[20]

[15] Paragraph 296.

[16] OJ L 96, 12/4/2003, pp.16–25.

[17] OJ L 339, 24/12/2003, pp.70–72.

[18] The Market Abuse Directive was the first Directive to be implemented under the "Lamfalussy process" which involves four levels or stages for properly implementing EU legislation.

[19] See para.1.11 of the Committee of European Securities Regulators, *Level 3 – second set of CESR guidance and information on the common operation of the Directive to the market* (July 2007, CESR/06–562b).

[20] See para.1.11 of the Committee of European Securities Regulators, *Level 3 – second set of CESR guidance and information on the common operation of the Directive to the market* (July 2007, CESR/06–562b).

However, in the absence of such an argument being run successfully, the wording of the new legislation means that, in terms of price sensitivity, the Supreme Court judgment in *Fyffes* may have significantly less impact going forward than the High Court judgment it overturned. Regardless of the unanimous rejection of the reasonable investor approach in the Supreme Court judgments, that is the approach required under the wording of the new statutory regime. The obvious question in this regard is whether the test as formulated in the new provision is the same as that adopted by Laffoy J. in the High Court in *Fyffes*.

The test in the Market Abuse Regulations can be construed from reg.5(1), in conjunction with the definitions in reg.2, and is as follows: Was the information such as a reasonable investor would be likely to use as part of the basis of his investment decisions?

The reasonable investor test employed by Laffoy J., as quoted above, was as follows: Would the information have impacted on the judgment of the reasonable investor in relation to an investment decision about the shares to the extent that he would have concluded that the information probably would have a substantial effect on the shares?

It is submitted that there is a subtle, yet potentially significant, difference between the test adopted by Laffoy J. and that set out in the Market Abuse Regulations. While those Regulations ask whether the information would have been *used* by the reasonable investor in his decisions, Laffoy J.'s test merely asks whether the information would have *impacted* on the judgment of the reasonable investor. It could be argued that, for a piece of information to be price sensitive under the new statutory test, it is not enough that it would have been a mere "factor in the mix" with all other market factors at the time of the reasonable investor's decision. It would have had to have been positively used by the reasonable investor and formed part of the basis of his decision. By contrast, Laffoy J.'s test might be considered to cover such information. As can be seen below, this distinction may have some bearing on the issue of "offsetting".

It will be interesting to see the approach taken by the courts on this issue in any future claim of insider dealing brought under the Market Abuse Regulations. While it is true that the Supreme Court rejected the use of the reasonable investor primarily on the basis that it was not required by the statute and focused on the formulation of the test adopted by Laffoy J., the judges undoubtedly also expressed more general criticism of the principle of the reasonable investor being employed as a tool in measuring price sensitivity.

(e) Offsetting against other market factors

While Laffoy J. found that the information at issue in *Fyffes* was "unquestionably bad news about Fyffes' trading and earnings performance in the first quarter",[21]

[21] Paragraph 441.

and was of a type and quality that was potentially price sensitive, she refused to accept that this was the end of the matter. She refused to adopt what she called an "intuitive" approach, stating:

> "… [T]he court was invited to conclude that intuitively the information appeared on its face to be price-sensitive. The statutory test does not warrant drawing any conclusion in relation to the information contained in the trading reports standing alone. The furthest the court can go is that the information was of a type and quality that was potentially price-sensitive. Whether it was or was not, falls to be judged by applying the principles which I have adumbrated earlier."[22]

Laffoy J. went on to hold that the negative impact of the information would have been "offset" by certain factors which, she found, negated the price sensitivity of the information. For instance, she held that the reasonable investor would have concluded that it was too early in the financial year to make a judgment about the outcome for *Fyffes*. Further, she found that the reasonable investor would have concluded that the impact of the information would have been offset by the prospects of a merger or a major acquisition, as well as the potential of an internet-based venture that was being pursued by Fyffes and had been the main driver of the share price.

The Supreme Court rejected the approach taken by Laffoy J. in this regard. It held that the court could not "offset" the hypothetical impact of the information on the market against certain factors already in the market. Denham J. stated:

> "The legal principle of 'offset', applied by the learned trial judge, to determine what the reasonable investor would have concluded of the market, and then used to determine share price and price-sensitivity, is not in the statute, and there is no legal authority for it in this jurisdiction. Nor is it in the Council Directive.
>
> … The learned trial judge referred to four factors, as set out above, but this is an arbitrary choice. There are myriad factors at play in a market. Experts analyse and differ each day. I am satisfied that the High Court erred in choosing factors and then applying them to 'offset' the information in the Trading Reports. The information disclosed a risk, and bad news for Fyffes, and this was not altered by making it generally available to the market. Other information, including the 'offsets' was already in the public domain."[23]

The court took the view that Laffoy J. had been wrong to reject what she had called the "intuitive approach". In this regard, Denham J. stated:

> "First, the term 'intuitively' more appropriately may be termed as the 'common sense' approach. This is in keeping with the common law approach

[22] Paragraph 442.
[23] Paragraphs 61 and 62.

to commercial issues. Applying that term the effect is that the High Court held that applying common sense, the information was of a type and quality that was price-sensitive. There is nothing in the statute that excludes common sense from the analysis as to whether or not information would be likely materially to affect the price of the shares. Consequently, it was an error to exclude common sense from the analysis.

Secondly, the High Court appeared to exclude consideration and application of the Trading Reports standing alone. This is not an appropriate approach, as the issue is whether the information in the Trading Reports would be likely materially to affect the price of Fyffes' shares. The information does require to be considered specifically. The information in the documents disclosed a risk, and that is not altered by putting it on the market."[24]

Fennelly J. further explained:

> "The very notion of offset supposes that there is something to 'offset'. It suggests a balancing of one influence against another. If the effect of the worldoffruit.com venture was to counteract or to cancel the effect of the 'bad news', it would still have materially affected the price. The statutory test does not postulate a fall in price."[25]

There is no reference to the "offsetting" of factors in the statutory test provided under the Regulations. However, it is submitted that this process is a legitimate step in applying the reasonable investor test and that the rejection by the Supreme Court of this process might be distinguished as only applying to the test under the 1990 Act, as interpreted by that court.

Under that "market effect" based approach employed by the Supreme Court the question to be answered is whether the piece of information is a factor having an effect, whether positive or negative, on market price. As Fennelly J. emphasised, in this approach there is no requirement to balance the influence of the information against any other market factor. The effect of the information can be looked at in isolation from a common sense point of view, as endorsed by Denham J.

By contrast, under the reasonable investor test, as formulated in the Market Abuse Regulations, the question is whether the information would have been likely to have been *used* by the reasonable investor as part of the *basis* of his investment decisions, taking into account the various other factors at play in the market which are influencing the price of the relevant instrument. In this test, a process of offsetting is essential if one is to assess whether a piece of information would have been positively put to use by the reasonable investor in his decisions and would have formed part of the basis of those decisions. It is not enough that it would have been a mere factor going into the mix. In this way,

[24] Paragraphs 64 and 65.
[25] Paragraph 218.

despite the fact that a piece of information is found to be objectively negative news about the issuer of shares, the court may find that, when offset against other stronger factors playing on his mind, it would nevertheless not have been used by the reasonable investor in his investment decisions in relation to that issuer.

The above argument is based on the formulation of the reasonable investor test as set out in the Market Abuse Regulations. As discussed above, there is a potentially significant difference of emphasis between that formulation and the one employed by Laffoy J. which focused on what would have *impacted* on the judgment of the reasonable investor, rather than what would have been *used* by him in his investment decisions. It would appear that the process of offsetting lends itself even more readily to the new statutory formulation of the reasonable investor test.

Support for such practice under the new regime might be found in the related Market Abuse Rules, which have been adopted by the Financial Regulator.[26] Rule 5.1 of those Rules requires issuers to disclose inside information. Rule 5.3 defines "inside information" in the same manner as the Market Abuse Regulations, however it expands on the reasonable investor test as follows:

> "In conducting the reasonable investor test, the issuer is required:
> (a) to take into account that the significance of the information in question will vary widely from issuer to issuer depending on a number of factors such as the issuer's size, recent developments and the market sentiment about the issuer and the sector in which it operates; and
> (b) to assume that a reasonable investor will make investment decisions relating to the relevant financial instruments or related derivative financial instruments to maximise his economic self interest.
>
> In undertaking such an assessment, the issuer is required to take into consideration the anticipated impact of the information in light of the totality of the issuer's activities, the reliability of the source of information and any other market variables likely to affect the related financial instrument or derivative financial instrument in the given circumstances."

Thus, when conducting the reasonable investor test under the Market Abuse Rules, the issuer is specifically required to take account of the fact that "the significance of the information" will vary depending on "recent developments" and "market sentiments". Further, the issuer must account for "any other market variables likely to affect" the financial instrument in the circumstances. This suggests that the process of offsetting other factors influencing the investment decisions of the reasonable investor against the information in question is a valid step in determining whether, in the words of the Market Abuse Regulations, the

[26] Adopted in March 2006 under s.34 of the Investment Funds, Companies and Miscellaneous Provisions Act 2005.

reasonable investor would be likely to use that information as part of the basis of his investment decisions.

Support for a process of offsetting under the Market Abuse Regulations might also be garnered from the first recital in the Implementing Directive which states that, in assessing whether information would have been used by the reasonable investor in making his investment decisions, one must:

> "... [T]ake into consideration the anticipated impact of the information in light of the totality of the related issuer's activity, the reliability of the source of information and any other market variables likely to affect the related financial instrument or derivative financial instrument related thereto in the given circumstances."

Furthermore, in its second set of implementing guidelines, the CESR, focusing on the statutory hypothesis simpliciter rather than the reasonable investor test, lists as factor that might be taken into consideration "market variables that affect the price of the financial instrument in question".[27]

Of course, it remains to be seen how the courts will approach this issue under the Market Abuse Regulations and whether the expanded test set out in the Market Abuse Rules, and the European sources mentioned above, will have any impact on the approach of the courts. Clearly, much will depend on the view taken of the applicability of the reasonable investor test and the formulation of same. However, it is reasonable to conclude that, given the change in the law affected by the Market Abuse Regulations, the question of offsetting would at the very least be a live issue in any future claim of insider dealing.

(f) Use of post-disclosure market event as proxy

A crucial aspect of Laffoy J.'s judgment in *Fyffes* was her decision to exclude the evidence of the market reaction to a profit warning given by Fyffes between four and six weeks after the share sales the subject of the insider dealing claim. The judge set out the relevant legal principles as follows:

> "... [A] post-market event is only of evidential value for the purpose of resolving the statutory hypothesis if two factors are present: that there is parity of information between the alleged price sensitive information and the information which precipitated the putative proxy share price effect; and that the market conditions were the same on the date the hypothesis is being applied and the date of the putative proxy event."[28]

[27] Paragraph 1.13.

[28] Paragraph 580.

Laffoy J. refused to allow the profit warning to be used as a proxy as she found that it failed to satisfy both elements of the two-part test set out above. In coming to her decision that the two pieces of information were not sufficiently similar, Laffoy J. interposed the reasonable investor in the above test, as follows:

> "To properly assess whether there is parity, what is relevant is what the impact of the information would have been in the market on the date of the Share Sales. That impact would have been conditioned by what the market already knew about Fyffes ... Viewed in the context of the other information available to him, the reasonable investor might well have deduced at the beginning of February, 2000 that Fyffes' management had not formed the view that its own expectations for the first half or for the full year would not be met. In that respect, the information contained in the March 2000 trading statement was fundamentally different because, by that information, Fyffes was formally telling the market that it had revised downwards its expectations in relation to the first half and was uncertain whether it would meet its target for the full year."[29]

The Supreme Court unanimously held that the High Court Judge had erred in excluding this evidence and found it to be of evidential value in assessing the price sensitivity of the information in issue. Finnegan J., having analysed the foreign jurisprudence opened to the courts in this regard,[30] stated:

> "I am satisfied that these cases are not authority for the proposition that the court is precluded from looking at post disclosure share movement as having evidential value in relation to the materiality of the non-disclosed information unless there is parity of that information and the information coming to the market at both relevant dates and the market conditions are the same. In assessing the weight to be attributed to such share price movement clearly the court must have regard to any discrepancies between the non-disclosed information and the information disclosed which affected the market. Again regard must be had to any differences in the state of the market generally and the market for the particular share at the relevant dates. In the present case regard should be had to the enthusiasm which existed at each of the relevant dates for dot.com shares."[31]

Thus, the Supreme Court favoured a more relaxed attitude to the use of a subsequent market event as a proxy or comparator in assessing the price sensitivity of a piece of information. Any differences in the information and the

[29] Paragraph 589.

[30] *Chase Manhattan Equities v Goodman* [1991] B.C.L.C. 897; *Securities and Exchange Commission v Bausch & Lomb Inc.* (1977) 565 F.2d 8; *Elkind v Liggett & Myers Inc.* (1980) 635 F.2d 156; *Securities and Exchange Commission v Lund* (1983) 570 F. Supp. 1397 and *Securities and Exchange Commission v Falbo* (1998) 14 F. Supp. 2d 508.

[31] Paragraph 321.

market conditions would be matters affecting the weight afforded to the evidence, rather than requiring its exclusion. Macken J. set out the less strict test in the following terms:

> "As to the question of parity, this requires, not that the information in question should be identical, but according to its ordinary dictionary meaning, that there should be 'functional equivalence' between the two sets of information. It is therefore necessary to see whether in the present case there was some sufficient similarity between the information released by the plaintiff on the 20th March, 2000 and that appearing in the November/December, 1999 trading reports. If there is, then even taking parity as an appropriate test, the High Court Judge ought not to have rejected the former as having no evidential value whatsoever."[32]

As regards the use by Laffoy J. of the "reasonable investor" to assess the parity between the two pieces of information, Macken J. stated:

> "I find no equivalent approach in the jurisprudence cited … It is not the view of the reasonable investor which is the key factor in determining whether the later information lacks parity with the earlier information. Rather this is a fact finding exercise for the court to undertake, so as to enable it properly to assess whether the drop in share price following the release of the later information, constitutes a good pointer to what would have happened in the market at the earlier relevant dates. In my view, interposing the reasonable investor into that exercise was also an error in law on the part of the High Court Judge."[33]

Given the importance placed by the Supreme Court in *Fyffes* on the evidence of the market reaction to the profit warning, and the fact that the new legislation does nothing to restrict such evidence, it would seem that the use of evidence of a post-disclosure market event as a proxy in assessing price sensitivity will be a key factor in any future claim of insider dealing.[34] The more permissive, weight-based approach of the Supreme Court will thus apply. Such evidence will not be automatically excluded where there are differences between the non-disclosed information and the information later disclosed, nor where there are differences between the market conditions at the time of the alleged insider dealing and the market conditions at the time of the disclosure. Rather, such differences will affect the weight to be attached to the evidence.

However, it should be pointed out that, while the court will not automatically exclude such evidence by reason of differences in information or market conditions, it will nonetheless exercise extreme caution before allowing such

32 Paragraph 257.

33 Paragraphs 261 and 262.

34 This would seem to be supported by the second recital in the Implementing Directive which states that "ex post information may be used to check the presumption that the ex ante information was price sensitive".

evidence to be a determinative factor in a claim of insider dealing. This caution can be seen in the following passage from the judgment of Fennelly J. in the Supreme Court:

> "It is, of course, dangerous to draw inferences from any piece of evidence relating to events on different dates. The court must be astute to see that the evidence is genuinely of value."[35]

It would also follow from *Fyffes* that the reasonable investor will not be used as a tool in assessing parity of information in this regard. The Market Abuse Regulations do require that the reasonable investor be used as a tool in the final decision of whether or not the information in question, if made public, would have been likely to have had a significant effect on the price of the financial instrument. However, it would not seem to follow that this tool should also be used in assessing parity between the information in question and information later disclosed.

As Macken J. stated, this is a fact-finding exercise for the court. It is a ruling by the court as to the evidence which will be permitted to assist it in making the final determination as to price sensitivity, based on the reasonable investor approach. It is premature to be looking at the impact of any information on the reasonable investor at this stage. If the court decides that the evidence of the market reaction to the disclosed information has some evidential value, it may be used by the court in gauging the hypothetical reaction of the reasonable investor had the non-disclosed information been disclosed at the relevant time.

(g) Fundamental incongruity

A curious facet of the *Fyffes* litigation was raised in the following passage from the judgment of Laffoy J.:

> "… [I]n my view, in this case there is an inherent incongruity in reason and common sense between the plaintiff's assertion that, on receipt of the November and December trading reports on the 25th January, 2000, Mr. Flavin had in his possession information which, if generally available, would be likely to materially affect Fyffes' share price, on the one hand, and the fact that at no time did Fyffes determine that, or even consider whether, if made public, the very same information would be likely to lead to a substantial movement in Fyffes' share price, thus triggering its duty of disclosure under the Listing Rules. In order to justify that proposition I do not consider it necessary to determine that the hypothetical tests posited in s. 108(1) and Rule 9.2 of the Listing Rules are precisely the same. In my view, they are essentially the same."[36]

[35] Paragraph 209.
[36] Paragraph 560.

As well as Fyffes' failure to make a disclosure under the Listing Rules, the defendants in *Fyffes* highlighted other apparently contradictory actions on the part of Fyffes, such as the purchase of a congratulatory bottle of champagne for the alleged insider dealer, Mr Flavin. The defendants did not pursue an estoppel argument in their final submissions to the court, but rather argued that the conduct on the part of Fyffes which they highlighted was evidentially significant in the determination as to whether the information in issue was price sensitive. The High Court was not, in the end, required to deal with this issue. Having concluded that the information in issue was not price sensitive, Laffoy J. stated:

> "That outcome on the price sensitivity issue obviates the necessity to confront the fundamental incongruity in the plaintiff's position, which I have highlighted earlier. However, it is difficult to see how a statute outlawing, and providing a remedy for, insider dealing could accommodate such a fundamental incongruity. That it could, would seem to be at variance with fairness and justice."[37]

The Supreme Court acknowledged this fundamental incongruity, but found that it did not affect its finding of insider dealing. Finnegan J. stated:

> "There may be many reasons for this incongruity. The trial judge in the evidence before her found that it exists. However, the subjective appreciation of Fyffes' directors will not be determinative as the test to be applied is an objective one. The subjective appreciation of Fyffes and its directors should go into the mix of evidence available as showing that experienced responsible executive and non-executive directors of a public company had reached that appreciation. The weight to be attached to that evidence will depend on their knowledge and experience and all the circumstances. Other than to remark on the incongruity it does not appear that the trial judge attributed any evidential value to the same."[38]

Fennelly J. suggested that the fundamental incongruity was a quirk which arose from the unusual nature of the proceedings, in which the plaintiff was not a disgruntled shareholder, but rather the company which had issued the shares the subject of the claim. He stated:

> "One can only conclude that the 'fundamental incongruity', if there is one, is just that. It may arise from the remedy provided by the legislature to the company itself. The Directive does not require member states to provide a civil remedy to a company against those trading in its shares in breach of s. 108(1). The incongruity would not exist if the plaintiff were another party to a share

[37] Paragraph 602.
[38] Paragraph 306.

> transaction, not in possession of the relevant information, and suing by virtue of s. 109(1)(a) for loss sustained by him.
>
> Part V provides a statutory remedy, which is not defeated by incongruity."[39]

It would seem that such a fundamental incongruity is liable to arise again under the new legislative regime. Section 33(1) of the 2005 Act, which governs liability under reg.5(1) of the Market Abuse Regulations, provides:

> "If a person contravenes a provision of Irish market abuse law (being a provision the purpose of which is expressed by that law to be for the implementation of Article 2, 3 or 4 of the 2003 Market Abuse Directive) the person shall be liable—
>
> ...
>
> (b) to account to the body corporate or other legal entity which issued the financial instruments concerned for any profit accruing to the first-mentioned person from acquiring or disposing of those instruments."

Thus the statute clearly envisages cases being brought by issuing companies such as Fyffes. Where a statutory remedy is provided to such companies, the same fundamental incongruity is bound to arise. It was open to the legislature to condition the availability of relief by reference to the conduct of the plaintiff, but, once again, it chose not to so.

The *ratio* of the Supreme Court in *Fyffes* in relation to this matter will thus apply. While the evidence of the plaintiff's actions and reactions may, as stated by Finnegan J., "go into the mix of evidence available as showing that experienced responsible executive and non-executive directors of a public company had reached that appreciation", the statutory remedy will not, as stated by Fennelly J., be "defeated by incongruity".

3. Acquiring Price Sensitive Information

Regulation 5(1) of the Market Abuse Regulations provides that:

> "[A] person *to whom this paragraph applies who possesses* inside information shall not use that information by acquiring or disposing of, or by trying to acquire or dispose of, for the person's own account or for the account of a third party, directly or indirectly, financial instruments to which that information relates". (Emphasis added)

Thus, in order to be subject to the prohibition on using inside information, one must be a person to whom the Market Abuse Regulations apply. Regulation 5(3) sets this out.

[39] Paragraphs 225 and 226.

(a) The insider

Regulation 5(3)(a) states that reg.5(1) applies to any person who possesses the insider information concerned by virtue of:

i. membership of the administrative, management or supervisory bodies of the issuer of the financial instrument;
ii. the person's holding in the capital of the issuer;
iii. having access to the information through the exercise of the person's employment, profession or duties; and
iv. the person's criminal activities.

For the purpose of this article, persons who fall under this section will be referred to as "insiders". These are the persons who acquire the inside information by virtue of the fact that they are closely connected to the issuer company (or by virtue of some illegal activity whereby they become privy to inside information in relation to the issuer's shares). Thus, for example, a person who acquires the information by virtue of being a director on the board of the issuer company will be prohibited from using that information for the purpose of dealing with the shares.

A key issue which arises here is the extent to which another company might be deemed to be an insider.[40] For example, if Company A owns shares in issuer Company B, it may be the case that Company A might nominate a director to sit on the board of Company B. In these circumstances, could Company A be deemed to be in "possession" of inside information by virtue of the fact that one of its directors, who sat on the board of Company B, acquired this information? This is an issue which arose in *Fyffes* and involved detailed discussions in relation to the principles of agency in company law. In order to understand the arguments made in this context, it is necessary to understand the background facts pursuant to which the DCC group acquired and sold the shares in *Fyffes*.

Mr Flavin was chief executive of DCC and a director of its wholly-owned subsidiary S&L Investments. Both these companies had acquired a stake in Fyffes dating back to 1981 and by the late 1980s the DCC group's stake had reached approximately 10.5 per cent. In August 1995, DCC and S&L Investments sold their shares to Lotus Green Limited, another company wholly-owned by the DCC group.[41] However, Mr Flavin was *not* a director of Lotus Green. Two weeks later, Lotus Green became resident in the Netherlands and it was fully acknowledged by DCC that these arrangements were wholly tax-driven and were done with a view to mitigating tax liability on a future disposal

[40] It should be noted that the wording of reg.5(3)(b) appears to expressly recognise that the persons who might fall within reg.5(3)(a) could be legal persons in addition to being natural persons.

[41] In fact Lotus Green was a wholly-owned subsidiary of DCC International Holdings BV which in turn was a wholly-owned subsidiary of DCC plc. In addition Lotus Green held the beneficial title to the shares whilst legal title remained with DCC and S&L.

of the holding. When the shares were eventually sold, they were sold by Lotus Green, to whom the profit from the transaction accrued.

In *Fyffes,* there was no evidence that Mr Flavin had formally communicated the alleged price sensitive information to any of the above companies. To get around this, the plaintiffs argued that Mr Flavin had come into possession of price sensitive information and that his knowledge of the information should be imputed to DCC as he was a director of this company.[42]

In support of this, the plaintiffs referred to *Meridian Global Funds Management Asia Ltd v Securities Commission*,[43] a case which discussed the general rules whereby the acts of the officers of a company could be attributed to the company itself. The traditional test is that acts of officers could be deemed acts of the company where those officers constitute the directing mind and will of the company.[44] One of the main points of that case was that if a statutory obligation was intended to apply to *a company*, that company should not be allowed to evade this obligation by delegating the responsibility of compliance to a person down the ranks who was not the company's "directing mind and will". Therefore a special rule of attribution would apply to make that person's acts the acts of the company. By way of analgous reasoning, the plaintiffs argued that the knowledge of Mr Flavin should be attributed to DCC so the policy behind the statute could be properly effected.

In the High Court, Laffoy J. rejected this argument, due to the wording of s.108 under the old statutory regime.[45] In particular, she pointed out that s.108(6) specifically provided for a scheme of attribution by stating that a company cannot deal in shares of another company where its own officer was in possession of price sensitive information. She said it was therefore clear that the legislature was conscious of the necessity to bind a company where an officer of the company was found in possession of the inside information and provided a method of addressing this.

It is submitted that, if this case was fought under the new market abuse regime, a different approach might need to be taken to this issue of attribution. This is because the regulations do not provide for their own scheme of attribution (unlike s.108(6) under the old statutory regime). This could lead to a company arguing that whilst their director may have been in possession of the price sensitive information, the company, as a separate entity, was not and therefore its dealing in the shares could not be caught by reg.5(1), even if those dealings were influenced or orchestrated by the director in question. Therefore,

[42] If the plaintiffs were successful in this argument then they could then argue that DCC was a shadow director of Lotus Green, by virtue of which liability for insider trading could be attributed to Lotus Green under s.108(6).

[43] [1995] 2 A.C. 500.

[44] *Lennards Carrying Company Limited v Asiatic Petroleum Company Limited* [1915] A.C. 705, which was applied by the Supreme Court in *Superwood Holdings Plc v Sun Alliance and London Insurance Plc* [1995] 3 I.R. 303.

[45] This aspect of the judgment was not appealed to the Supreme Court.

in accordance with the principles set down in *Meridian,* it might be necessary to attribute possession of information to the company in question.

However, this position might itself lead to an injustice. What if a company decided to sell shares in ignorance of the fact that one of its directors had in his possession price sensitive information relating to those shares because he was a nominee director in the issuer company? To impute this possession to the company might seem to be unfair considering there is no link between the information and the decision to sell. A possible solution to this might be in the wording of reg.5(1) which does not prohibit "possession" of price sensitive information per se but "use" of that information by dealing (discussed further below.) In these circumstances, it could be argued that if the company has not *used* the information when dealing, no liability could accrue to it.

As we have seen above in the context of the test for price sensitivity, the incorporation of this word "use" is one of the key differences between Pt V of the 1990 Act and the new Market Abuse Regulations. This might suggest that the insider or dealer must have some knowledge of the sensitivity of the information or is motivated to deal as a result of the information. In *Fyffes*, Laffoy J. expressly ruled out that knowledge or motivation was relevant to attach liability to the insider under Pt V of the 1990 Act.[46]

(b) The tippee

Regulation 5 also applies to a "tippee". This was used in *Fyffes* to describe the person who acquires insider information from the "insider". A *form* of "tippee liability" is catered for under reg.5(3)(c), which provides that the prohibition on insider dealing applies to:

> "... [A]ny other person who possesses the insider information concerned while the person knows, or ought to have known, that it is inside information."

It appears that this provision was designed to capture those persons who happen to acquire inside information but who are not necessarily "insiders" as catered for under reg.5(3)(a). The key point here is the knowledge requirement. A person can only come under this section if they are aware (or ought to be aware) of the price sensitive nature of the information and the fact that it is inside information.

In *Fyffes*, the nature of the knowledge requirement was examined by Laffoy J. In particular she noted the distinction that the old statutory regime made between the "insider" and the "tippee". Under the old statutory regime, the wording of s.108 did not expressly make knowledge a requirement for liability to attach to an "insider". However, this was a requirement for the "tippee" in that the "tippee" could not be liable unless they knew or ought to have known that the information was price sensitive.[47]

46 Paragraph 91.

47 This aspect of the judgment was not appealed to the Supreme Court.

Similarly, under the new Market Abuse Regime, it appears that the prohibition against using inside information applies to persons under reg.5(3)(a) (the insiders) regardless of whether they know the information is price sensitive. However, under reg.5(3)(c) there is an express knowledge requirement.

The knowledge requirement is particularly pertinent to the issue of whether a company or body corporate can be deemed a "tippee" by virtue of the simple fact that one of its directors was an "insider". This arose for deliberation in *Fyffes*.

As already stated, there was no evidence before the court that Mr Flavin had formally communicated the alleged price sensitive information to DCC and S&L. However, it was alleged by the plaintiffs that as he *knew* the price sensitive information, and as he was chief executive and director of DCC and S&L respectively, his knowledge could be attributed to those companies which in turn made them "tippees" under s.108(3). As Laffoy J. put it, the plaintiffs were attempting to argue that the "information in the possession of the source can be attributed to the body corporate tippee".[48]

Laffoy J. rejected this argument. One of the reasons for this was that the wording of s.108(3) precluded such an interpretation.[49] This was because to become a "tippee" under s.108(3) one needed to have received the information and known (or ought to have known) that it was price sensitive information. If Mr Flavin's possession of the information could be simply imputed to DCC then this would obviate this knowledge requirement on behalf of DCC. As Laffoy J. put it:

> "If the principle of attribution could be applied in that manner, the effect would be to give DCC some type of quasi insider status and render the knowledge requirement superfluous. In my view, that is not what the legislature intended."[50]

It would seem that the reasoning here would be apposite in interpreting the wording of reg.5(3)(c) of the Market Abuse Regulations.

4. The Test for Dealing

Regulation 5(1) of the Market Abuse Regulations provides that a person possessing inside information:

> "… [S]hall not use that information by acquiring or disposing of, or by trying to acquire or dispose of, for the person's own account or for the account of a third party, directly or indirectly, financial instruments to which that information relates".

48 Paragraph 101.
49 This aspect of the judgment was not appealed to the Supreme Court.
50 Paragraph 102.

In addition, reg.5(2)(b) also states that a person with inside information cannot:

> "[R]ecommend or induce another person, on the basis of inside information, to acquire or dispose of financial instruments to which that information relates."

This can be compared with the prohibition against "dealing" under the old statutory regime, which was defined in s.107 of the Companies Act 1990 as:

> "([W]hether as principal or agent) acquiring, disposing of, subscribing for or underwriting the securities, or making or offering to make, or inducing or attempting to induce a person to make or to offer to make, an agreement—
> (a) for or relating to acquiring, disposing of, subscribing for or underwriting the securities; or
> (b) the purpose or purported purpose of which is to secure a profit or gain to a person who acquires, disposes of, subscribes for or underwrites the securities or to any of the parties to the agreement in relation to the securities;".

In addition, s.108(4) of the 1990 Act stated:

> "It shall not be lawful for a person at any time when he is precluded by subsection (1), (2) or (3) from dealing in any securities, to cause or procure any other person to deal in those securities."

There is a certain degree of overlap between the new regime and the old statutory scheme in respect of the meaning of "dealing". The dealing provisions were examined in detail in *Fyffes* and this was mainly based on the defence mounted by *DCC* and the other defendants. In particular, the defendants' contended that even if the information in Mr Flavin's possession was price sensitive the defendants could not be liable because:

a. Mr Flavin did not deal in the shares. He merely acted as a facilitator passing on unsolicited offers to the beneficial owners of the shares, Lotus Green;
b. Mr Flavin did not cause or procure the dealing; and
c. Lotus Green *did* deal in the shares and all the profit accrued to Lotus Green. However Lotus Green dealt *lawfully*. It did not receive any price sensitive information from Mr Flavin and so was not a "tippee". Nor was Mr Flavin an officer of Lotus Green.

As a result of these propositions, there was significant discussion in the judgment of Laffoy J. in respect of the meaning of "dealing". It should be noted that her findings in this regard were not appealed to the Supreme Court.

(a) Factual background to the dealing issue in *Fyffes*

There were three share sales in issue. The first was for in excess of 17 million shares for a price of €3.20 and was executed by Davy Stockbrokers as the dealing agent. The second and third sales were on February 8 and 14, and were executed by Goodbody Stockbrokers. The predominance of the evidence in respect of the dealing related to the first share sale and the transcripts of telephone conversations between Mr Flavin and representatives from Davy Stockbrokers and Goodbody.

The negotiation for the sale of the shares began with unsolicited phone calls from Davy and Goodbody stockbrokers directly to Mr Flavin in late January and early February 2000 expressing interest in the shares. During the course of the conversations, Mr Flavin said they (DCC) would consider a bid for the entire holding in Fyffes or exactly half the holding at €3.20.

At 16.00 on February 3, 2000, Mr Ronan Godfrey of Davy Stockbrokers, phoned Mr Flavin and stated:

> "I will bid you for 17,895,697 ordinary shares at three twenty."

Mr Flavin responded that he would come back to Mr Godfrey and said:

> "... Ronan it may be that you get a call not from me but from a guy from ING Bank in Holland, Tom Diepenhorst, and if it's not him you can take it that they have authority to give an instruction."

Mr Godfrey indicated that that was not a problem and Mr Flavin then said:

> "I have no authority on the matter."

There then appeared to have been a laugh audible on the tape and Laffoy J. recorded the fact that, "Mr. Flavin explained this on the basis that it was a mannerism of his when he was nervous and that he felt discomfiture about only telling Mr. Godfrey that he had no authority at that stage".[51]

Mr Flavin indicated further to Mr Godfrey that in fact doing the deal "wouldn't be with us at all" and that "we really want the trail of instruction entirely from Holland ... in correspondence to you there and back". In this regard, Mr Flavin's evidence was to ensure that all the paperwork should reflect the factual situation that he had no authority in the matter. As Laffoy J. stated, "his concern was driven by tax considerations".[52]

It was the defendant's case that ultimately the key decisions in respect of the sale of the shares were made by the board of Lotus Green, and not Mr Flavin,

[51] Paragraph 235.
[52] Paragraph 235.

and that final authority came from them as beneficial owner of the shares. Mr Flavin was merely the conduit passing on unsolicited bids.

The board of Lotus Green consisted of four directors, three Dutch directors and Mr O'Dwyer, the chief financial officer of DCC plc. On January 31, 2000, Mr Flavin informed Mr O'Dwyer of an increasing level of interest in the Fyffes holding and, following from this, Mr O'Dwyer made arrangements to hold a board meeting of Lotus Green. At that meeting a resolution was passed that Lotus Green would accept offers of €3.00 or higher for all or part of Lotus Green's shareholding in Fyffes. It was also resolved that any of the three Dutch directors would have authority to accept an offer, with Mr Tom Diepenhorst ranking first.

After the bid made by Mr Godfrey on February 3, 2000, Mr Flavin told Mr O'Dwyer about the bid and Mr O'Dwyer phoned Mr Diepenhorst giving him details of the offer and the name and telephone number of the contact in Davy. Mr Diepenhorst then rang Mr Godfrey in Davy stating that Lotus Green in Amsterdam "confirm[s] the data … that is 17,895,697 ordinary shares in Fyffes at a price of 3 point 20 cents".

(b) Meaning of "dealing"

The definition of dealing under s.107 of the 1990 Act was extremely broad (see above). On the facts of the case, Laffoy J. had to have regard to the interpretation of the concepts of "inducing" and "making an agreement" as set out under s.107. In respect of inducement she agreed with the defendant that:

> "… [I]n order to prove that a person induced the making of an agreement, it must be proved that the person persuaded or exerted influence over the contracting party in a manner which materially contributed to the outcome, the making of the agreement."[53]

In respect of "an agreement" in the context of making or offering to make an agreement she agreed with the proposition that:

> "… [T]hose words denote an agreement as a whole or the entire of an agreement, in the sense of all of the essential elements … However, in the case of the sale of shares in a listed company, as a general proposition, the essential elements will be the identity of the purchaser, the number of shares, the price and, perhaps, the type of shares."[54]

Under the Market Abuse Regulations, the "dealing" aspect is defined in more succinct terms in that it simply states at reg.5(1) that one cannot use inside information:

[53] Paragraph 117.
[54] Paragraph 120.

> "[B]y acquiring or disposing of, or by trying to acquire or dispose of, for the person's own account or for the account of a third party, directly or indirectly, financial instruments to which that relates."

However, it is arguable that the words "trying" to acquire/dispose would encompass the similar concepts of "offering" or "inducing an offer" to make an agreement to acquire/dispose. Furthermore, reg.5(2)(b) also states that a person with inside information cannot:

> "[R]ecommend or induce another person, on the basis of inside information, to acquire or dispose of financial instruments to which that information relates."

In this regard, Laffoy J.'s interpretation and application of the meaning of the word "induce" are apposite to the new market abuse regime.

5. Conclusions in Respect of Dealing in *Fyffes*

Ultimately, Laffoy J. rejected the arguments of the defendants and concluded that Mr Flavin did deal in the shares. First, she held that the conversations which took place between Mr Flavin and representatives from Davy and Goodbody did amount to a process of negotiation which she defined as "discussion aimed at reaching an agreement".[55] She then determined that, as a result of this negotiation, the following terms were agreed—who the buyers were, the number of shares, the type of shares, the price, late delivery and late settlement in relation to some of the shares.[56]

The next and crucial question was who decided these terms—Lotus Green or Mr Flavin? She concluded it was Mr Flavin. This was for a number of reasons. First, Mr Flavin had complete control over what offers to pass on and what offers to reject, as no one knew Lotus Green owned the shares. Therefore "the only offers which were going to come to Lotus Green were offers which Mr. Flavin chose to pass on".[57]

Secondly, Lotus Green had no real input into the process whereby the agreed terms were arrived at. Mr Flavin was the one who decided how many shares would be sold and he did so on the basis of tax advice. Lotus Green did not make this decision.[58] Thirdly, Mr Flavin and not Lotus Green decided on which types of shares would be sold and in particular how the preference shares would be dealt with. Again this was on foot of tax advice passed on by Mr O'Dwyer and in doing so Laffoy J. concluded that Mr O'Dwyer was "acting as chief financial officer of DCC".

55 Paragraph 270.
56 Paragraph 272.
57 Paragraph 274
58 Paragraph 275.

Fourthly, the resolution of the board of Lotus Green deciding to accept a price of €3.00 or higher for all or part of the shares within the next month was commercially unrealistic because it was clear that the shares were around €3.20 and rising. This resolution was taken with the view of allowing DCC to determine the actual price at which the shares would be sold while trying to maintain the appearance that Lotus Green was the entity deciding the price. As Laffoy J. put it:

> "I have no doubt that it was understood by all involved that, if an offer was passed on, it could be assumed that the price was acceptable to DCC."[59]

She went on to say that Mr Flavin did not need ultimate authority from Lotus Green. In reality it was him who accepted the offer and although Mr Diepenhorst had to formally signify acceptance from Holland there was no question but that this was going to happen.[60] She also concluded that in this regard Mr Flavin dealt "as agent for the DCC group".[61]

6. Causing or Procuring Dealing

Having concluded that Mr Flavin "dealt" there was no need to deliberate on the issue of whether Mr Flavin caused or procured any of the corporate defendants to deal. However, for the purpose of completeness Laffoy J. examined this issue.[62] In particular she looked at the meeting of "causing" and "procuring" for the purpose of s.108(4) of the 1990 Act which stated:

> "It shall not be lawful for a person at any time when he is precluded by subsection (1), (2) or (3) from dealing in any securities, to cause or procure any other person to deal in those securities."

Again, a parrellel can be drawn between this provision and reg.5(2)(b) which states that a person with inside information cannot:

> "[R]ecommend or induce another person, on the basis of inside information, to acquire or dispose of financial instruments to which that information relates."

It is submitted that the words "recommend" or "induce" are broader than the words "cause" or "procure". If the Market Abuse Regulations prohibit a person

[59] Paragraph 277.
[60] Paragraph 279.
[61] Paragraph 289.
[62] Paragraphs 131 to 134.

recommending or inducing another person to deal in shares then, a fortiori, they must prohibit a person causing or procuring another to deal.

In respect of the meaning of "cause", Laffoy J. put it simply:

> "In my view, the test in relation to 'causing' is whether the alleged causer brought about the dealing engaged in by the other person."[63]

She rejected the contention that the person in question must be the direct cause of the dealing or that intention or reasonable foreseeability in relation to the result is required.[64]

As regards the test in relation to "procuring", Laffoy J. adopted a passage from Lord Widgery C.J. in *A-G's reference (No.1)*,[65] which states:

> "To procure means to produce by endeavour. You procure a thing by setting out to see that it happens and taking appropriate steps to produce that happening."[66]

In light of the evidence, Laffoy J. determined that "Mr. Flavin both caused and procured the dealing which resulted in the Share Sales".[67]

7. Using Inside Information

As already stated, reg.5(1) of the Market Abuse Regulations provides that a person possessing inside information:

> "... *[S]hall not use that information* by acquiring or disposing of, or by trying to acquire or dispose of, for the person's own account or for the account of a third party, directly or indirectly, financial instruments to which that information relates". (emphasis added)

The incorporation of these words could be interpreted as constituting a significant distinction between the old statutory scheme and new Market Abuse Regime. The old statutory scheme operated so that dealing was prohibited if the dealer happened to be a person who was directly or indirectly in possession of price sensitive information in certain defined circumstances. However, there was no requirement to investigate into the knowledge or motivation of the dealer.[68] In particular, no causal link was required between the possession of the information and the decision to sell. As Laffoy J. put it in *Fyffes*:

[63] Paragraph 134.
[64] Paragraph 134.
[65] [1975] 2 All E.R. 684.
[66] [1975] 2 All E.R. 684 at 686.
[67] Paragraph 293.
[68] The only possible exception to this was where the dealer was a "tippee" who was prohibited

> "I can see no basis for implying a requirement of knowledge as to the price sensitivity of the information into subs. (1) or subs. (6) [of s.108 of the 1990 Act], *nor can I see any basis for implying a requirement as to motivation in using the information*. That conclusion is enforced by taking an overview of the legislative scheme in which the civil liability is created. Where knowledge is not expressly made a requirement, the legislative scheme is that a person deals while in possession of price-sensitive information on pain of illegality unless the factual circumstances come within one of the exceptions, thereby obviating illegality. The fact that the legislature included the exceptions suggests that its intention was that the preceding provisions should be interpreted without any implied qualification as to knowledge or motivation."[69]

This may prove to be a vital distinction in the Market Abuse Regulations. These Regulations are open to the interpretation that they do not apply to a person who deals in the shares for reasons entirely unrelated to the inside information which might be in their possession. However, from a practical perspective, this interpretation may undermine the effectiveness of these Regulations. Proving motivation is difficult in the extreme and might provide a convenient defence to those who trade whilst knowingly in possession of price sensitive information.

8. Conclusion

The change in the law relating to insider dealing may not appear significant on first reading of the old and new legislative provisions. However, on closer inspection, it is apparent that, in litigation concerning complex transactions involving many parties and intricate corporate relationships, even seemingly minor changes in wording can have profound effects on the applicable legal principles. From a regulatory point of view, market players should take note of the shifts in emphasis resulting from the change in the law as regards the test for price sensitivity, the scope of persons capable of insider dealing and the actions which might be considered to be "dealing".

From a legal point of view, the new statutory regime would benefit greatly from the sort of judicial scrutiny afforded the old regime by the Superior Courts in *Fyffes*. A number of issues dealt with in the judgments of the courts in that case have been blown wide open again with the introduction of the Market Abuse Regulations. Considering the volatility which the markets have experienced in recent times this is one area of the law that desperately needs clearly defined principles if it is to have any influence on the activities of those dealing in the market.

from dealing where he or she knew or ought to have known that the information was price sensitive.

69 Paragraph 91.

Part IV

Looking to the Future

CHAPTER 9

REVOLUTIONISING IRISH COMPANY LAW—THE PROPOSED NEW COMPANIES CONSOLIDATION AND REFORM ACT

Brian Conroy, B.L.

1. Introduction

(a) Background

The General Scheme of the new Companies Consolidation and Reform Bill (the "Bill") was presented to Minister Micheál Martin on May 11, 2007, and approved by the Cabinet in late July 2007. The Bill is still undergoing the rigours of amendment by parliamentary counsel and has yet to pass through the Oireachtas, but, even with the prolonged scrutiny which a Bill of this magnitude invariably receives in the Dáil and Seanad, all looks set fair for it to become law by 2011.[1] The Company Law Review Group—the expert body responsible for drafting the General Scheme—has promised that its enactment will entail "the most dramatic modernisation and simplification of company law in the history of the State."[2] This claim cannot be dismissed as mere hyperbole. While large swathes of the Bill consist of little more than coherently structured and worded reproductions of provisions that appeared in the prior legislation, the Bill does propose far-reaching changes to both the form and the substance of Irish company law. Accordingly, it is important that practitioners, students and all others affected by company law on a day-to-day basis appraise themselves of the practical changes set to be wrought by the new legislation in advance of its enactment.

(b) Objectives

This article does not purport to offer a comprehensive guide to the proposed legislation. If enacted as it currently stands, the Bill will become the longest Act in the history of the Irish state, and therefore its provisions are not amenable to

[1] Some guidance as to how long this Bill might take to wend its way through the Oireachtas may be gleaned from a comparison with the Companies Act 1963, which was initiated on July 19, 1962 and received its final reading on December 10, 1963, a period of one year and five months.

[2] See press release on the Review Group's website at *www.clrg.org*, posted on May 11, 2007.

summary in a piece of this nature. Company law is inherently complex and technical, and it is likely that even experienced practitioners will take years to become entirely familiar with the intricacies of the new legislation. This article will have fulfilled its modest ambitions if it alerts readers to the most practically significant innovations outlined in Pillar A of the Bill, the portion of the Bill which makes the most sweeping reforms.

2. Structural Changes

(a) A break with the past

Unsurprisingly, given our history, Irish company law has long struggled to move out of the long shadow cast by its UK progenitor. For example, the Companies Act 1963 was in large part inspired by the content of the British legislation which preceded it—the UK Companies Act 1948—and many of its provisions are identical to their equivalents in that legislation.[3]

The proposed new Companies Act represents a clear break with this pattern of flattery through imitation. The General Scheme of the Bill arrives as the culmination of years of discussion, drafting and redrafting by an expert body specially appointed to consider legislative reform suitable to the Irish context. Of course, many of its reforms do mirror provisions incorporated in the most recent consolidation of UK company law, the Companies Act 2006. An example of such a provision appears at s.2, Pt A4 of Bill, which draws on the British legislation by permitting single-director companies for the first time in the history of Irish law. However, here as elsewhere, the Company Law Review Group eschewed the easy option of slavishly following the law in the UK, instead recommending the inclusion of a new provision—incorporated at s.3 of Pt A4—retaining a measure of oversight on the activities of the director by requiring a single-director company to have a separate company secretary. There is no such safeguard in the British legislation.

There are several provisions in the Bill which are influenced by foreign legislation from as far afield as the United States, Canada, New Zealand and Australia. For example, s.20 of Pt A2 opts for the approach to abolition of the ultra vires doctrine adopted at s.16(1) of the New Zealand Companies Act 1993, going further than s.39(1) of the UK Companies Act 2006, which simply prevents a company's acts from being invalidated on the basis of the ultra vires doctrine, rather than abolishing it altogether.[4]

[3] The Companies Act 1963 was preceded by the Kenny Report, but that report was not supported by anything like the time and resources devoted to the various Reports of the Company Law Review Group that preceded this Bill.

[4] These provisions are discussed in detail at para.10.9.2 of the CLRG's First Report.

(b) The Company Law Review Group

The Company Law Review Group (the "CLRG") was established pursuant to Pt VII of the Company Law Enforcement Act 2001, with s.68(1) of this Act listing the amendment and consolidation of the existing companies legislation as two of the most important aspects of the Group's brief. The General Scheme of the Bill ultimately drafted by the CLRG—available online at *www.clrg.org* or in hard copy directly from the offices of the CLRG—achieves both of these tasks by bringing the areas covered by the 12 Companies Acts and numerous statutory instruments comprising the prior law within a single piece of legislation, and implementing quite a number of substantive changes to the prior law.

The outcomes of the CLRG's various work programmes are set forth at some length in the various reports it has published over the last number of years. Its First Report, published on December 31, 2001, delineated the overall structure of its proposals for its proposal to reform and consolidate the companies legislation and also discussed potential reforms to the following specific areas of company law: shareholder protection, creditor protection, corporate criminal acts and omissions, corporate governance, prospectuses and public offers, auditors, directors and other company officers, corporate litigation, the regulation of insolvency practitioners, strike-off and investment companies. Its proposals in relation to corporate litigation have already led to the establishment of the hugely successful Commercial Court within the Four Courts in Dublin. A Second Report was published on March 31, 2004, and dealt with the following areas: shares and shareholders, liquidations, charges and security, company management regulations, EU developments and accounts and audit. The CLRG has also published a 2005 Report dealing with the contentious Directors' Compliance Statement required under s.45 of the Companies (Auditing and Accounting) Act 2003, as well as a Report accompanying the General Scheme presented to the Cabinet in May 2007.

(c) Shifting the focus of the companies legislation

The cornerstone of the CLRG's First Report (the "Report") was its recommendation that private companies limited by shares should be brought centre stage in the companies legislation. The rationale behind this recommendation is set out at some length in Ch.3 of the Report, where the private company limited by shares is described as "the most important type of company". According to the Report, 88.8 per cent of companies incorporated in Ireland are private companies limited by shares, while just 0.6 per cent are public limited companies. However, the prior legislation was drafted in such a way as to suggest that the public limited company was the "default" mode of incorporation, and readers were required to scrutinise the legislation with some care to ascertain which of the provisions also applied to private limited companies. Ironically, as the Report points out, it is the shareholders and directors of private limited companies, most of which in this jurisdiction are family companies with just a small number of shareholders and a relatively small turnover, who are worst equipped to engage expert advisors to assist them in navigating the statutory provisions.

Accordingly, the new Bill is structured so as both to prioritise and to simplify the law governing private companies limited by shares. The Bill is divided into two Pillars, and Pillar A is devoted exclusively to the law governing private companies limited by shares, or "CLSs". The law relating to other corporate entities, such as the public limited company (Pt B2), the guarantee company (Pt B4) and the unlimited company (Pt B5), along with certain newly created company types such as the designated activity company (Pt B3) is placed within Pillar B of the Bill, which operates by way of reference to Pillar A. In short, any provision of Pillar A which is not applicable to one of these alternative corporate entities is specifically disapplied in the Part of Pillar B devoted to the relevant form of company, with any additional provisions not included in Pillar A but applicable to the form of company in question being incorporated within the relevant Part of Pillar B.

To illustrate how all of this works in practice, s.2 of Pt B2 of the Act provides that the provisions of Pt A will apply to Plcs except to the extent that they are misapplied or modified within the body of Pt B2 itself. So, for example, the provisions of Pillar A of the Bill permitting single-director companies are specifically misapplied in s.62 of Pt B2 of the Bill which relates to public limited companies, while provisions specific to public limited companies dealing with matters such as market abuse and public offers of securities are incorporated within Pt B2.

3. The Private Company Limited by Shares

(a) Incorporating a CLS

Part A2 of the new Bill provides for substantial changes to the law governing the incorporation of a private company limited by shares (now to be known as a "CLS", a phrase that is likely to become common parlance following the enactment of the Bill). Instead of the traditional memorandum and articles of association, the member or members of a CLS will now subscribe to a single document of incorporation known as a constitution.[5] This document will perform most of the functions previously fulfilled by the articles and memorandum, although significantly, as explained below, it will not contain an objects clause.

(b) The abolition of the ultra vires doctrine

Section 20 of Pt A2 of the Bill provides that, subject to the general law, a CLS will have full and unlimited legal capacity, hence abolishing the ultra vires

[5] As recommended by the CLRG at para.7.2.2 of the First Report.

doctrine in relation to this type of company. This is a massive change to the prior law which gives effect to the CLRG's recommendation that, in light of the reality that the objects clauses of most private companies were drafted as widely as possible and that the ultra vires doctrine constituted an unnecessary hindrance both to the company's promoters and to third parties (see, for example, *Northern Bank Finance Corp. Ltd v Quinn*,[6] where the plaintiff company was a creditor which was prevented from enforcing an otherwise valid guarantee because the company's memorandum denied it the power to enter into the relevant transaction), a CLS should have the legal capacity of a natural person.[7] Any company that wishes to retain an objects clause will be obliged to convert to a "designated activity company" or "DAC", a new form of corporate structure created under Pt B3 of the Bill which is intended to accommodate special-purpose vehicles such as those formed for certain financial transactions as well as companies whose stakeholders wish to retain the safeguards comprised in an objects clause. This conversion must take place within six months after the Bill is enacted, placing the onus on a company's stakeholders and their advisors to move quickly to consider their options once this happens.

(c) The incorporation of Table A, EU Regulations and other provisions

There will continue to be a pro forma model constitution scheduled to the Act. However, the CLRG recommended that the common modes of internal governance of a company formerly contained in Table A of the Companies Act 1963 should be readable immediately from the main body of the statute, with the proviso that a company should be able to opt out of any of these provisions via its constitution.[8] Hence, numerous provisions of the Bill state that certain rules should apply to a company's operations "save to the extent that the constitution of company provides otherwise", e.g. the provision in s.55, Pt A3 permitting CLSs to issue bonus shares. It is submitted that this is preferable to the prior position under the Companies Act 1963 (the "1963 Act") whereby the provisions of Table A were scheduled to the Act and a company had to expressly adopt its provisions in order for them to apply, since most companies did this in any event, and it renders the law applying to those companies more accessible both to third parties and company stakeholders.

For similar reasons, the CLRG recommended that company law measures which were formerly to be found solely in regulations transposing EU legislation into domestic law should be imported into the body of the legislation, and this recommendation has been carried through to the Bill: see, for example, ss.142–150, Pt A11, which implement arts 5–13 of the EC (Corporate Insolvency) Regulations 2002 (S.I. No. 333 of 2002).[9] Numerous provisions that were solely

6 [1979] I.R. 149.

7 At para.10.9.2 of the First Report.

8 Paragraph 4.7.2 of the First Report.

9 The recommendations appear at para.3.12.7 of the First Report.

to be found in the Rules of the Superior Courts have also been brought into the main body of the legislation, for example the power currently set forth in Ord.42 r.32 of the Rules of the Superior Courts to attach and commit company officers for wilfully ignoring a judgment, which now appears at s.36, Pt A2.

4. The Transition

(a) A note of caution

As flagged previously, the rules applying to the transition from the current company law regime to the "new dawn" heralded by the Bill are of particular importance to company stakeholders eager to ensure that the enactment of the Bill does not prejudice their rights or interests, as well as to practitioners seeking to advise company officers of their options and obligations in this regard. The manner in which it is proposed to phase in the Bill's provisions is reasonably complex, and it seems inevitable to this writer that there may be recriminations and possibly litigation arising from a failure on the part of certain companies to respond appropriately to the changeover.

(b) Converting to a CLS or a DAC

At any time between the commencement of the Bill and the date six months after the date of commencement (the "status date"), private companies limited by shares will have the option under s.37, Pt A2 to (by ordinary resolution) adopt a new constitution and so convert to a Designated Activity Company. Private companies that have published a prospectus or been admitted to trading for their debentures on a recognised market are obliged to take this step. Companies that have thus converted are then to be subject to the provisions applying to DACs set out in Pt B3 of the Bill. Special Purpose Vehicles established to engage in a particular transaction or transactions are most likely to wish to avail of this option, and it is important that they are advised to proceed quickly in this regard. A company which does not avail of this option will be subject to the law applicable to DACs from the status date until such time as it re-registers as a CLS.

At any time between the status date and the end of the transition period (12 months after the status date and 18 months after the Bill's enactment), a company may by special resolution adopt a new constitution and choose to re-register as a CLS (s.40, Pt A2). In the event that the shareholders do not proceed to take this step, the company's directors are obliged to adopt a new constitution and re-register as a CLS within the relevant time, subject to the condition that the new constitution so adopted must not alter the rights and obligations of existing members of the company (s.41, Pt A2). Section 37, Pt A2, provides that any company which has not so converted by the end of the transition period will be automatically converted into a CLS with the pro forma constitution provided for in the Bill (similar to the default constitution set out in Table A to the 1963 Act).

(c) Understanding the changeover

The transitional provisions set out in the Bill mean three different legal regimes (the current law, the law applying to DACs and the law applying to CLSs) will apply to most private companies within an 18-month period. Practitioners will need a reasonable understanding of the mechanics of the transition process in order to advise their clients of the precise provisions governing a company's behaviour at any given point in time. In addition, it will be important to ensure that companies either convert to DAC status or (more commonly) adopt an appropriately adjusted CLS constitution within the relatively tight time-frame provided for under the Bill, unless the company's stakeholders are happy to be governed by the pro forma constitution set out in the Act. This imperative should be underscored by the fact that the Bill provides specific civil remedies for creditors and shareholders aggrieved by a failure in this regard on the part of the company's officers (at ss.38 and 43 of Pt A2 of the Bill). It should be noted, however, that s.1(2) of Pt A2 permits the Minister to extend the relevant periods by regulation, and one assumes this may well be done in the event that many companies are adversely affected by the speed of the changeover, drawing on Hannah Arendt's famous aphorism stating that "if everybody is guilty, nobody is guilty."

5. Corporate Governance

(a) Single-director companies

The Bill departs from its predecessors by permitting single-director companies, with the proviso that the director and the company secretary must be different people in the case of such companies. This change was recommended by the CLRG on the basis that the prior requirement for a minimum of two directors often led to family members with little or no involvement in the running of a company being appointed, a situation which only served to "devalue and trivialise the office of a director".[10] One spin-off from this amendment is that it may eradicate the hitherto relatively common problem of spouse directors being subject to enforcement measures such as restriction proceedings in circumstances where their role in a company existed on paper only (for one such case, see the decision of MacMenamin J. in *Re Cooke Events Company Ltd*[11]). By

[10] Paragraph 11.8.4 of the First Report.
[11] Unreported, High Court, MacMenamin J., June 29, 2005.

extension, this might encourage a stricter judicial approach to compliance by directors with their obligations.

(b) The role of a secretary

The role of a company secretary is placed on a firmer footing than in the current legislation, which is significant in circumstances where the company secretary will be the only person other than the director with the capacity to oversee the management of a single-director company. Section 8, Pt A5 of the Bill incorporates a general definition of the duties of a company secretary, something that was hitherto absent from Irish law. However, this definition is somewhat circular, in that it refers to the secretary's statutory and other legal duties, as well as "such duties and responsibilities as are delegated ... by the board of directors". This coheres with the CLRG's recommendation in its First Report, which had considered but rejected a more legalistic definition of the company secretary's role as provided for, for example, in s.268 of the South African Companies (Amendment) Act 1999.[12] Also in accordance with the CLRG's recommendations, s.8 imposes a duty on a company's directors to appoint a suitably skilled secretary, and obliges a company secretary to sign a statutory declaration acknowledging his or her duties.

(c) Other changes

In keeping with the CLRG's policy of ensuring that the entirety of the law applying to CLSs is readily ascertainable from the body of the statute,[13] the possibility of a single-member company is also recognised (in s.2, Pt A2) for the first time within the body of the Bill, although provisions permitting this form of company were previously contained in reg.4 of the EC (Single-Member Companies) Regulations 1994. In tandem with the provision for single-director companies, this ensures that sole entrepreneurs are facilitated to a greater degree than in the prior legislation. Further flexibility is provided by the increase in the number of members permitted in a CLS from 50 in s.33 of the 1963 Act to 99 (originally the CLRG had proposed the raising of the threshold to 150, but this was revised downwards in light of the EU Prospectus Directive, which requires a company with a membership of 100 persons or more to issue a prospectus).

(d) Responsibility and accountability of directors

Section 5, Pt A4 resolves an anomaly in the prior law by fixing the minimum age for directors at 18. Previously there had been no minimum, leading to several

[12] Paragraph 11.7.11 of the First Report.
[13] This policy is discussed at a little length in Ch.3 of the First Report.

reported instances of company directors who had not yet learned to walk or talk! This highlights the trend towards ensuring that company directors are persons who can actually be held accountable for the running of a company.

There are several provisions in the Bill which appear to be aimed towards ensuring greater responsibility from those who are permitted to assume the role of a director. This can be seen as a continuation of a legislative policy begun in the form of the Company Law Enforcement Act 2001, one which has perhaps given added impetus in the light of high-profile cases disclosing dubious corporate governance such as *Fyffes v DCC*,[14] and indeed of the current climate of discontent with corporate culture arising from the banking crisis.

An important innovation in this regard is that s.9, Pt A5 for the first time lists the fiduciary duties of directors in statute law. This was recommended by the CLRG on the basis that it would encourage greater awareness in the layman of the responsibilities of a director's role.[15] The CLRG recommended against a very detailed statement of the nature of these duties (as outlined, for example, at ss.170–177 of the UK Companies Act 2006), and so the provision simply sets forth the following broad categories of duty recognised in the prior case law and/or legislation either in this jurisdiction or elsewhere: the obligation of good faith (*Clark v Workman*[16]); the duty to act honestly and responsibly in respect of the company's affairs (as required, for example, under ss.297 and 297A of the 1963 Act and s.150 of the Companies Act 1990); the duty of obedience to the company's constitution (*Punt v Symons & Co.*[17]); the duty of avoidance of secret profits (*Regal Hastings v Gulliver*[18]); the duty of independence of judgment (*Clark v Workman*, as modified in *Fulham Football Club Ltd et al v Cabra Estates PLC*[19]); the duty to avoid conflicts of interest (*Gabbett v Lawder*[20]); the duty of due skill, care and diligence (*Re City Equitable Fire Insurance Ltd*[21]); and the duty to have regard to the interests of the company's employees (s.52(1) of the Companies Act 1990) and its members (*Re Frederick Inns Ltd*[22]). It would appear, therefore, that the prior case law will continue to be of great assistance in determining the precise contours of these duties.

(e) The directors' compliance statement

To the same end, s.7, Pt A5 requires CLS directors to complete a declaration signalling their awareness of their company law obligations on assuming office,

14 Unreported, Supreme Court, July 27, 2007.
15 At para.11.3.7 of the First Report.
16 [1902] 1 I.R. 107.
17 [1903] 2 Ch. 506.
18 [1942] 1 All E.R. 378.
19 [1994] 1 B.C.L.C. 363.
20 (1883) 11 L.R. Ir. 295.
21 [1925] Ch. 407.
22 [1991] I.L.R.M. 582.

as well as an annual compliance statement. A directors' compliance statement was inserted into s.205E of the Companies Act 1990 pursuant to s.45 of the Companies (Auditing and Accounting) Act 2003 (the "2003 Act") but never subsequently commenced. The reason for the failure to commence the compliance statement set out in s.45 of the 2003 Act was because of widespread criticism from the business community, which cited concerns related to the cost for individual companies and the impact on national competitiveness of requiring directors to sign up to a statement in what was perceived to be the overly demanding form set out in that provision.

The CLRG itself was subsequently requested to complete a 2005 Report on the Directors' Compliance Statement, on foot of which its primary recommendation was that s.45 should not be brought into force because of its potential negative impact on Irish business in circumstances where an equivalent regime was not in place in competing jurisdictions. It was also recommended (by a narrow majority of the CLRG) that the compliance statement set out in that provision should not be replaced, even with a less prescriptive compliance statement. However, in the event that the legislature did not accept this latter recommendation, the CLRG proposed the introduction of a revised version of the compliance statement differing from the s.45 statement in a number of respects, including the following:

(i) the threshold monetary requirements in relation to a private company for triggering the requirement for a compliance statement should be increased from a minimum annual balance sheet total of just over €7m and a minimum annual turnover of over €15m so that a greater number of companies would be excluded;

(ii) the definition of "relevant obligations", i.e. the number of statutory obligations with which directors were required to state their acquaintance, should be narrowed by removing the third limb incorporated in s.45 relating to "any other enactments that provide a legal framework within which the company operates and that may materially affect the company's financial statements" (the gravamen of the objection to this limb was that it encompassed an almost infinite variety of legislative requirements, and that no non-lawyer could reasonably be expected to spend the time which might be required to fulfil this obligation), while the first and second limbs relating to the obligations created by Companies Acts and the tax acts, respectively, should be retained;

(iii) the first limb of the definition of "relevant obligations" should be narrowed so as only to cover requirements under the Companies Acts breaches of which constitute serious criminal offences, rather than all provisions under the Acts which create criminal offences; and

(iv) the requirement that the company's auditors must specifically opine on the reasonableness or otherwise of the compliance statement should be removed.[23]

[23] A number of other amendments to the s.45 compliance statement were also recommended.

The revised compliance statement set out in s.7, Pt A5 of the Bill, if carried through to the Act, represents a decision to embrace the compromise solution of adopting a revised directors' compliance statement, contrary to the CLRG's primary recommendation in its 2005 Report on the Directors' Compliance Statement, but along the lines recommended in the alternative therein. In particular, the financial thresholds in relation to balance sheet totals and turnover are increased to €12.5m and €25m, respectively, and the suggestions made in the Report in relation to the definition of "relevant obligations" and the involvement of company auditors are followed.

(f) The removal of the requirement for an AGM

The Bill should help to render company administration—particularly in the case of small companies—less onerous by minimising the need for face-to-face meetings. This is a significant change from the prior position under s.131 of the 1963 Act, whereby all companies are—at least in theory—required to hold oral, face-to-face meetings to approve the various matters which must be dealt with at an Annual General Meeting. In practice, the degree of formality attending an AGM and the seriousness with which its business is taken tends to vary greatly depending on the nature of the company involved, and in many instances the meeting itself is—in the words of the CLRG—an "empty gesture".[24] The reality at present in a typical small family company is that the members in their capacity as directors will already have approved the accounts, the level of dividend, the re-election of themselves as directors (where required) and the continuance in office of the auditors in advance of the AGM. Accordingly, the CLRG recommended in its First Report that the requirement for an oral meeting be removed provided that certain written procedures were followed to deal with the business that would otherwise have been dealt with at the AGM.[25]

In accordance with the above recommendation, s.46, Pt A4 of the Bill states that an Annual General Meeting will no longer be required where a unanimous written resolution is signed by all members acknowledging receipt of accounts, confirming no change in the audit appointment, and approving all other matters that would otherwise have been dealt with at the AGM.

(g) Permitting resolutions in writing

The administrative burden on those involved with companies is further eased under s.65, Pt A4, by permitting ordinary and special majority resolutions to be passed in writing provided the appropriate procedures are followed. Written resolutions are currently permitted under s.141(8) of the 1963 Act only where

[24] At para.4.5.6.1 of the First Report.
[25] At para.4.5.6 of the First Report.

members are unanimous. A safeguard is provided by placing a moratorium on the coming into effect of a majority resolution so that the dissenters can take steps to challenge the resolution, most commonly by convening an extraordinary general meeting where the matter can be debated.

Section 47 also facilitates company administration, particularly in relation to companies where a significant number of controlling figures reside or do business abroad—an aspect of the Irish corporate landscape which appears to be becoming ever more prominent in a globalised economy where our low corporation tax rate continues to constitute a major attraction to international investment—by permitting company meetings to be held outside the State, or partially outside and partially within the State (this was prohibited under s.140 of the 1963 Act). This is facilitated by permitting company meetings to be held at two or more venues using "any technology that provides members as a whole with a reasonable opportunity to participate" (presumably this is intended to refer to tele- and video-conferencing and similar technology).

(h) The new universal validation procedure

Another innovation introduced by the Bill which should streamline the running of companies is the provision set out in s.71, Pt A4 for a single universal procedure which can be used to validate several different "restricted activities" (including, inter alia, the provision of financial assistance in connection with the purchase of a company's shares, certain financial transactions with directors, the reduction of a company's capital and the voluntary winding up of a solvent company) that a CLS proposes to carry out. This replaces the distinct, though similar, procedures now provided for in various provisions of the Companies Acts, including s.60 of the 1963 Act (in relation to the provision of financial assistance in connection with the purchase of a company's shares), s.34 of the Companies Act 1990 (in relation to certain transactions with directors) and ss.72–73 of the 1963 Act (in relation to the reduction of a company's capital). The procedure itself is to a great extent an amalgamation of the procedures set forth in s.60 of the 1963 Act and s.34 of the Companies Act 1990, and involves a special resolution and a declaration by the directors in a preceding meeting complying with specified conditions. The declaration is not a statutory one, unlike the position under the prior statutory regime, since the CLRG felt that a statutory declaration was a burdensome and unnecessary step in circumstances where it is already a criminal offence under s.12, Pt A13 of the Bill to give false information in compliance with any provision of the Bill.[26]

One assumes that the existence of a single validation procedure will eventually lead to the minimisation of legal and other administrative costs

[26] The removal of the various requirements for statutory declarations in the prior legislation was recommended by the CLRG at para.7.4.1.2 of the First Report.

involved in embarking upon one of these restricted activities, since company officers will be more likely to have a reasonable grasp of the required steps without needing further legal advice. This appears to have been the intention of the CLRG in recommending the measure.[27]

6. LIQUIDATIONS

(a) The scope of the proposed changes

The Bill proposes sweeping reforms to the court-initiated mode of winding up (official liquidation). The changes envisaged in relation to the voluntary modes of winding up are more modest, being predominantly structural in nature. The majority of the changes implemented in relation to court-initiated windings up appear to reflect a view on the part of the CLRG that the High Court had too great an involvement in overseeing official liquidations, leading to excessive costs.

From a structural perspective, the most notable feature of Pt A11 of the Bill is that, insofar as reasonably possible, the differences between the three separate modes of winding up are eliminated so that many of the same procedures apply regardless of the route taken to wind up a company. There is also an attempt in s.60 of Pt A11 to succinctly summarise the scope of a liquidator's role as follows: "to administer the property of the company",[28] although this effects no substantive change to the existing position at common law. The CLRG considered but ultimately rejected more radical changes such as establishing a State insolvency service or abolishing the preferential status of Revenue debts on insolvency.

The option of abolishing Revenue preference or reducing the 12-month preference period in respect of Revenue debts was considered in light of the decision to abolish Crown preference in the UK under Pt 10 of the Enterprise Act 2002. However, the CLRG concluded that there was no basis for any change to the current position, particularly given the important contribution that the Revenue's preferential status allows it to make to the liquidation process.[29] The option of establishing a State-funded insolvency service along the lines of the Insolvency Service in the UK was also rejected, on the ground of the prohibitive cost involved, and the fact that there was no evidence that it would necessarily improve the position of creditors in a winding up.

[27] At paras 5.2.6–5.2.14 of the First Report.

[28] The term "property" is defined extensively in s.1, Pt 11 to encompass "all real and personal property", including "any right of action by the company or liquidator".

[29] At para.4.20 of the Second Report.

(b) Initiating the winding up process

One change that will be of some significance in practice is that, pursuant to s.11, Pt 11 of the Bill, the minimum debt required to ground a petition for compulsory liquidation has been increased to €10,000. An increase was recommended by the CLRG in its Second Report, on the basis that the previous figure of €1,269.74 (IR£1,000) was "much too low", being a figure that is well below the civil jurisdiction of the Circuit Court and that would generally be regarded as insignificant in commercial practice. Section 11(b) creates an entirely new mechanism, intended to permit groups of small creditors to jointly initiate the court winding-up process, whereby two or more creditors who are owed cumulative amounts totalling a minimum of €20,000 can collectively petition for a winding up. This was recommended by the CLRG in its Second Report on the basis that it would constitute a cost-efficient means of initiating the process for smaller creditors, since it would permit the legal and other expenses involved to be pooled between such parties.[30] Interestingly, the figures recommended by the CLRG were €5,000 in the case of an individual creditor, and €10,000 for a group of creditors, respectively; the uplift on these figures in the Bill may to some extent reflect the decrease in the value of money since the publication of the Report.

(c) Winding up on the public interest ground

A new ground for winding up is added to the legislation. The High Court is now permitted pursuant to s.10, Pt A11, to order a liquidation where the Director of Corporate Enforcement has established that it is in the public interest for a company to be wound up. This provision is similar in many respects to the Director of Corporate Enforcement's power to apply for the winding up of a company on the public interest ground contained in s.12(2) of the Companies Act 1990, as amended by s.14 of the Company Law Enforcement Act 2001, on foot of information obtained following an investigation carried out under Pt II of the Companies Act 1990. The sole example in practice of this power actually being exercised to date (it involved an exercise of the power by the Minister for Industry and Commerce, since the power to initiate an investigation was only transferred to the Director of Corporate Enforcement pursuant to s.14 of the Company Law Enforcement Act 2001) was the subject of the High Court decision in *Conroy v Corneill*.[31] The CLRG recommended the extension of the prior provision to include circumstances where there had been no investigation by an authorised officer in its Second Report, and this recommendation is duly implemented in the Bill.[32]

[30] At paras 4.15.21–22 of the Second Report.
[31] [2003] 3 I.R. 588.
[32] At para.4.13.6.

(d) The qualifications of liquidators

On the recommendation of the CLRG in its *First Report*,[33] new qualification requirements have been introduced for liquidators to rectify the anomalous position under the prior legislation whereby no specific professional qualification was required from a liquidator. Section 68, Pt A11 now requires a liquidator to be a member of a prescribed professional organisation. To avoid individual cases of injustice, transitional provisions have been inserted with the objective of ensuring that persons who have achieved appropriate qualifications through working in the profession can continue to act as liquidators provided they have obtained authorisation from the supervisory authority within two years from the coming into force of this provision and pending the outcome of their application for authorisation, and that persons appointed as liquidators prior to the coming into force of the provision can continue to act in those liquidations. For the first time, liquidators are also required to have in place professional indemnity insurance on such terms as may be fixed by the Irish Auditing and Accounting Supervisory Authority. This obviates any need for the court to have a role in fixing security for a liquidation, as currently required under s.228(a) 1963 Act.

(e) Reducing the High Court's role in court-ordered liquidations

As flagged above, the most discernible policy of Pt 11 of the Bill is to greatly reduce the involvement of the court itself in court-initiated liquidation. The provision noted above whereby the court will no longer become involved in fixing the liquidator's security is simply one aspect of this general policy. The court's primary role in fixing the liquidator's remuneration, as provided for in s.228(d) of the 1963 Act, is also removed. Under the new regime set forth in s.79, Pt 11, the same basic mechanism applies to the remuneration of liquidators in all modes of winding up, although the scheme preserves the role of the court in fixing the remuneration of provisional liquidators. The terms of remuneration of liquidators proper will be set either by the creditors/committee of creditors (in a creditors' voluntary winding up or a court-ordered winding up) or by the members (in a members' voluntary winding up), with a residual power for the court to intervene where remuneration is not set. The liquidator must seek to have his remuneration set as soon as possible following his appointment, and the parties obliged to set the terms of remuneration are to be given notice of those terms in advance of the meeting to approve same. Further approval will be required where payment is sought on foot of those terms of remuneration. The remuneration set can be reviewed by the court or by an arbitrator at the instance of either the liquidator or other interested parties. As recommended by the CLRG in its Second Report, the criteria in accordance with which such review

[33] See Ch.13 of the First Report, which deals with the regulation of insolvency professionals.

is to be exercised are similar to those recommended in the UK by Mr Justice Ferris's Working Party on the Remuneration of Office-holders and Certain Related Matters.[34]

The court's role in overseeing the conduct of an official liquidation is also reduced. Unlike the current position pursuant to s.232 of the 1963 Act, neither an initial court direction nor a subsequent application to court will be required for a committee of inspection to be appointed in a liquidation. Instead s.96, Pt 11 provides for the committee of inspection in a court-winding up to be appointed on the initiative of the liquidator or a minimum proportion of the creditors. Similarly, s.104, Pt 11 transfers to the liquidator in a court winding up the power formerly vested in the court under s.241 of the 1963 Act to fix the time within which the creditors may prove claims. Again, however, a residual power to intervene is reserved for the court in cases where this is necessary. A new safeguard is also created in that the provision specifies that the period specified for the making of claims cannot be less than 28 days.

There are various other provisions which transfer certain powers formerly reserved for the court in official windings up to the liquidator, among them the power to settle the list of contributories (s.87, Pt 11, formerly dealt in s.276(c) of the 1963 Act), the power to make calls on shareholders in respect of amounts unpaid on shares (s.88, Pt 11, formerly dealt with in s.276(d) of the 1963 Act), and the power to adjust the rights of contributories and to distribute any surplus among the persons entitled thereto (s.89, Pt 11, formerly dealt with in s.242 of the 1963 Act). Nor does the court necessarily have a role any longer in dissolving the company at the conclusion of a liquidation, as it did under s.249 of the 1963 Act, since s.130, Pt 11 of the Bill ensures that the court will only have a role if it so directs.

Accordingly, once the initial order for winding up has been made and the liquidator appointed, the court's role will in general be restricted to making orders and giving directions in relation to the liquidator's powers, when requested to do so (the power to apply for such directions is retained and expanded at s.66, Pt A11). It would appear, therefore, that the liquidator will have more freedom in relation to how the liquidation is conducted than under the current regime. This is subject, however, both to s.117 of Pt 11, which is a new provision that requires the liquidator to have regard to the directions of the creditors and contributories, and to the various provisions that allow applications to be made to court for directions in respect of the liquidator's conduct.

(f) Reducing the Court Examiner's role

The role of the Examiner of the High Court is similarly displaced. The Examiner's current power to adjudicate on debts and liabilities and settle a list of contributories is now transferred to the liquidator pursuant to ss.63 and 87 of

[34] Report of July 1998.

Pt A11. Furthermore, the liquidator's account need no longer be settled by the Examiner's Office (s.111, Pt A11).

7. Compliance and Enforcement

(a) The four-tier classification of criminal offences

The CLRG focused to a significant extent in its First Report on the need to ensure that the quality of the provisions contained in the Bill would be supported by the quality of their enforcement. In furtherance of this objective, Pt A13 of the Bill codifies the law relating to compliance with company law. Section 57 of this Part of the Bill provides for the following four-level categorisation of the criminal offences created under the Bill and the penalties available for their breach:

- Category 1 offences, which are subject to a maximum fine of €5,000 and/or a term of imprisonment of up to 12 months in cases taken summarily, and to a fine not exceeding €500,000 and/or a term of imprisonment of up to 10 years in cases taken on indictment.
- Category 2 offences, which are subject to a maximum fine of €5,000 and/or a term of imprisonment of up to 12 months in cases taken summarily, and to a fine not exceeding €50,000 and/or a term of imprisonment of up to five years in cases taken on indictment.
- Category 3 offences, which are subject to a maximum fine of €5,000 and/or a term of imprisonment of up to six months, and which can only be taken summarily.
- Category 4 offences, which are subject to a maximum fine of €5,000 and which cannot attract a term of imprisonment, and which can only be taken summarily.

All but a handful of the most serious criminal offences provided for under the Bill are classified under one of the four categories. The offences excluded are those sections of Pt B2 of the Bill which implement the Market Abuse Regulations and the Prospectus Regulations.

It is to be hoped that this new simplified regime will encourage a more consistent and rigorous approach to the implementation of company law. While the number of criminal offences in existence under the Companies Acts has multiplied in recent years, this increase does not appear to have been matched by a commensurate increase in enforcement. In particular, it is exceptionally rare for a prosecution on indictment to be mounted in relation to offences under the companies legislation. The only very recent example that springs to mind is the prosecution of Stuart Fogarty, a director of a Dublin advertising company who was made subject to a two-year suspended sentence and a heavy fine before the Dublin Circuit Criminal Court in June 2008 following breaches of the provisions of the Companies Act 1990 relating to loans to directors.

(b) The restriction and disqualification of directors

There are a couple of important changes in relation to the heavily litigated area of the restriction and disqualification of directors. In particular, s.52 of Pt 13 permits a person to give an undertaking to be restricted or disqualified rather than be required to face court proceedings. The introduction of this procedure is intended to avoid the unnecessary use of resources in the course of court proceedings on the part of liquidators, directors and the courts. The procedure set forth in the provision is based on that already operating in the UK under s.1A of the Company Directors Disqualification Act 1986, as inserted by s.6 of the Insolvency Act 2000. According to the CLRG, approximately 80 per cent of disqualification cases in the UK are now dealt with in this manner. It is likely that a similarly high proportion of directors will accede to undertakings here rather than incur the cost and public odium that tends to attend court proceedings. The option is likely to be particularly popular among company directors who have little interest in continuing in commercial life following their restriction or disqualification.

Another new requirement is incorporated in s.32(3)(b) of Pt 13, which requires directors to demonstrate that they have co-operated with the liquidator in relation to the conduct of the winding up in order to avoid a restriction order, as well as demonstrating that they have acted honestly and responsibly in relation to the company's affairs (as currently required under s.150(2)(a) of the Companies Act 1990). In addition, the same section abolishes the defences set out in subss.150(2)(b) and (c) of the Companies Act 1990 in relation to directors who were appointed to directorships solely as representatives of a financial institution or venture capital company.

All of this suggests that it may become even more difficult for directors of insolvent companies to avoid restriction once the Bill is enacted. However, it should be noted that it was suggested by Shanley J. in the High Court in *Re La Moselle Clothing*[35] that the requirement under s.150(2)(a) 1990 that there be no other reason why it would be "otherwise just or equitable" to impose a restriction order even where a company director had shown himself to have acted honestly and responsibly prior to the winding up order should permit a court to restrict a director where he had failed to co-operate with the winding up. Furthermore, there are no recorded instances of the defences set out in subss.(2)(b) and (c) of the 1990 Act actually succeeding.[36] Accordingly, the change in the statutory position may have little effect in practice.

35 [1998] 2 I.L.R.M. 345.

36 Although, in *Kavanagh v Delaney*, Hardiman J. did refer to the two defences in drawing an analogy between persons who would covered by the defences and the defendant, who "went on

The General Scheme of the Bill was drafted prior to the swingeing criticisms articulated by Hardiman J. in the Supreme Court in *Re Tralee Beef and Lamb; Kavanagh v Delaney*[37] both of the statutory mechanism for the restriction of directors and of the manner in which the mechanism has been applied in practice by the Director of Corporate Enforcement. It is notable that the Director of Corporate Enforcement has asked the Government and the Attorney General to review the restriction scheme in the light of this decision.[38] Accordingly, it is very possible that the provisions relating to these matters that are finally enacted may differ significantly from those set out in the General Scheme.

8. Debentures and Charges

(a) The priority of charges

The most fundamental change proposed to the law relating to debentures and charges, dealt with at Pt A7 of the Bill, relates to the date on which charges acquire priority. The current legislation is silent as to the date on which a charge, once created, acquires priority. However, it has long been recognised in practice that priority is acquired on the date of *creation* of the charge rather than on the date of its registration with the Companies Office. This situation carries with it an obvious but significant anomaly: a creditor can file a charge over an asset at a time when a CRO search reveals no pre-existing charges over that asset, but a charge created earlier in time and registered later but still within the required 21-day period has priority over this charge. This situation can have unfair consequences for creditors, who have no way of achieving certainty as to their charge's priority at the date of its registration. The present position also creates the potential for fraudulent abuse by company officers, who can assure a creditor that its charge will have priority in the full knowledge that the charge will rank behind another, hitherto unregistered, charge. Accordingly, the CLRG recommended in its Second Report that the law should be changed to specify that priority runs from the date of registration,[39] and this recommendation is implemented in s.10(1), Pt A7 of the Bill.

The change in the law relating to priority is facilitated by s.7(3) of the Bill, which provides for a mechanism for the preliminary filing of notice of a charge. This permits notice of the creation of a charge to be filed in the Companies Office on a given date. That charge will then gain priority from that date so long as full particulars of the charge as required under the legislation are filed within

the Board solely because someone had to represent the interest of the BES investors so that he was in a position not unlike that of a director who might have been exempt from restriction under [subparagraphs 150(2)(b) and (c)]".

37 Unreported, Supreme Court, February 1, 2008.

38 See *Irish Times*, March 12, 2008, "Government to review restrictions on directors".

39 At para.8.3.5.

21 days thereafter. A preliminary filing system has existed for more than 50 years in the United States, and similar systems also operate in Canada and New Zealand. The establishment of such a system here is, again, in accordance with the CLRG's recommendations in its Second Report.[40]

Section 10, Pt A7 ensures that the ordinary rule as to priority will not apply in circumstances where it is inappropriate. In particular, this rule is made subject to any contrary agreement between the creditors such as an inter-lender agreement often entered into between financial institutions where more than one such institution lends to a particular company.[41] The general rule as to priority is also made subject to any over-riding priority applicable to certain categories of assets, such as those created under the principles applicable to the Registry of Deeds, the Land Registry, the Shipping Registry or the Chattel Registry.

(b) The obligation to file

Under ss.100–102 of the 1963 Act, the obligation to file particulars of both charges and judgment mortgages in the Companies Office rests on the debtor company, with criminal penalties for its officers in case of non-compliance. In practice, the creditor tends to take responsibility for registration, since it is in its interest to ensure the charge's priority and validity. In accordance with the CLRG's recommendation in its *Second Report*,[42] the criminal penalty for breach of this duty is abolished pursuant to s.9, Pt A7 in light of the reality that the duty is shouldered primarily by the creditor in practice. The statutory obligation on company officers to register charges remains in place, however, in light of the overriding importance of ensuring that a company's file reflects the reality of its financial position.

Under the prior legislation, company officers were required to register a judgment mortgage and a judgment mortgage was invalidated by a failure to register. This created an opportunity for unscrupulous company officers to defraud creditors by failing to register, since the criminal penalty for a failure to register was a relatively small fine pursuant to s.102(2) of the 1963 Act. To counter this problem, the obligation to file details of judgment mortgages has been switched from the company to the creditor under s.11, Pt A7, and a failure to register will no longer invalidate the mortgage. This provision also brings the law on the priority of judgment mortgages into line with the law on the priority of charges by providing that priority as regards a judgment mortgage will run from the date of its registration, rather than from its creation.

[40] At paras 8.3.6–8.3.8.

[41] As recommended by the CLRG at para.8.13.5 of the *Second Report*.

[42] At para.8.9.1.

9. Auditing and Financial Statements

(a) Overview

The new Bill implements relatively few changes to the law governing auditing and financial statements, since this area has been amended significantly through a number of pieces of legislation enacted in the past few years, including the Companies (Auditing and Accounting) Act 2003, the Investment Funds, Companies and Miscellaneous Provisions Act 2006, and the statutory instruments implementing EU provisions requiring a shift from our traditional accounting standards to Fair Value Accounting and International Accounting Standards. The most important impact of the Bill in this area is simply to bring together all of the prior legislative provisions in relation to auditing and financial statements, and to structure these in a systematic fashion so that they can be easily read and—hopefully—easily understood. Previously, even by company law standards, the law in this area was contained in a bewildering number of statutes and statutory instruments.

Notably, s.11 of Pt A6 of the Bill contains a general requirement that a company's statutory financial statements as approved by its directors are required to give a true and fair view, and that the company's auditors are to have regard to this requirement in carrying out their statutory functions. While it implements no substantive change to the existing position as provided for by the EU's Fair Value Directive (2001/65/EC) as transposed into Irish law by the European Communities (Fair Value Accounting) Regulations 2004 (S.I. No. 765 of 2004), this provision is significant from the point of view of the "optics" of this Part of the Bill in that it highlights the core philosophy now underpinning our accounting regime.

(b) Revision of defective financial statements

There are a number of important substantive changes to the present law. Notably, ss.69–82, Pt 11 are devoted to the details of a procedure for the voluntary revision of defective financial statements, something which does not currently exist in Irish law. At present, in the event that it comes to light that a set of statutory financial statements that have already been filed are defective, there is no procedure to govern their revision. The new provisions governing the making and delivery of revised financial statements are very similar in substance to the provisions governing the making of the initial financial statements, and further directors' and auditors' reports will be required in the event that this step is taken.

(c) Exemptions from requirement to deliver statutory financial statements

Section 58, Pt A6 helps to further one key objective of the Bill, that of minimising insofar as possible the red tape attending company administration, by raising the thresholds below which a company can be treated as a small or medium company. These were formerly an annual turnover of €3m or €12m and a balance sheet total of €1.5m or €6m, for small and medium companies, respectively, as provided for in the European Communities (Accounts) Regulations 1993. Section 58 raises these thresholds to €5,000,000 and €2,500,000, for small companies, and to €20,000,000 and €10,000,00, for medium companies, respectively. Such companies are subject only to the special requirements set out in ss.59–65 of Pt A6 in relation to furnishing certain financial information to the CRO together with the annual return, rather than being subject to the full impact of the requirements of Pt A6 in relation to financial statements.

(d) The failure to extend the audit exemption

Section 67 of the Bill does not propose any change in relation to the current position whereby holding companies that are obliged to prepare group financial statements are excluded from the audit exemption, as currently provided for under s.32(3)(a)(v) of the Companies Amendment (No.2) Act 1999. Holding companies continue to be subject to a general requirement to have their accounts audited, even where the overall size of the various companies within the group is well below the audit exemption for an individual company. This appears anomalous, and it creates an unnecessary administrative burden for groups of small companies. After all, the group structure is a common and perfectly legitimate manner in which to organise the operations of a business, regardless of the size of that business. The author would suggest that the legislature should consider inserting a provision within the final Act that would extend the audit exemption to holding companies where the overall size of the group is such as would permit it an exemption if it was a single company.

10. Conclusion

The new Companies Bill is perhaps the most ambitious and thorough piece of law reform ever attempted in this jurisdiction. While the detail of certain provisions may change—in some cases considerably—before it is enacted, there appears little doubt now that the Bill will become law. It is not as yet clear whether this will to happen in the short or medium term: it was initially anticipated that the Bill might come into force in 2007 or 2008, but at the current slow rate of progress in placing it before the Oireachtas, it appears more likely now to become the Companies Consolidation and Reform Act 2010 or 2011. But whatever the date of its coming into force, company law practitioners will have to be well versed in the Bill's provisions in advance of its enactment if they are to advise their clients as to its impact on their companies with any degree of assurance. Company directors and shareholders would also do well to acquaint themselves with at least the broad outline of the Bill's provisions at an early stage, given the practical importance of many of the changes it makes to the current law, and the potentially embarrassing consequences of getting it wrong.